THOMAS FLANAGAN is a member of the Department of Political Science at the University of Calgary. He has edited *The Diaries of Louis Riel* and *Louis Riel: Poésies de Jeunesse.*

Louis Riel believed that on 8 December 1875 he received a divine commission which authorized him to save the métis and reform the Catholic Church. He was a prophet, inspired by the Holy Spirit, and the métis were the new Chosen People. A new branch of the Catholic Church would be founded in North America, with its Holy See first in Montreal, then in Riel's birthplace of St Vital.

When Riel expressed these views in 1876, he was confined to a lunatic asylum. After his release, he concealed his ideas for several years, but revealed them to the métis during the North-West Rebellion, which was as much a religious as a political movement. He believed himself a prophet to the end of his life, and he went to his death thinking that he, like Christ, would be resurrected on the third day.

Earlier writers about Louis Riel have noted his religious beliefs but have not taken them seriously. Riel's attempt to found a new religion has usually been dismissed as the symptom of a deranged mind. This book takes Riel's religion seriously and analyses it using categories developed in the literature about millenarian movements. It is shown that Riel's religion, far from being simply individual madness, is typical of the nativistic and millenarian movements described by Vittorio Lantenari as the 'Religions of the Oppressed.'

The book is biographical in method. It traces Riel's thinking on religious subjects from his childhood to the end of his life. It pays particular attention to events in Riel's life which influenced his thinking. This developmental approach is necessary because Riel's ideas changed frequently; he never arrived at a fixed 'system.'

The book relies on primary manuscript sources throughout. Much new documentation has become available since the publication of G. F. G. Stanley's standard biography in 1963. In particular, new information is presented about Riel's youth in Montreal, his time in the insane asylums, and his years in Montana. In addition to using new manuscript sources, the book also re-evaluates well-known documents in the light of the hypothesis that Riel was a genuine religious figure, not just a madman on the loose.

THOMAS FLANAGAN

Louis 'David' Riel:
'Prophet of the New World'

UNIVERSITY OF TORONTO PRESS
Toronto   Buffalo   London

© University of Toronto Press 1979
Toronto Buffalo London
Printed in Canada

Library of Congress Cataloging in Publication Data

Flanagan, Thomas.
   Louis 'David' Riel: prophet of the new world.

   Includes bibliographical references and index.
   1. Riel, Louis David, 1844-1885.   2. Revolutionists – Northwest Territories
  – Biography.
   F1060.9.R53F57   971.05'1'0924   78-18497
   ISBN 0-8020-5430-7

Contents

Preface

Louis Riel came to believe during the course of his life that he was endowed by God with a special mission as 'Prophet of the New World.' His task was to announce a new era in the Kingdom of God, in which spiritual primacy would pass from Europe to America. After the mid-1870s, Riel's mission became the controlling force of his mind. All his actions, whether political or religious, revolved around it.

Little attention has been paid until now to the religious dimension of Riel's career, except by psychiatrists who have considered it proof that he was insane.[1] Historians have noted some of Riel's religious beliefs but have made little attempt to analyze them, preferring to emphasize his importance as a political and constitutional figure.

This book takes Riel's prophetic mission as its focus. His beliefs are presented in their origin and step-by-step development. At every stage, an attempt is made to explain how they were influenced by the events of his life.

It was necessary to make a fresh study of the documentary sources because existing biographies do not say much about the religious question. This allowed me to take advantage of several new manuscripts which have become available to researchers since the publication of George Stanley's *Louis Riel* (1963). As a result, this work contains some new information about Riel, particularly about his youth and his years in Montana.

The first seven chapters are primarily narrative; the last is theoretical. It tries to show that Louis Riel's religion was a form of millenarianism and can be understood through use of the concepts w
veloped in the study of that field. The major comp
Riel is the psychiatric thesis that he was mentally i

gious ideas were symptoms of his disease. That thesis is not directly challenged here, but readers who accept it are asked to suspend their belief in it, at least temporarily. I assume that Riel's religion, regardless of labels, is important enough to deserve a serious and sympathetic inquiry.

This book has been published with the help of a grant from the Social Science Federation of Canada, using funds provided by the Canada Council. A publication subsidy was also received from the University of Calgary. Financial support for the research was provided at an earlier stage by the University of Calgary, the Canada Council, and the National Museum of Man. This assistance is gratefully acknowledged.

Thanks are also due to the many libraries and archives which have made available their manuscript collections and given permission to quote from them: Archives of the Archdiocese of Montreal, National Archives of Quebec, Archives of the Archdiocese of St Boniface, Archives of the Seminary of Quebec, Archives of the Seminary of Trois-Rivières, Archives of the Union St Jean-Baptiste (Woonsocket, Rhode Island), Bibliothèque Nationale du Québec (Montreal), Glenbow-Alberta Institute, Historical Society of St Boniface, National Archives of the United States, Provincial Archives of Alberta, Public Archives of Canada, Provincial Archives of Manitoba, Archives de la Compagnie de Jésus (St-Jérôme, Quebec), Archives of the Diocese of St-Hyacinthe, Archives of Ontario, University of North Dakota Library (Grand Forks), St Norbert Parish (Manitoba), University of Saskatchewan Library, Queen's University Library, University of New Brunswick Library, Archives of the Archdiocese of Quebec, Archives des Sœurs Grises de Montréal, Queen Street Mental Health Centre (Toronto), Hôpital St Michel-Archange (Beauport), Centre Hospitalier St Jean-de-Dieu (Montréal-Gamelin), McCord Museum (McGill University), Minnesota Historical Society, Parks Canada (Prairie Region), and the College of Montreal. My research could never have been done without the co-operation of these institutions.

It is impossible to list all the individuals who have helped me in the study of Louis Riel. However I would like to mention the names of George Stanley, John Bovey, Cyril Greenland, Dr Jack Griffin, Léon Pouliot, SJ, and Lionel Dorge. Special thanks are also owing to my colleagues and collaborators Glen Campbell and Gilles Martel, who have assisted me in ways too numerous to mention. Finally I must acknowledge the loyal and cheerful support of Marianne Flanagan, who has never failed to encourage my work. It goes without saying that if I have committed any errors, in spite of all this help, the responsibility is mine alone.

TF

Abbreviations

PJ   Gilles Martel, Glen Campbell, Thomas Flanagan, editors,
            Louis Riel: Poésies de jeunesse, St Boniface 1977
QvLR   Desmond Morton, editor, *The Queen v Louis Riel*,
            Toronto 1974. Transcript of Riel's trial for high
            treason, 1885

LOUIS 'DAVID' RIEL:
'PROPHET OF THE NEW WORLD'

1
Preparation

Louis Riel's emergence as the 'Prophet of the New World' was a gradual process, although it seemed sudden to those who witnessed only the final stage. Hindsight, aided by the modern availability of documents depicting Riel's inner life, can trace the pattern of development. That development began in his childhood and youth.

FAMILY AND CHILDHOOD

The story of the Riel family in western Canada begins with Louis Riel's grandfather, Jean-Baptiste Riel, a voyageur for the Northwest Company. At Ile-à-la-Crosse in northern Saskatchewan, he married Marguerite Boucher, who was half French and half Chipewayan Indian. Their son Louis (father of the more famous Louis Riel who is the subject of this book) was born in 1817. Jean-Baptiste brought him back to grow up in Lower Canada, where he learned to read and write and acquired the trade of a wool carder. At the age of twenty-one, he took a term of service with the Hudson's Bay Company. He lived with a métisse in a common-law marriage at Rainy Lake and fathered a daughter by her.[1] Returning to Lower Canada, he entered the novitiate of the Oblate Fathers, who were engaged in missionary work in the West. But his religious vocation lasted only a few months.[2] He soon went back to the West, to settle in the Red River colony.

His attention was drawn to Julie Lagimodière, one of the few white girls in the colony. Her parents had come west in 1807. Like the few other French-Canadians in Red River, they were part of the métis community, and Julie grew up a métisse.

She was thinking of becoming a nun when Louis Riel asked her parents for her hand. According to legend, she refused to marry until a vision convinced her to follow her parents' will rather than her own. Leaving church, she saw high in the heavens an old man surrounded by flames who cried down at her, 'disobedient child!' whereupon she agreed to her parents' wishes.[3] Louis Riel and Julie Lagimodière were married on 21 January 1844. Their eldest child, Louis, was born almost exactly nine months later, on 22 or 23 October of that year.[4] This prompt conception and early arrival of her first-born must have embarrassed the mother, for she later told her children that her wedding had taken place on 21 January 1843.[5]

More children came quickly, as the Riel family settled down to farming on the Seine River. Two babies died in infancy, but eight more survived. It was a close family, and Louis seems to have been deeply and genuinely attached to his brothers and sisters. Virtually nothing is known about Louis' early childhood except a few family anecdotes. He was said to be remarkable for his affection for his parents and for his piety, and was so generous that when he was old enough to go to school he would give away his lunch to poverty-stricken Indians, so that his mother had to ask the bishop's residence to feed him at noon. One time, challenged to fight by another boy, he is supposed to have said: 'Stop! Tonight when I get home I'll ask my mother for permission to fight, and if she says yes, we will meet again.'[6]

An important influence on Louis' formative years must have been his father's image. The elder Riel was a vigorous, restless man, one of the most forceful spirits among the métis. He played a memorable role in the incidents of 1849 which broke the monopoly of the Hudson's Bay Company and legalized, at least to some extent, the southward flow of furs. Four métis had been caught and charged by the Company with selling furs to American buyers. Three hundred armed métis, led by Louis Riel, surrounded the courtroom on Ascension Thursday, when Guillaume Sayer was tried. The intimidated jury found the defendant guilty but recommended mercy, and Sayer was discharged without punishment. 'Le commerce est libre!' shouted the métis, and Louis Riel was a hero. Recalling these events at the end of his own life, his son wrote:

And you, my father, who overthrew a colossus of iniquities through your courage and intelligence, your name will become more famous in the whole North-West over the years. To the extent that the commerce of its peoples becomes prosperous and flourishing, your accomplishments and your sacrifices will be celebrated.[7]

Louis Riel idolized his father, and he conceived of his own political activities as a continuation of his father's work.

Yet the elder Riel was not really, over the long term, one of the leading métis. He had married into the Lagimodières, who were one of the prominent families of St Boniface; and he definitely belonged to that small, settled métis bourgeoisie which engaged in agricultural and commercial pursuits instead of the buffalo hunt and boat brigades. He farmed and raised livestock on a modest scale; and he also operated at various times a grist mill, a fulling mill, and a carding mill on the Seine River. But he was always deeply in debt to the Hudson's Bay Company, and his best efforts did not succeed in elevating him above the bottom layer of the métis bourgeoisie.[8] The insecurity of this marginal position may have helped produce his son's soaring ambition.

In a different way, Louis' mother also inspired him towards high achievement. She told the children that her name was really 'De la Gimodière,' and that they were descended from one of the noble families of France.[9] The grain of truth in this tale is very small indeed. The great-great-great grandfather of Louis Riel on his mother's side was Samuel Lecomte, sieur de la Vimaudière (as the name was then spelled). Although only a surgeon, he must have received the title of 'sieur' in recognition of some service to the French crown.[10] This is a far cry from actual descent from a wealthy and powerful house of the aristocracy. However, Louis grew up believing his mother's stories, which eventually attained major importance in his thinking.

Not surprisingly, considering that both parents had once pondered religious vocations and that the family was closely associated with bishops Provencher and Taché, the atmosphere of the home was pious. Almost the first words Louis learned to say were Jesus, Mary, and Joseph.[11] He wrote about his childhood:

My earliest years were scented with the sweet perfume of faith, for my beloved father permitted no one to speak evil in my presence. Family prayers and the rosary were always before my eyes. They were part of my nature like the air I breathe.[12]

His education was naturally conducted under religious auspices. Attendance at school and commencement of Latin studies were points of accomplishment comparable to spiritual achievements such as the first reception of the sacraments of confession, communion, and confirmation. In later life, Riel regarded these steps of Christian initiation as the preparation for his prophetic calling.[13]

His confirmation, administered on the Feast of Pentecost, 1858, was especially significant to him. He later described it to Taché in these words:

When I ascended to the railing to genuflect before you, Monseigneur, and to be confirmed, my preparation had been so well directed that there was, to the best of my knowledge, no blemish on my conscience. You yourself know with what faith we approached each other.[14]

According to one legend, when Bishop Taché administered the sacrament, he told Louis that he was a boy with a mission ahead of him, which he must not falter in performing.[15] The story is plausible, for Louis Riel was one of three métis boys chosen to be sent east to study in the seminaries of Lower Canada. Bishop Taché had made arrangements with the colleges and with certain wealthy families for the expenses to be met. It was hoped that the boys, after completing the classical curriculum, would continue on to the priesthood, and return as missionaries to the North-West. There was no native clergy in Rupert's Land, a deficiency which Taché hoped to overcome. Of the three boys who were sent, two returned to Red River within a few years, leaving Louis to carry the hopes of the community, expected to become the first métis to graduate from college and to enter the priesthood. Louis' sister Sara entered the Grey Sisters of St Boniface in 1866. When she later went to the mission at Ile-à-la-Crosse, she became the first métisse missionary nun. The inclination of the two oldest children towards the religious life suggests a powerful influence from the religious ambitions of the parents.[16]

So there was much about Louis' boyhood that he could interpret retrospectively as preparation for his mission: his parents' piety and their dreams of entering the service of the Church; his sister's vocation; his father's exploits in the Sayer affair; his mother's stories about his noble ancestry; the intellectual precocity and suitability of character which had attracted the attention of the bishop; the great favour displayed by Taché in sending him east for an education; and the hopes of the entire métis community that he would return as a missionary.

COLLEGE OF MONTREAL

Louis and his companions left St Boniface on 1 June 1858. They traveled by cart train to St Paul, a trip of twenty-eight days. When they crossed the Mississippi River, Louis met his father returning from a trip to

Montreal, where he had sought to acquire the equipment to set up a fulling mill in the Red River colony. It was the last meeting of father and son. We do not know what passed between them, save for Louis Schmidt's comment that their encounter was 'very touching.'[17]

After reaching St Paul, the boys continued their journey by steamboat and railway until they reached Montreal on 5 July. They were received at the convent of the Grey Sisters, where Riel was to be a frequent visitor in subsequent years. While the other two went on to other destinations, he stayed in Montreal to study at the College of the Sulpician Fathers.

The College of Montreal was the oldest college in the city. The Gentlemen of St Sulpice imparted with strict discipline almost the same classical education that had been taught in seventeenth-century France. An eight-year curriculum, with heavy emphasis on languages, literature, philosophy, and theology, led to the baccalaureate.[18] The program of instruction made few concessions to the modern world. It offered a great deal of Latin and Greek, of philosophy and theology, but only a smattering of natural science. Modern literature was chiefly defined as the French classics of the seventeenth century, such as the works of La Fontaine and Molière. In the eyes of an American visitor, the curriculum was '200 years behind that generally pursued in France, and 50, at least, behind that pursued in the United States.' He felt that 'lads acquire, in this institution, almost no knowledge which is of any consequence to them in subsequent life.'[19] But in education everything depends upon one's definition of utility. The Sulpicians were training their pupils as a Catholic and French-Canadian élite, proud of their difference from the English majority of North America. The classical curriculum was not only a means of education, it was a bulwark of patriotism and religion.

Riel considered it a privilege to study at the College. It was another stage in the preparation for his calling.

To the age of twenty I had the good luck to grow up not only surrounded by learned and pious teachers and by good students, but also under the guidance of one of the wisest directors of conscience in the world, the Reverend Father Delavigne, my confessor. ... the seven years I spent in that wonderful institution taught me good principles, so that my soul was filled with them.[20]

During the academic year, Riel boarded at the College. His holidays were spent with his father's sister and her husband, John and Lucie Lee of Mile End, a suburb of Montreal; with the Grey Sisters at their resi-

dence at Chateauguay; or at the mansions of the Taché family of Bouch-
erville and the Masson family of Terrebonne. He associated with the
wealthy and the powerful, he learned good manners and social polish,
and he made acquaintances who would be useful in his subsequent career.

Louis entered the second level of the College. In his first year, handi-
capped by his sketchy prairie education, he was in the lower half of his
class; but thereafter his natural endowment moved him ahead. From
week to week he was almost always in the top ten; sometimes he was
even first or second – no mean achievement for a boy from the frontier.[21]

Two schoolmates have left descriptions of his personality and character. Riel was apparently well liked by his fellows, though he held himself
slightly aloof from all except his closest friends. He tended towards dignity and gravity of bearing. He had an unusual passion for fair play, often protecting weaker students from bullies. One story about this side of
his character is particularly interesting. When once he intervened to defend an ungainly Irish youth whom the others were teasing, he said:
'Let him alone, the poor fellow, he hasn't done anything to you. Anyway
if England had made you eat as many potatoes as he has had to, you
wouldn't be any more solid on your legs than poor Quinn.'[22] In Riel's
later life, compassion for the Irish as fellow unfortunates alongside the
French Canadians within the British empire was to be a hallmark of his
thinking. The less attractive side of Riel's character was his considerable
pride and obstinacy. He became irritated when he was contradicted; 'he
never understood how someone could fail to agree with him, so convinced was he of his personal infallibility.'[23]

Until recently, this was about all that was known about Riel as a
young man, but discovery of an important manuscript now makes it
possible to say a good deal more. The Provincial Archives of Manitoba
acquired a large number of Riel family papers in 1966, including a notebook of poetry composed by Louis in the years 1864-6. Eighty pages
long, the notebook contains about three dozen poems, all but two of
which are in Riel's hand (the exceptions appear to have been written by
the girl to whom he became engaged after leaving the seminary). The
first entry is dated 15 January 1864; the last concerns Riel's departure
from Montreal, which took place on 19 June 1866. This material affords
precious insights into his youthful thinking and attitudes.[24]

One item in the collection stands out because it is in Latin. Entitled
'Incendium' or 'Fire,' it consists of seventy-eight lines of classical
hexameters.[25] Probably it was a classroom exercise which Louis pre-

served and later copied into his notebook. The poem, which describes the burning of Montreal, is based on historical fact. Details show that Riel had in mind the great fire of 7-8 June 1852, which ravaged downtown Montreal, even threatening the ships in the harbour. This fire would have been particularly memorable to the Sulpicians because it threatened their famous church of Notre Dame. The students of the College were called out to fight the fire, and formed a bucket brigade to wet down the roof of the nearby hospital, the Hôtel-Dieu. Even though he did not come to Montreal until six years later, Riel would have heard about these exciting events.

'Incendium' sheds considerable light on Riel's way of looking at the world. The first fifty lines vividly describe the devastation caused by the fire. The citizens, 'contrite for their sins,' implore God to stop the fire. 'But the judgments of heaven must first be fulfilled. The flames increase.' In Riel's poem, the fire is not only a natural disaster but a divine punishment for sin. The fire spreads because the debt of sin is not yet paid. However, the flames do not consume the whole of Montreal. When the church of Notre Dame is threatened, the people, 'their hands joined in prayer, pay homage to the ordinances of Heaven and beg Mary's aid.' She finally intervenes to save her church. The moral is that mercy comes only after men submit to Providence and acknowledge the decisions of God. Not mere regret but complete submission to heaven's decree is required. Then, and only then, do men get another chance.

Rather similar in mood is another piece entitled 'Les hommes après le déluge.'[26] Imagine the scene as the waters of the great flood recede and Noah's ark finally touches ground. The eye meets a sight of horrible destruction. 'Once smiling fields are no more than an abyss of mud scattered here and there with debris, even with human bodies half-buried in the mud.' Riel seems to take almost sadistic satisfaction in this grim spectacle. 'Everywhere tree trunks, twisted and piled up, show only a few branches, but decorated with scraps of flesh and human limbs which rot together with the foul remains of wild animals.' Noah realizes that mankind deserved this punishment for their wickedness, and that God in His mercy has saved him and his family to be the nucleus of a better race of men. In eighty lines of rather bombastic verse, he explains to his family why this catastrophe has befallen them, and consoles them by saying: 'It is from you that a happier world will be born.'

Not all the poetry in the notebook is so heavy-handed. About twenty of the pieces are fables in imitation of La Fontaine. It is not surprising that Riel tried his hand at writing fables, for the curriculum of the Col-

lege was saturated with them. The students read Aesop in Greek, Phae-
drus in Latin, and La Fontaine in French. The fable is a form of light
verse, but Riel did not think of his poetry as mere diversion or entertain-
ment. He was attracted to the fable because of its moral seriousness.
There is always a lesson to be gained from a fable, a *moralité*. In a short
piece entitled 'Fables,' Riel set forth his poetic theory.[27] He wanted his
fables to imitate those of La Fontaine, to be 'simple, good-hearted,
sincere.' The chief attraction of the fable was its candour. If it became
too subtle, too sophisticated, it might not be understood by those whom
it was intended to instruct. Riel liked fables because they depict a morally unambiguous world. The good or the clever are always rewarded,
the bad or stupid always come to a bad end. Riel understood the world
of the fable much as he apparently thought of divine Providence. He
saw a mechanism working in the universe to establish justice in the long
run, even if injustice seemed to have the upper hand at the moment.

It is ironic that Riel should have attributed this simplistic moralism to
La Fontaine when the latter, of all fabulists, managed to rise above it.
Riel faithfully imitated La Fontaine's stories and diction, but he did not
have the latter's capacity either for irony or for sadness. Riel always imposed a happy, or at least an edifying ending (of course Riel was writing
at age nineteen or twenty, while La Fontaine did not begin to compose
fables until he was almost fifty).

Let us briefly consider a few of Riel's fables. 'The Spaniel and His
Master' relates the story of an owner who will not feed his dog
properly.[28] The famished creature finally gulps a piece of poisoned meat
and dies on the spot, a proper reward for the master's stinginess. In 'The
Ant and Her Mother,' an ant ungraciously refuses to share her food with
her old mother.[29] The mother dies, but the young ant too comes to a
suitably bad end. In 'The Thief and the Wind,' one of the best written
fables, a thief, attempting to burglarize a rich farmer's house, is blown
through the trap door in the roof.[30] His fall makes so much noise that
the farmer awakes and traps him. The moral is that fortune can ruin the
most carefully laid plans.

One piece, which captures the quintessential Riel, makes a particularly good comparison with La Fontaine. Riel's poem is entitled 'The
Cat and the Mice.'[31] A tribe of mice who have been for years terrorized
by a cruel cat finally plan a concerted attack against him. They surprise
him one night and, in a fearful struggle, put out his eyes. The cat creeps
away to die while the mice 'could at least once savour the joys of
vengeance.' 'The cause of right,' concludes Riel, 'is always avenged!'

This composition may well have been inspired by La Fontaine's 'The League of Rats,' as there is a similarity of racial theme in the two poems. La Fontaine's was written about the Dutch, who made an alliance to fight France; while Riel's was a parable of conflict between English and French. In the first draft of his poem, Riel described the cat as 'anglais par la naissance' and called him 'notre saxon,' phrases which were later crossed out by another hand and replaced by 'noble par la naissance' and 'notre héros.' The unknown friend and critic wanted him to be a bit more subtle; La Fontaine's poem does not openly refer to the Dutch and French. La Fontaine is not only more subtle, he is also ironic where Riel is earnest. La Fontaine lets the rats make their league, but when it comes to a fight they are intimidated by the cat and stay in their holes. The poem thus works in two directions at once. La Fontaine celebrates the natural superiority of the French over the Dutch, while he also ironically points out that might sometimes seems to make right in this world. But such subtlety was foreign to Riel. His poem is a straight morality play. Those who abuse their power by preying on the weak are overturned in the end.

The fables are then not so very far in spirit from 'Incendium' and 'Les hommes après le déluge.' In all cases, Riel is depicting a morally deterministic world, in which Providence sees to it that good and evil get their appropriate deserts. Gilles Martel has recently dubbed this mode of thought Riel's 'conscience némésiaque.'[32] In Greek mythology, Nemesis was the goddess who carried out the sentences passed by the gods against mortals who broke divine commandments. She represented a kind of automatic balance in the universe by which man's pride was brought low. Of course Riel's 'conscience némésiaque' was Christian, not pagan. He thought not in terms of goddesses or forces but in the categories of Providence; and he believed that punishment and reward might come after life, in heaven, hell, or purgatory, as well as on earth. But, although distinct from one another, the Greek and Christian views are variations on the same theme of a reasonable universe where goodness is rewarded and wickedness brings retribution.

Riel never lost his faith in Providence. He never ceased to believe that God would punish the oppressors and comfort the afflicted. He always interpreted his own sorrows not as tragic misfortune but as a deliberate trial set up by God to test him. If he could endure and submit to 'heaven's decrees,' success would be his. These attitudes became the basis on which he later built his new religion, which predicted that redemption would come as a reward for his sufferings.

ALLEGED INSANITY

The first sharp test of Riel's confidence in Providence was the death of his father on 21 January 1864. Louis was so shattered at the news that he was advised not to write home until he had regained his composure. When after some days he did send a letter to his family it was an out-pouring of grief, but sorrow was tempered by faith.[33] Riel found consolation in the old adage that the Lord loves those whom He chastises. 'Let us weep,' he wrote, 'but let our hearts be strong; let us think of God: He loves us, for He has terribly afflicted us.' And further: 'You know, dear mother, brothers, and sisters, when God acts it is always with generosity. Let us adore him then! May He be blessed, glorified! ... Love the hand of God; whatever it does, it is always paternal.' Although Riel was very sad, he was able to keep up with his school work. He wrote to his mother on 21 March that he had just passed his trimester examinations with good marks, thanks to the help of St Joseph.[34] He received a report of 'très bien' in philosophy and 'bien' in physics and chemistry. Even if he was profoundly shaken by his father's death, he must have retained his presence of mind and self-control.

During the first half of 1864 he also spent time relaxing with his aunt and uncle, the Lees. John Lee later recalled:

That death [of Riel's father] caused him extraordinary sorrow. He was then at the College of Montreal, and my wife and I brought him out to give him consolation. [But] that death had so touched his heart that he was inconsolable. I perceived then that this profound sorrow was affecting his brain and that he was delirious [battait la campagne]. That was obvious in his exaggerations and religious eccentricities; for he threw himself into excesses of piety and spoke in language on religious matters which I found unreasonable. My wife noticed the same thing and mentioned it to me. Afterwards, he remained very melancholic; I observed that to last about a year or a year and a half, after which he became his old self again.[35]

This episode, said Lee, presented the first 'signs of mental alienation' in his nephew. It raises the question of whether Riel did in fact go through a period of unusual behaviour after his father's death.

Obviously the death was much on Riel's mind, as is evident in the notebook of poetry discussed above, almost all of which was written after it. There is an almost morbid fascination with death in 'Les hommes après le déluge,' and about ten of the fables deal explicitly with death. This may not seem unusual since death is a common occurrence in the fables of all authors. But three of Riel's poems deal with a certain kind of death, namely the unhappy end of the unrepentant sinner. In 'The Sexagenarian' (1 July 1864), an old man decides that he will die as sinfully as he has lived: 'Do you think I can die/otherwise than I have lived?'[36] In 'The Dying Lion' (3 July 1864), the king of beasts, who has long terrorized all the lesser animals, gets the kind of death he deserves, 'a tyrant's reward.'[37] And in a verse story without a title, written 1 May 1865, Riel narrates the death of a hypocrite.[38] His external piety does not save him; the priest arrives too late to give absolution, and the hypocrite's soul goes to hell. Riel had written to his mother that he had no doubts that his father's soul was now in heaven; but was he as confident as he tried to appear?

Riel's fables also emphasize another theme which may possibly be autobiographical, the relation of child and parents. I have already mentioned 'The Ant and Her Mother,' which deals with filial ingratitude. Another example is 'The Rat and His Mother,' which describes a young rat who unintentionally injures his mother's eye.[39] He is overcome with sorrow and indeed, in the long run, suffers more than his mother. The moral holds this up as an example of filial piety, and says that men would become more human if they would imitate the good conduct of the rat. Riel ends by cautioning children in strong terms against ingratitude.

Other poems about relations between generations are 'The Young and the Old Cocks,' in which a young rooster proves to be just as vain as his father; and 'The Son and His Father,' in which a young man, desirous of becoming rich, ignores his father's advice about generosity and ends by becoming 'more avaricious than Harpagon,' Molière's famous miser.[40] Having become rich, he lets his old father end his days in poverty. This conclusion seems to thrust close to home for Riel. Was he perhaps reproaching himself for pursuing his own career in Canada while his father was dying in Red River?

All of these poems portray situations of discord between parent and offspring. Either the child is ungrateful and injures the parent, or the parent himself has given a bad example to the child. It is common for children to have ambivalent feelings about their parents; resentment of the older generation is a normal part of growing up. But Riel's moral code did not allow any open expression of hostility towards his parents. If he had such emotions at times, he may have been put in an exceedingly painful position by his father's death. He had not seen his father since he left Red River at fourteen, and now he would never have another opportunity to atone for his adolescent feelings against paternal authority. His deep grief, undoubtedly genuine, was perhaps pushed to exaggeration by disquieting feelings of guilt.

However, in all of this there is nothing particularly unusual or even remotely insane. Riel tried to master his sorrow, and his poetry provided a valuable outlet for ambivalent emotions that otherwise could not be expressed. What then do we make of the remark of his uncle that Riel showed signs of 'mental alienation' at this time? Should it be given much weight? It was made twenty years after the fact and in the context of a polemic in which Lee was trying to prove that Riel should not have been executed in 1885. Given the circumstances, the remark about signs of insanity might be taken as an exaggeration.

However, the question cannot be settled so quickly. It is now accepted in the literature that around 1865 Riel became deranged, believing himself to be someone other than Louis Riel, and endowing himself with a messianic role. This story seems to have its origin with Dr Daniel Clark, the Toronto alienist who testified at Riel's trial. According to Clark:

In 1865 he wrote to a clerical friend in the northwest, that he was not Louis Riel, but somebody else. He claimed that he was David Mordecai, a Jew, and was born in Marseilles, France. He came over to Canada when he was only a mere child. His appearance was so like that of Louis Riel that they might be taken for twins. *The* Louis Riel was thrown overboard from a steamer on the Mississippi and he was put in his place. So alike were they that even those in charge of the child did not detect the deception. His guardians did the foul deed, because his parents had left him immense wealth, and they wished to secure the property for themselves. He was not Louis Riel, and not the rightful heir of an immense estate, which had been acquired in this way. Being a Jew it was his duty to redeem the race, and rectify the wrongs which had been done. He was a second Saviour sent in these latter days to not only succour Jews but also Gentiles, from temporal, political and spiritual bondage.[41]

Clark is also the source of several other anecdotes about Riel's youth. The doctor claimed that Bishop Taché showed him letters from Riel 'of a boastful and presumptuous nature,' in which the young man asked for money to carry out missionary work. These letters contained such 'monstrous demands' and were full of such 'hare-brained projects' that Taché decided to have him dismissed from the seminary and sent home. Before returning to Red River, Riel was guilty of some 'fantastic tricks' in Montreal. Making himself out to be a 'second Loyola,' he demanded money from numerous people, old friends and benefactors as well as strangers on the street. Then he wrote to his widowed mother, telling her to 'sell all the chattels she could' and meet him in St Paul, Minnesota. The foolish woman complied, but when she arrived Louis was still in Montreal.[42]

Since Dr Clark is the only witness for these tales, their authenticity should be carefully examined. Let us begin with a few considerations about Clark himself, who was then superintendent of the Toronto Asylum for the Insane. A well-known alienist and frequent expert witness at trials involving the plea of insanity, he was called as a witness by Riel's attorneys in 1885. He left Toronto on 25 July, examined the prisoner on 28 and 29 July, testified on 30 July, and was back in Toronto on 6 August.[43] He stopped in Winnipeg on the way back and met Archbishop Taché, as well as certain friends and relatives of Riel. Subsequently Dr Clark made several long statements to the Toronto press about Riel and read two papers to psychiatric audiences in the United States.

There is no question that Clark felt strongly about the case. He firmly believed Riel insane, he wished to prevent the execution, and afterwards he used the case as an example in his crusade for abandonment of the McNaghten Rules. Clark's involvement was polemical, and he would naturally have been receptive to any information tending to support his diagnosis of lunacy. His ideas on the etiology of mental illness favoured physical causation. He called for a post mortem autopsy of Riel's brain, and he thought it relevant to say that Riel was an 'inveterate masturbator,' which he learned from 'those well qualified to know.'[44] He described Riel's mother as 'semi-imbecile' and Riel's father as 'ill-balanced, whose hot passions bordered on insanity,' implying that the insanity might be inherited.[45] Furthermore, Clark held that insanity usually manifested itself in delirious episodes alternating with periods of normality. Thus it would have been congenial to his view to find evidence of youthful aberrations in Riel, which would establish the alternating pattern supposedly characteristic of insanity.

Unfortunately for Clark's credibility, there are several difficulties in his account. First, he claimed to have seen letters written by Riel when the latter was about seventeen. Clark did visit Taché, and the bishop did show him correspondence from Riel, for three existing letters can be identified from the description Clark gave of them.[46] But there are no letters in St Boniface written by Louis Riel before 1869, except the two he sent to his family after his father's death. If Clark did see correspondence from this early part of Riel's life, the documents have now vanished. Second, at least one thing Clark said is demonstrably false. Riel was not withdrawn from the College of Montreal at Taché's request, he was dismissed by the director for infractions of house rules. Third, other of Clark's stories are improbable, to say the least. In the mid-1860s, Julie Riel was a poor widow with eight children on her hands. There is not a shred of evidence that she agreed to 'sell all the chattels she could,' and cart her youngsters off to St Paul. (Perhaps Clark got this idea from examination of some of Riel's correspondence from the mid-1870's, when a move to Minnesota was actually discussed.) Fourth, the stories about Louis' conduct in Montreal are not impossible, but they appear to be a distorted account of his attempt to find a career for himself after leaving the seminary. Considering all this, one would want independent corroboration before accepting anything reported by Clark.

By this criterion, most of Clark's material can be dismissed except the Mordecai story, which is supported by fragmentary evidence. There is a communication from Riel to Taché dated 8 January 1878, in which he wrote that God was punishing him 'for having called himself a Jew' when he was 'still young.'[47] The rest of the letter relates how Riel decided not to enter the priesthood, and how his conscience was plagued by that decision for years. But there are no further details reminiscent of the Mordecai story. Dr Clark was apparently shown this letter, but he could not have found all his 'facts' there. Where did he gather his information?

In the notebook of poetry discussed earlier, there is a piece entitled 'Le Juif de Marseille.'[48] The text is undated but its location in the notebook suggests that it was composed in late 1865 or 1866. The poem describes a foundling, 'born on the beach of Marseilles,' who is raised by wealthy Jewish parents. Naturally he also becomes a Jew, an 'enemy of Jesus Christ.' But then God, wishing to redeem him, deprives him of his wealth while, in some unknown way, also converting him to Christianity. Now the Jew carries a new name, and no one knows of his Jewish upbringing. He has suffered a great deal, and sometimes regrets his lost family and wealth. But he prefers the grace of Christ to the 'favours of a sullied people.' He trusts in Providence and submits himself to Jesus Christ.

The contents of this poem bear some resemblance to Clark's story of David Mordecai. Common to both are the reference to Marseilles and the themes of wealth, inheritance, a change from Judaism to Christianity, and concealed identity. Yet there is a good deal in Clark's account that is absent in Riel's youthful composition: murder, twins, the Mississippi River, and the messianic role. Either Clark invented these details, or he had access to documents which have disappeared.

If Clark's Mordecai story is true, Riel must have gone through a very grave emotional crisis. To believe such things about oneself is at least as great a departure from rationality as Riel's later prophetic inspirations. If he struck people as mad in 1876, he should have given a similar impression in 1865. But no one who knew Riel at that time recorded anything so unusual, with the exception of his uncle; and that brief reference is far removed from the flagrant delusions of the Mordecai story. Other people who knew Riel in these years called him taciturn, melancholy, concerned about his future, rebellious, a bit excitable and feather-brained but not mad. A final consideration is that years afterward, when Riel developed unconventional religious views, they bore little or no resemblance to the Mordecai story. He did affirm a special connection with the Jewish people, but not in the way reported by Clark. All in all, given the paucity of primary evidence and the unreliability of Dr Clark as a witness, Riel deserves the benefit of the doubt.

This is a matter of considerable importance, because if such fantastic delusions were produced in young Louis by word of his father's decease, he would seem to have been naturally rather unstable and prone to mental disorder. Indeed, the Mordecai story has been used to support this thesis in a recent psychoanalytic commentary on Riel.[49] But in the absence of solid evidence, such a theory is conjectural at best.

RIEL'S 'FALL'

What happened to Riel between his father's death and his return to Red River in the summer of 1868? The critical event in these years, which in large measure determined the further course of his life, was his departure from the College of Montreal on 8 March 1865, a few months before completion of his baccalaureate. Historians have usually assumed that his exit from school was somehow connected with his father's death. Stanley writes: 'It would almost seem that he became completely obsessed with the weight of his new responsibility as head of the family, and yielded to the nagging anxieties of what he would do with his life.'[50] There is probably some truth in this view, but there is another dimension to the question, as the recently discovered poetry makes clear.

The notebook includes four consecutive love poems which seem to concern Riel himself. Unfortunately none is explicitly dated. However, they follow a piece which is marked 3 July 1864; and the next dated entry, several poems later, is 9 March 1865. It is reasonable to deduce that the love poems were composed in the interval, since almost all dates in the book are entered in proper chronological order.

It has long been known that Riel became engaged to Marie-Julie Guernon of Mile End; but for lack of other evidence, it was assumed the romance began only after Riel's dismissal from the College. However, the poems make it seem likely that Riel fell in love in 1864, probably during the summer holidays, when he would have spent time with his aunt and uncle, neighbours of the Guernon family.

The poems follow a logical progression. The first, 'Un jeune malade,'[51] depicts a dying young man who calls to his love not to forget him after he is gone. He asks her to visit his grave and shed a tear in memory of what might have been. The sickness which prevents the young man from fulfilling his love is a metaphor for Riel's religious vocation. As a future priest, he should not let himself yield to the attractions of concupiscence.

The second composition shows him having overcome his reluctance and wooing the girl, who resists his suit.[52] Marie, as she is named in the text, tells him that love is too fickle, and that she is afraid to be tied down to vows which last too long. She also says that her mother is opposed. But Riel finally overcomes her reluctance by resorting to the ancient stratagem of flattery:

> Aimable et fière demoiselle,
> Vous pouvez compter sur vos traits.
> Comme vous, lorsqu'on est si belle
> Les amants ne trompent jamais.

The girl blushes at these words, and the poet knows that he has won her heart.

The third poem, which is very brief, perhaps only a fragment of a longer piece, continues the theme of the mother's opposition. She says that her daughter is too well bred for the suitor, whom she calls a 'bandit.'[53] The cause of the mother's hostility is not specified, but we may presume it was Riel's mixed blood, his poverty, or both.

The fourth poem is a lyrical expression of happiness called 'Le Merveilleux.'[54] Riel does not directly refer to his love affair, but in the context of the other pieces the implication is that he has finally won the girl's consent. Perhaps drawing on the memory of visits to the country estates of his benefactors, the poet pictures himself as a rural bumpkin privileged to enjoy the luxuries of a grand château. He has grasped the secret of happiness: love.

Louis' feelings were reciprocated. Another hand, presumably that of Marie-Julie, has entered two love poems in the notebook. Both are farewell pieces, perhaps written on occasions when Louis was getting ready to leave Mile End to return to the College. The poems, conventional in their imagery and phrasing, are written with numerous errors of grammar and spelling. For example:

Premier Couplait

Comme l'éperle et les étoiles
Horne d'ége le font des cieux,
La nuit étant partout c'est voile
Le sommeille me fermis mes yeux
Reviendera tu. Dans un doux songe
Haut mon bell ange[55]

Translated into conventional French, this would read:

Comme les perles et les étoiles
Ornent déjà le fond des cieux
La nuit étend partout ses voiles
Le sommeil me ferme les yeux
Reviendras-tu dans un doux songe
O mon bel ange?

One can hardly help wondering why Riel, with his excellent education, would have been attracted to a girl of such spectacular illiteracy.

It is unclear whether Riel was impelled more by his love or by concern for his family in Red River, but in any case he began seriously to consider a secular career. At the end of 1864, he went to see John Atkinson to inquire about employment. Atkinson was the commercial agent of Madame Sophie Masson, who had long been one of Riel's patrons. Atkinson wrote to Madame Masson:

He informed me that it was his intention, if approved by his friends, to remain in Montreal for some years, and he was undecided whether to take a profession or enter a store. I told him that I was under the impression that he would enter the Church. He told me no, that his tastes led him into the world as he hoped at some future day to be able to assist in settling his young brothers and sisters.[56]

By February 1865 Riel had become so preoccupied with his future that he refused to live any longer at the College. He wished to move in with the Grey Sisters, where he would be freer to come and go and to look for work. The director of the College opposed this plan but finally gave in. However, Riel's behaviour at the Sisters' did not improve. Sometimes he did not come back to the convent at night. He even stayed away from classes for fifteen days, saying untruthfully that he was sick. When interrogated by the director, he admitted he was actually spending his time in Montreal looking for a job. He was warned once, and when his absences recommenced, the director dismissed him 'for continual infractions of the rules of the institution.'[57]

Why did Riel act so strangely, both furtive and defiant at the same time? He had told John Atkinson that he was concerned about supporting his younger brothers and sisters; but that reason is not convincing because it fails to explain his sense of urgency. Once he was dismissed from the College, he made no particular effort to help his family in Red River. He went instead to his aunt and uncle, where he could also be near Marie. It is more sensible to suppose that Riel began his frantic search for a job because he knew that establishing himself was his only chance of overcoming Madame Guernon's opposition. The delicate state of his love affair prevented him from being candid with people about his intentions.

Riel's actions were certainly foolish and hasty, but youth is prone to rashness. He must have found the disciplined environment of the College hard to bear once he had given up his notions of a religious vocation. He may have half-intentionally provoked his expulsion; for trimester examinations were coming up in mid-March, and he could not hope to do well because his mind had not been on his school work. The day after his dismissal he wrote a poem which exhibits his feeling of rebelliousness. The poem is about the director of a college who unfairly condemns a student 'notwithstanding perfect innocence.'[58] The pupil's only fault is a small one – he is too independent and self-reliant. But that is enough to get him in trouble. The director, hardly able to restrain himself in his authoritarian prejudice ... Unfortunately the text breaks off here, several pages having been ripped from the scribbler.

Riel remained in Montreal for over a year after leaving school. Not very much is known about what he did in these months, but obviously his first concern had to be to secure his future. One may guess he explored many possibilities in the summer of 1865, but the only plan of which we have any record is that he wanted to set himself up as a fur trader in Red River, backed by Montreal capital. Our slim knowledge of this scheme comes from two letters by Father Vandenberghe, inspector of the Oblate missions, who happened to be in Montreal. 'Riel also came to see me,' Vandenberghe wrote on 16 July to Bishop Taché:

He told me his history and how he finds himself in possession of a thousand pounds sterling for doing business in furs at Red River. I must say his story seems extraordinary to me, I don't know whether to believe it or not. An Englishman is supposed to have offered him a thousand pounds on the simple word of an unknown. Poor boy! When I saw him with his shaggy hair and his too fashionable airs, I accorded him little confidence. He should have written to you.[59]

On 18 August, Vandenberghe reported that Riel had come to see him again, and was planning to leave Montreal on 8 September. The priest added that he felt only pity for the young man. 'I see he wants to make his fortune and I greatly fear that he will cast his net in waters he has not sounded.'[60]

Riel's activities in the summer of 1865 may be the basis of Dr Daniel Clark's anecdotes about his eccentric behaviour in Montreal. He may have done some foolish things if he was trying to raise money and launch himself in business on little more than bravado.

Riel did not depart on 8 September. On the 13th of that month the Superior of the Grey Sisters of Montreal wrote to St Boniface, where Sara Riel lived as a nun, that Louis had not fulfilled his intention. She commented: 'That young man is incomprehensible and his conduct is really dubious. I believe the poor child has no sense. He needs someone to guide him and follow him, and here he is left to himself. None of his former friends has confidence in him now; I'm afraid he will do himself harm. Pray for him.'[61]

By November, if we may judge from a verse epistle which he sent to the director of the Petit Séminaire de Montréal, Riel was beginning to regret his precipitous departure from the College.[62] Most of the poem is a mournful lament about the passage of time:

Le temps vole et se précipite
Hélas! Rien ne peut l'arrêter!

Il entraîne tout dans sa fuite.
En vain veut-on lui résister.

These are melancholy sentiments for a young man who has just had his twenty-first birthday. Riel was probably depressed about his prospects since he could not find suitable employment. The college, which had once seemed so restrictive, now appeared in the haze of nostalgia as a secure refuge which he had been foolish to leave. Others had come to take his place and receive the privileges which had been his. 'You who follow in my footsteps,' he admonished the younger students, 'be sure to enjoy what I enjoyed.'

The poem was a peace offering. It was written on 4 November, the feast of St Charles Borromeo, namesake of Father Charles Lenoir-Rolland, director of the College. Riel addressed him as 'Honoré-Directeur' and signed: 'I remain, Monsieur le Directeur, with the deepest respect and a great gratitude, he who cherishes your protection, Louis Riel.' This humble demeanour was far removed from the defiance he had displayed in March. Perhaps he hoped that the Sulpicians might help him in some way.

Riel tried another plan early in 1865. Through his poetry he would approach the leading French-Canadian politician, George-Etienne Cartier, to ask for work. Most government jobs were then filled by patronage, and people in power were accustomed to letters from young men. Cartier, with his railway connections as well as his cabinet position of attorney-general, was well situated to find something for a job-seeker. Poetry, it seemed to Riel, might be the ideal way to gain the great man's favour; for from his college days Cartier had been in the habit of writing verse. He was the author of the famous song, 'O Canada, mon pays, mes amours,' as well as 'Avant Tout Soyons Canadiens,' which was sung by the Sons of Liberty in 1837. Cartier had attended the College of Montreal and it is also said that Riel had met Cartier socially, an occurrence which is not improbable but is not verified.[63] In any case, Cartier was a logical target for Riel's petitions.

The first letter, written on 5 January 1866, struck a confident note.[64] Riel compared himself to Vergil and Cartier to Macaenas, the famous Roman patron of the arts. After a couple of pages of this sort of thing, Riel came to the point. He requested a white-collar job of the type that politicians were accustomed to fill through patronage appointments:

S'il est à la douane un service vacant,
A la poste aussi bien, à quelque banque autant.

Riel waited for seven weeks but received no reply from his intended patron, so he wrote again, this time in a more subdued vein, to ask for an interview.[65] 'When the hour is opportune, could I have the privilege of a short audience?' Much of the poem is devoted to celebrating the greatness of Cartier's achievements and the honours he has gathered. Riel took the opportunity to congratulate him on just having been received into the Bar of Upper Canada. He also sympathized with him over the criticism heaped upon him by the opponents of Confederation, and told him not to pay attention. He frankly contrasted his own miserable position to that of Cartier:

Mais quoi! Je ne suis rien! Je languis et j'attends!
La triste oisiveté consume tout mon temps.
Et que puis-je? Ignoré, sans aucune assistance
Désœuvré seul, réduit à vivre d'espérance?

When even this pathetic confession produced no results, Riel wrote a third time.[66] He pictured himself as a tragic hero afflicted by fate, condemned to suffer amid his uncaring fellow men. Riel was indeed caught in a painful quandary. He had given up his future in the Church, but he had not yet managed to launch a secular career. Yet he vowed that he would never give up, no matter how hopeless matters seemed. 'Tenacity will be my God,' he declared. In this mood of melancholy defiance he wrote this third letter, his last, despairing appeal to Cartier.

While Riel was seeking to establish himself in Montreal, his family in the West naturally was worried about him. No letters survive from this period; it may be that Riel wrote infrequently, or not at all. His sister Sara, now a novice with the Grey Sisters of St Boniface, wrote to the nuns at Montreal to see if they knew what Louis was doing. The sister superior replied on 13 March 1866:

It is natural that you share the concern of your good mother about your dear brother Louis. In fact, the poor child worries us too and we do not know what to think of him. He was supposed to leave for Red River in the month of September, but it does not appear that he has yet left Montreal, and God knows what he's doing. Pray hard for him that he does not go astray, for young people here are very exposed to temptation.[67]

Even as these words were written, Riel was fulfilling their prophecy. He took a position reading law in the firm of Rodolphe Laflamme, *rouge*, anti-clerical, anti-Confederationist, and a strong opponent of Cartier.[68]

It would be intriguing to know more about this, since for Riel to associate himself with a man like Laflamme meant a break with the principles under which he had been educated by the Sulpicians. Perhaps he was so anxious for work he would have taken anything regardless of political implications.

There is an unsubstantiated tradition that Riel did not like legal work. It rests on a statement of a friend that 'Louis, as a lawyer, would have had his office in his hat and would have received his customers on the top of Mount Royal.'[69] Even if Riel was not too happy reading law, it seems he was prepared to see it through; for he began to take steps towards his marriage. On 12 June 1866, he and Marie-Julie Guernon signed a marriage contract, which he would probably not have done if he had not expected to continue with Laflamme. The contract called for separation of property, specifying that 'there will be no community of goods between the said future spouses, whether of those which belong to them now or whether of those which will accrue to them hereafter.' Neither of the partners would be responsible for the other's debts, and Riel gave up any right to demand a dowry from the bride's family.[70] But Marie's parents were not mollified. They forbade the marriage, and Riel left Montreal for good on 19 June exactly one week after the contract had been signed.

There is reason to believe that the entire romance was secret. Although Riel had a number of friends in Montreal, none of them later referred, at least in public, to his romance. The existence of Riel's engagement was only discovered a century later by George Stanley through a descendant of Marie-Julie.[71] Probably Riel explained to his friends that his abrupt departure from Montreal was caused by homesickness; at least that is what they subsequently said. But that reason would be more plausible if Riel had gone directly home to Red River, which in fact he did not do for two more years. His departure was an expression of chagrin at his defeat, at his failure to make a place for himself in Canada. The collapse of his marriage was the ultimate symbol of his rejection.

Riel did not leave Montreal without filling up the last two pages of his notebook. He composed two farewell poems, one to his friends and one to his beloved.[72] The first speaks of his sorrow at leaving the city where he had spent eight years, and of his desire to see his native land, his family, and the tomb of his father. The second poem makes clear that he had no intention of returning. His romance was finished:

Adieu! Adieu! ma fiancée
C'est en vain que tu m'attends.

Consider the significance of these events in Riel's life. He had left the College and given up his religious vocation for a life in the world: marriage and a career. But then his marriage plans collapsed, causing him to give up the legal career which it had been so difficult to begin. He who had come to Montreal with such high hopes at fourteen departed at twenty-one with nothing to show for his years of effort.

How did Riel himself interpret these bitter disappointments? We cannot be certain of what he thought at the time, but two texts demonstrate his retrospective view. In 1885, he portrayed these years as a fall from grace:

It is true that subsequently [ie, after attending the College of Montreal] I fell, sadly and profoundly. But my first communion, my holy confirmation, the good education given me by my family and college, had their good effects. The tempest of passions raged and wanted to seduce me so that I might be lost, but I remained, thanks to God, anchored in the port of salvation. Thanks to divine grace, I was led at the right time to approach the confessional and the Eucharist. I am confident this will save me.[73]

Unfortunately we are not told what constituted this 'fall.' Was it his love affair, the renunciation of his vocation, expulsion from the College, or something else?

A statement of 1876 is somewhat more explicit. Riel wrote to Taché in dramatic terms reminiscent of St Paul's description of his famous experience on the road to Damascus:

At the age of twenty [Riel's twentieth birthday was 23 October 1864], when I was just about to stray from the correct path, I was one day suddenly struck and thrown almost lifeless to the ground. Not having yet made a retreat about my decision and being disturbed about the subject of my vocation, I was afraid; but in falling I had time to say to God: 'Lord, give me ten years in the world and I will leave it.'[74]

This passage makes clear that Riel was deeply troubled about giving up his vocation to the priesthood. Yet it is hard to accept as authentic his promise to stay in the world only ten years; this seems like a retrospective embellishment. If he was in love and contemplating marriage, he can scarcely have intended to return to the priesthood after a decade.

In any event, it is apparent that his actions, particularly the renunciation of his vocation, produced in Riel a powerful sense of guilt. But the guilt was tied to an equally powerful desire for greatness. In Riel's providential view of life, his fall could be a *felix culpa*, a 'fortunate sin,' if he obediently accepted the suffering it entailed. It could be a preparation for even greater achievement in the future. The hopes of his youth could still be fulfilled.

RETURN TO RED RIVER

We know almost nothing of Riel's life between his departure from Montreal on 19 June 1866, and his return to Red River on 26 July 1868. He apparently did not communicate with his family for much of this time. On 25 January 1868, Sara Riel wrote to her sister Marie: 'Louis hasn't written to me, I can't imagine what's causing this long silence, let's pray for him.'[75] Riel's 'long silence' may well have been the result of embarrassment over his lack of accomplishment in the East.

According to Louis Schmidt, Riel 'lived for some time with Louis Fréchette in Chicago. There they both wrote poetry, Fréchette trying to imitate Hugo and Riel Lamartine.'[76] There is no other confirmation for this statement, which moreover is suspect because of its wording. Riel's schoolfriend Eustache Prud'homme published a brief memoir in 1870 in which he reminisced about how he and Riel used to write poetry together. They had agreed that his verse resembled that of Lamartine, while Riel's bore a similarity to that of Hugo.[77] Schmidt seems to have drawn on this statement while distorting the details. Riel's own description of these years is anything but informative:

Left Montreal 19th June 1866. Came to St Paul, lived in Minneapolis, St Anthony and Saint Paul 2 years. Left St Anthony in July 68 and came to St Joe, Dakota.[78]

Nothing further is known for certain. Riel must have worked to support himself; it is said that he was for a time a clerk in a dry goods store.[79]

Although his prospects in the States were not particularly bright, there was no future in Red River to draw him back. When he did finally return, on 26 July 1868, it was because the disastrous years of 1867-8, when grasshoppers picked the fields clean and the buffalo herds retired beyond the Missouri, threatened the very survival of his mother and the younger children.

Once more united with his family in St Vital, Riel invited Louis Schmidt to come for a long visit. Schmidt accepted, and the two naturally discussed the changes impending for the colony as a result of

Canada's intention to purchase it from the Hudson's Bay Company. They resolved to 'become involved in public affairs' when the time came.[80]

Riel took his first step in that direction by sending a letter to a Montreal newspaper, *Le Nouveau Monde*. It was a reply to the poet Charles Mair, who had published an open letter in the English newspapers praising the fertility of the soil in Red River and inviting settlers from Ontario to come. He had also made some deprecatory remarks about the métis who, he said, were suffering famine only because of their own improvidence. Riel defended his people, at the same time pointing out that life in the West would not be as easy and pleasant for white settlers as Mair made it seem.[81]

Public affairs aside, Riel had to help provide for his family. On 7 September, we find him ready to leave for St Cloud, the southern terminus of the cart trains.[82] Louis Schmidt has bought a few oxen to set himself up as a freighter, and has invited Riel to join the venture. Louis agrees at first but later withdraws.[83] Why? His sister notes that he is afflicted with 'sad and tormenting thoughts,' but we get no clue as to what they are.[84]

The winter is severe but not fatal for the Riels. Their harvest of grain and potatoes has failed two years in a row, but they still have three bulls, three milk cows, and five calves, as well as five horses – a goodsized herd of livestock by métis standards. They can feed themselves, although they are compelled to accept seed grain in the spring from the famine relief committee. Over the winter Louis buys a plot of land, paying in barter with a two-year-old ox, 100 pounds of beef, twenty-two aspen logs, and one pelt.[85] He must be planning to farm. Yet his friends in St Paul are expecting to see him next summer.[86] He also writes in March to an unidentified 'Monsieur' that, if the latter is still prepared to hire him, he is ready to leave Red River.[87] His plans must have been uncertain; and had the sale of Rupert's Land to Canada not intervened, he might well have gone back to the United States to continue his search for suitable employment. Certainly, neither he nor anyone else could have suggested that within a year he would be President of the Provisional Government of Red River.

2
Testing

Louis Riel earned his first taste of glory in the insurrection of 1869-70. Those events have been well described by historians, so they will only be briefly recalled here. Our attention will be focused upon the effects which the insurrection and its aftermath produced in Riel's image of himself. He played only a political role in 1869-70. Although he was a loyal member of the Roman Catholic Church, his chief concerns were political, not religious. But by 1875 he conceived himself as more of a prophet than a politician. The story of those intervening years was one of repeated disappointments in politics, which eventually turned Riel's energies in the direction of religion.

RED RIVER 'REBELLION'

It had long been clear that the Hudson's Bay Company could not hold Prince Rupert's Land in perpetuity. Shortly after Confederation, a sale was arranged to Canada, with transfer of control to take place officially on 1 December 1869. The negotiations were conducted in London, and no effort was made to consult or inform the 10,000 inhabitants of the Red River colony. The métis were particularly worried about becoming part of Canada because they feared that the religious and linguistic balance of the colony would be upset by massive immigration from Ontario.

They formed a National Committee of the Métis of Red River, with John Bruce as president and Louis Riel as secretary, to defend their interests. In October they refused to allow William McDougall, the new Canadian governor, to enter the colony until the terms of transfer had been discussed with Ottawa. Early in November they seized control of Fort Garry. A convention was held later that month with delegates of the English-speaking parishes to seek a joint course of action. A tentative compromise was reached, but it dissolved when McDougall issued his famous proclamation of 1 December, declaring the transfer complete. Instructions from the prime minister to McDougall, forbidding him to make this pronouncement, were already in the mail but had not yet reached the West. In reaction against McDougall's proclamation, the métis declared a Provisional Government on 8 December. Louis Riel became president late that month.

A complicated series of events during the winter ratified Riel's control of Red River. Although Sir John A. Macdonald did not like it, he had little choice but to deal with the insurgents. The métis had made their move at the beginning of winter, and absence of suitable transportation made it impossible for Canada to put an armed force in the field before the next summer. Sir John feared that in the meantime the colony might invite the Americans in, making it impossible for Canada to take possession of her purchase. Thus he was compelled to send delegates to Red River, first the Abbé Thibault and Colonel de Salaberry, then Donald A. Smith, chief officer of the Hudson's Bay Company in Canada.

Smith was a clever adversary and almost undercut Riel's position, but the latter managed to maintain his power. A convention held in the bitter cold of January created a second Provisional Government, this time with the participation of the English. Riel was again named president. There were two attempts, led by the Canadian faction within the colony, to overthrow Riel by force of arms – one in December, one in February. Although both were successfully put down by the métis, they led to catastrophe for Riel through the execution of Thomas Scott. Scott participated in both uprisings of the Canadian faction. Imprisoned after the first attempt, he escaped and took part in the second, after which he was again jailed. In custody the second time, Scott was difficult to control and repeatedly antagonized his métis guards. Riel, on the request of his men, set up a court martial which condemned Scott to death.

Cooler heads advised against the execution. The Reverend George Young, Father Lestanc, and Donald A. Smith intervened on behalf of the condemned prisoner. But Riel was inflexible. He seems to have felt that an act of capital punishment would demonstrate the authority of the Provisional Government. 'We must make Canada respect us,' he told Smith.[1] He had earlier condemned to death Major Boulton, the leader of the abortive second uprising of the Canadian faction, but had relented when others pleaded for the major's life. Now Riel was determined to show that his government possessed the sovereign authority of a state.

He calculated that this act would put down internal resistance once and for all and would compel the Canadian government to negotiate in good faith. The sentence was carried out by firing squad on 4 March 1870.

The execution was a ghastly mistake. For one thing it was morally repugnant because of the procedures followed. Scott was hastily tried for an unclear offense; he had no legal assistance nor did he enjoy any other benefits of fair play. He could not even understand the proceedings, which were conducted in French. The alleged legal deficiencies of Riel's own trial fifteen years later pale by comparison. Furthermore the execution of Scott was unnecessary even on grounds of political necessity. The Provisional Government was well established by then, while the Canadian party was in disarray. No object lesson in intimidation was needed. If Scott was hard to manage, he could have been controlled by other means. In the long run, the Scott affair brought about Riel's downfall. When English Canadians learned of Scott's fate, there was widespread outrage; and Riel became such a controversial figure that he was prevented from having a future in Canadian politics.

But in March 1870, all this lay unforeseen in the future, while the pressing need was to conclude negotiations with Ottawa. A delegation of three, of whom the most forceful member was Riel's mentor Father Ritchot, set out for the East late that month. They carried with them a comprehensive set of demands. The new territory should enter Confederation as a self-governing province. There should be guarantees for the French language and Catholic religion modeled upon those prevailing in the Province of Quebec. The half-breeds should receive a land-grant settlement to extinguish the aboriginal land title they had inherited from their Indian forebears. Macdonald and Cartier, who conducted the discussions on behalf of the government, were quickly able to reach an acceptable compromise on everything except the one issue which the Scott affair had made the most urgent – the question of amnesty. Before 4 March, it would not have been difficult for the Canadian government either to grant an amnesty for all acts committed during the insurrection or to ask the imperial government to do so. But Scott's death and the clamorous reaction to it in Ontario made such an easy solution impossible. Ritchot insisted upon a complete amnesty, but in the end he was only able to extract verbal assurances from Cartier that no one would be prosecuted.

Riel continued to govern the country until Canadian authority could be established. At first he believed the promises of amnesty he had received from Ritchot and from Taché, but as the summer wore on he must have had second thoughts. Canada had sent out a military expedition under the command of Colonel Garnet Wolseley to establish peace in the new province. Riel was informed that the expedition, manned largely by Ontario volunteers, was spoiling for a fight and that his own safety would be in jeopardy. Wolseley would come before the arrival of political authority in the person of Governor Archibald, known to be a moderate and conciliatory man. At dawn on 24 August, Riel rode away from Fort Garry just before the arrival of the expeditionary force; he headed south and quickly slipped across the border to North Dakota. The wisdom of his retreat was proved by the words of Wolseley, who afterwards wrote that 'most of us felt that we had to settle accounts quickly with Riel, who had murdered the Englishman, Mr Scott. Had we caught him, he would have had no mercy.'[2] Wolseley apparently thought of Riel as a rebel to be captured, in spite of the official interpretation of the Canadian government that no treason had taken place.

Thus closed an action-packed chapter in Riel's life. He had been catapulted in less than a year from obscurity to national, even international prominence. He had in fact been head of a government, even if that fact was not legally recognized by other governments. He had demonstrated considerable political acumen, as well as the unfortunate streak of stubbornness that led him to disregard the sound advice he received not to have Scott executed. Unquestionably he enjoyed the role he played. Politics was his natural métier, for it allowed him to exercise his very great oratorical and persuasive gifts. He also relished the exercise of power and the prestige that went with it. The rebellion finally gave him the success for which he had been prepared in his youth.

Riel was an ambitious man, but his ambition was fused with his dedication to the cause of his people. Consider the following sentence from a letter he wrote to win the support of William Dease, a well-to-do métis who opposed his radical course:

Monsieur Dease, why do you oppose us when we have already worked for the same ideas? No, ambition is a thing which is not in my heart; and if I am capable of anything I do it for everyone. I don't demand any compensation, nothing but the support and the backing of all the métis. Help me, you can do a great deal. Help me and you will soon see that my heart is not wicked.[3]

This identification of the self with the cause is typical of gifted leaders. It is not necessarily bad, indeed it is a source of greatness; but it carries its own danger. If the self may be sacrificed for the cause, so may the cause for the self. If the two become identified in the mind of the individual, it becomes difficult, even impossible, for him to remain objective about himself. Any action, no matter how reprehensible it may seem to outsiders, can be justified for the sake of the cause.

Precisely this characteristic in Riel determined his reaction to the end of the insurrection. After thinking that all was settled and that an amnesty was forthcoming, he was confronted with Wolseley's hostile force, and had to flee for his life. Subsequently he waited in vain for the pardon to come. In righteous indignation he interpreted the government's actions as malicious, deliberate persecution, as reprehensible betrayal of a promise. He knew that his own motives were pure; had he not sacrificed everything for the cause? His reversal of fortune must be due to the machinations of his enemies. One will search Riel's life in vain for any sign that he ever felt remorse over the killing of Scott. He never saw that that tragic error was now the chief source of his problems. His guilt over taking another man's life was absolved by his identification with the cause, so he could not appreciate the historical nemesis he had brought upon himself. Instead, he came to conceive of himself as the nemesis of those who had betrayed him and his people. However, all of this did not happen at once. It took a long time and repeated disappointments before the possibilities implicit in Riel's equation of himself and the cause were realized.

YEARS OF WAITING

Initially, in fact, Riel showed remarkable patience. He went to stay with his old Latin teacher Father Lefloch, who was now at St Joseph in North Dakota, where there was a sizeable métis settlement. There Riel made a retreat, and Lefloch wrote to Taché that his guest was submissive to God's will although occasionally pride took over.[4]

The news from Red River was extremely disturbing. In the weeks following Wolseley's arrival there was a wave of reprisals against the métis and other old settlers who had been associated with the Provisional Government. The perpetrators were Ontario militiamen looking for the revenge that had been denied them. This reign of lawlessness, in which several men were killed or badly beaten, was a sign that the métis had not won the victory they thought.

Riel came back to Canada under cover of night on 17 September 1870, to chair a meeting at St Norbert, which resulted in a Memorial and Petition carried to President Grant by William O'Donoghue, the Irishman who had played a major part in the insurrection.[5] Riel asked the president to help obtain a public inquiry into the rights of the métis. Apart from this episode, he kept aloof from Manitoba politics. He refused an invitation to run for the provincial legislature, having indirectly heard from Sir George Cartier that it would be wise to imitate the example the latter had set in voluntarily accepting exile after the rebellion of 1837-8.[6] Riel may have felt that if Cartier could come back from exile for an illustrious career in politics, he could do likewise.

While biding his time in St Joseph, Riel fell so sick in February 1871 that his mother came to nurse him. At this new affliction he 'recalled' that when he had been considering his departure from the seminary in 1865, he had promised God that he would spend only ten years in the world and then enter the priesthood.[7] It is doubtful that Riel in fact made any such promise at the time; for he was planning to marry, which would have been a permanent barrier to entering the service of the Church. But in any event he now resolved to make a retreat to consider whether he should return to his abandoned vocation. That retreat was made two years later. Riel seems to have interpreted his sickness as a divine admonition about his political ambitions. He wrote that spring to his friend Joseph Dubuc: 'I am nothing. I must be nothing in order to do good.'[8]

When he was well enough to travel, Riel returned to St Vital. For several months he lived quietly, gathering his shattered strength. He did not appear on the public scene until September, when word came that William O'Donoghue was organizing an invasion of Manitoba. Governor Archibald, afraid the métis might support O'Donoghue, appealed to Riel for support. The latter, after some hesitation, threw his weight to the Canadian side by helping to raise a levy of métis volunteers. He was swayed, among other reasons, by Archibald's assurance to Father Ritchot that 'the co-operation of the French half-breeds and their leaders in the support of the Crown, under the present circumstances, will be very welcome and cannot be looked upon otherwise than as entitling them to most favourable consideration.'[9] Archibald even went so far as to meet Riel in public and shake hands with him. And indeed Archibald tried to move Ottawa to action, but to no avail. Once again Riel was disappointed.

Sir John offered a bribe instead of a pardon. With an election coming up in 1872, the prime minister was anxious not to be embarrassed by Riel's presence in Canada. The Liberals were already claiming that he was shielding a known rebel from justice. So Macdonald arranged through Bishop Taché to pay Riel and his friend Ambroise Lépine a stipend if they would leave the country for a year. Riel rather reluctantly accepted the deal, although he would have preferred an amnesty and redress of the métis grievances to any amount of cash. But he was also beginning to fear for his safety. While he was away from home on 8 December, his house had been invaded by armed men looking for him. So in February 1872 Riel and Lépine accepted the money (which, incidentally, was not enough and had to be amplified by cash from the pocket of Donald A. Smith) and set out for St Paul. They left under cover of night with police protection, so delicate was the operation.

Riel stayed in St Paul only about four months. He felt even less safe there than he had in Manitoba, where at least he was protected by loyal friends. Also he could not help being bored. His main interests in life were his family and the political struggle of the métis; and in Minnesota he was cut off from both. He wrote memoirs about the insurrection, but that was not enough to fill the void. 'I'm not bored,' he wrote to his mother, 'but neither am I without boredom. I'm between the two, between joy and vexation. I don't savour the joy, and I don't want the vexation.'[10] In this state of mind, political life came to seem increasingly attractive, and Riel decided to run for Parliament, certainly the last thing that Sir John wanted. In June he left St Paul, where time hung so heavy on his hands, and went to St Joseph, from where he could make frequent forays into Manitoba to prepare for the upcoming election.

His election was assured, since he planned to run in the constituency of Provencher, which comprised his area of greatest popularity. However, the opportunity arose for him to do one last favour for the government. Manitoba elections in those years were held several weeks after they had terminated in eastern Canada. That summer Cartier had lost his seat in Montreal East; and Macdonald, wishing to have him in the Cabinet, asked Governor Archibald to secure a seat for him in Manitoba. The latter felt that this could only be done without risk of failure in Provencher. So in spite of Macdonald's reluctance to be indebted to Riel, the ex-president of the Provisional Government now resigned his candidacy so that Cartier, the man who had once turned a deaf ear to his poetic appeals for employment, could be returned to Parliament. No firm commitments were made; but Riel, advised by Archibald and Taché, certainly thought the long-awaited pardon would be forthcoming.

This was the last time Riel put his faith in co-operation with the government. Cartier, so sick that he would die within a few months, was in no position to press for an amnesty, even if he had desired to. And the prime minister, unwilling to inflame the Ontario electorate, resisted all attempts by influential French Canadians to persuade him to act. Meanwhile Riel sat and brooded in St Vital. His mood can scarcely have been improved by an attempt to arrest him on 3 December 1872. Two and a half years after the passage of the Manitoba Act he was still not free to walk the streets of his home town.

The winter of 1872-3, which saw Riel's final disillusion with a strategy of conciliation towards Ottawa, also brought the beginnings, still very small, of his supernatural vocation. One incident which must have affected his thinking, although he wrote little about it, was the 'miraculous' cure of his sister Sara, who was a missionary nun in the inhospitable climate of Ile-à-la-Crosse. Late in November she was seized with such a severe inflammation of the chest that it appeared her death was certain. She had received the last sacraments and had resigned herself to die when her confessor begged her to pray to the Blessed Marguerite-Marie Alocoque, a French nun beatified in Rome eight years earlier. Marguerite-Marie had lived and died in the seventeenth century, but the cult of the Sacred Heart of Jesus, of which she was the great apostle, was just then gaining in popularity. Sara prayed to her and suddenly recovered. The cure was accepted as a genuine miracle by the Sisters, and Bishop Grandin wrote to Rome to pass on the information to the Association for the Propagation of the Faith, to be used as evidence in future canonization proceedings.[11] Sara promised in gratitude to adopt the name of her heavenly benefactor; she would become Sister Marguerite-Marie. She described the miracle in several graphic letters to her family after her recovery.[12]

The news must have strengthened Louis' belief that he came from a special family which was under divine protection. The idea of changing one's name may have also encouraged him to adopt the name of David, as he was to do a few years later. But there was another, more complex aspect to this affair. Louis would have been the first missionary of métis stock if he had entered the priesthood and returned to the North-West. Sara was the first métisse missionary nun. When she wrote her family about the miracle she referred to this, saying: 'Let us never forget the mark of love Our Lord put on our family by choosing the first métisse missionary among its members.'[13] She wrote to Louis a few months later about his own lost vocation:

Dear Louis – without reflection, I don't know why, I catch myself saying: 'Lord, grant that I may see my beloved brother mount to the altar.' Why that prayer?

God only knows. But I'm not trying to trouble you. March in the path that Providence will mark for you when the time comes.[14]

Louis must have been troubled in spite of Sara's admonition not to be. If, so soon after her miraculous return from death, she was nudging him towards the priesthood, this might be the will of God. Moreover, Riel himself fell seriously ill again during the winter of 1872-3. Sickness reminded him of his resolution to make a retreat about the subject of his vocation. The retreat was carried out in the early spring of 1873. With the encouragement of his spiritual director, Riel made a definitive choice 'for the world.'

This decision, easily predictable, was less remarkable than the rationalization for it. Riel had begun to reconsider his vocation when he fell gravely ill in 1871. But when he recovered, he realized that he did not 'have the strength to abandon the world.' He escaped this quandary by reasoning that perhaps he might be a more effective servant of God in secular than in ecclesiastical life. He prayed to God:

I love the world; I want to pass my life there. ... I beg You, give me as a layman the circumstances, the opportunity and Your help so that throughout my life even to the last breath I earn You more glory, I serve religion more, I save more souls from hell and deliver more from purgatory, I work more effectively for the good of society, I sanctify myself more than I could in the ecclesiastical state or in any other condition.[15]

His director put the seal of clerical approval on this logic during the retreat. Freed of his promise to become a priest, Riel now had an alternative, perhaps even a superior vocation as a layman, doing God's work in the world.

This, at least, was how Riel explained this phase of life in January 1876, when he was already convinced of being endowed with a special mission. It is probable that this conviction coloured his remembrance of the past, and that his thinking about his vocation in the years 1871 to 1873 had not been quite so clear-cut as he portrayed it in 1876. But the general line of thought is plausible enough.

Riel's decision to embrace the world was ratified by a peculiar experience in early May 1873. Passing by the convent of the Grey Sisters of St Norbert, where Sara had once resided, he stopped to spend the night. He retired early but could not sleep. His repose was troubled with visions of his family, of his father, of Sara, of his sister Marie who had died that winter. He arose at six o'clock, terribly tired, and went to the parish church, where he met Sister Sainte-Thérèse. Over breakfast he told her of his sleepless night, and she replied:

Louis, I see you are suffering ... Well, I have a treasure to give you which I have been saving for nine years. I have already seen you suffer often. But I thought a time would come when you would have even greater need of the help which has been reserved for you.[16]

Sister Sainte-Thérèse went on to tell how she had been present at the bedside of Louis' dying father. He blessed all the family, and she knelt before him and successfully implored a special benediction for his son absent in Canada. When he heard this, Riel fell to his knees to receive from the Grey Sister his father's last blessing.

He soon told the rest of his family about the incident, but he did not write to Sara about it until late July. He told her the story in the same letter in which he informed her he had given up all thought of entering the priesthood and was hoping to marry soon. He concluded the letter: 'I am certain that a divine force is guiding me.'

Years afterward, Riel interpreted the blessing conveyed by Sister Sainte-Thérèse as the first of a series of signs from heaven demonstrating the validity of his prophetic mission, and he recalled that he 'had been seeking' this benediction 'nine years without knowing if it had [been] left for him.[17] But this recollection is coloured by hindsight. Riel's experience was certainly important to him at the time, but he did not see it as the inauguration of a divine mission.

It is significant that this incident took place in such a strong familial context. The night before the blessing Riel's sleep was troubled by visions of family members, both dead and alive. The blessing, when it came, was a legacy from his father. When the episode was over, Riel communicated it only to his family. Caught in a net of personal and political difficulties, he returned for spiritual strength to the memory of his family. He could now be certain that his father approved of his course in life. His father's long-delayed blessing was a sign of forgiveness for abandoning his career in the Church, and thereby disappointing his family, Bishop Taché, and the métis in general. This vision, coming so soon after his retreat, eased his burden of guilt and allowed him to return to the political fray with renewed vigour.

There was a new election to prepare for. Sir George having died in London in the spring of 1873, the Provencher seat would have to be filled through a by-election. Riel began to campaign openly for the seat. It was obvious that he would be elected, but his troubles were just starting. A group of Canadians from Winnipeg, moved perhaps by a desire to embarrass Sir John A. Macdonald, succeeded in obtaining a warrant for Riel's arrest for the murder of Thomas Scott. Ambroise Lépine was taken into custody, but Riel, tipped off in advance, managed to hide himself in the woods across the river from St Norbert. He was still there a month later when he was unanimously elected *in absentia* as member of parliament for Provencher. Assisted by money raised by friends in Manitoba and Quebec, Riel was whisked out of the province and set on his way to Montreal.

While he was hiding in the woods, Riel was compared by his friend Dubuc to the David of the ancient Hebrews.[18] It was an apt metaphor. Just as David had won his victory over the Philistines while only a boy, and then had been forced to flee the wrath of Saul, so Riel had defied the power of Canada while still a young man, and then had to hide in self-protection. It was also an encouraging analogy, for David later became the king of the Hebrews. Within a few years, Riel would find new meaning in his resemblance to David, pushing it to the point of almost literal identification. For the time being, however, it was just an interesting comparison. Riel used the name 'David' as a pseudonym to throw pursuers off the track when he traveled east, but he does not seem to have attached mystical significance to it.[19]

Once in the Province of Quebec, Riel toyed with the idea of going to Parliament to take his seat; but he was afraid to enter Ontario because the brother of Thomas Scott had obtained a warrant for his arrest in that province, and the Ontario government had offered $5000 for his capture. There were bound to be attempts to take him if he spent any length of time south of the Ottawa River. In December Riel retreated to the safety of a home for priests of the Oblate Order situated at Plattsburgh, New York, on the shores of Lake Champlain. He rested there for a few weeks, seeking to regain his health, which had been badly taxed by the hectic life of the past few months. In his leisure, he wrote a memoir on the Red River insurrection and the amnesty question which was published in 1874 by the ultramontane paper *Le Nouveau Monde*. The pamphlet was a vigorous defence of the métis movement of 1869-70 and of his own conduct as president of the Provisional Government. Riel's account was as tendentious as most political pamphlets. He defended his judgment in the Scott affair, arguing that the prisoner 'was executed out of the necessity to establish order and to fulfill our duty by making that order respected.' He made a forthright plea for himself, for Ambroïse Lépine, and for all others who might face criminal charges as a result of the insurrection: 'What we demand is an amnesty, that is, the fulfillment in good faith of the Manitoba Act. Nothing more, but also nothing less.'[20] While staying with the Oblates, Riel was introduced to Father Fabien Barnabé, pastor of the French community in the nearby village of Keeseville. He was made welcome in the home of the kindly priest, who lived with his mother and his sister Evelina. Riel was to be a frequent visitor there in years to come.

On 8 January 1874 Riel was at the Hôtel-Dieu of Montreal, where Bishop Ignace Bourget had retreated to rest. Worried about his own health, Riel fell to his knees and asked Mgr Bourget to heal him. The venerable bishop spoke: 'Arise, arise, you are going to recover your health. Do what your doctor prescribes. I bless the medicines that are given to you.'[21] Riel's health did seem to improve, at least temporarily, after this encounter. He made a novena after returning to Plattsburgh, praying for his health, and he wrote to Bourget that he had recovered his serenity.[22] Years later, when he was fully convinced of being a prophet, he remembered the episode as a miraculous cure, another sign demonstrating the authenticity of his mission. '8th January 74, was miraculously [healed] from prostration and complete exhaustion of his strength, was miraculously saved by the prayer of Archbishop Ignace Bourget.'[23]

Ignace Bourget was nearing the end of a long, illustrious, and controversial career in the Church. Born in 1799, ordained at the age of twenty-three, he became coadjutor bishop of Montreal in 1837, the year of the Patriote agitation, and full bishop in 1840. He capably administered his diocese until 1876 in a period of rapid and turbulent growth. But he was much more than an administrator; he was deeply involved in politics, both ecclesiastical and civil. He was the acknowledged leader of the ultramontane tendency in Quebec public life, a school of thought which must be considered at some length because of its profound impact on Riel's thinking. When he came to Quebec at the end of 1873, Riel was beginning to think about himself in supernatural terms, but his ideas were largely personal – relating to himself and his family – or nationalistic – relating to the survival of the métis. He was lacking an overall framework, a world view, to support his nascent feeling of being endowed with a special mission. This need was supplied by ultramontanism.

Ultramontanism in France was an ancient term associated with the struggles between the king and the pope for control of the French Church. The ultramontanes were those who looked 'beyond the mountains,' ie, to Rome, for leadership. As a term in Quebec ecclesiastical politics in the mid-nineteenth century, ultramontanism also designated ardent advocates of Roman supremacy, but with differences of nuance compared to the meaning of the word in Europe. The French ultramontanes were historically opposed to the efforts of the state to gain power over the Church, to 'Gallicanize' it. Hence the French ultramontanes were 'internationalists' (on the side of Rome) rather than 'nationalists' (on the side of the French state). The distinction followed naturally from the conflict of interest between the international Church and the national state. But the Quebec ultramontanes were French-Canadian nationalists. At one and the same time, they could be loyal to Rome and struggle against the Canadian state, controlled by English Protestants, for the survival of the Catholic French-Canadian people.

Ultramontanism taught that the Church was an international army under the direct command of the Roman pontiff. This conception was well articulated by Bourget in his famous dictum: 'Let each say in his heart: "I hear my curé, my curé hears the bishop, the bishop hears the Pope, and the Pope hears Our Lord Jesus Christ".'[24] The ultras were strongly in favour of the doctrine of papal infallibility proclaimed in 1870. Mgr Laflèche, bishop of Trois-Rivières and a leading ultra, wrote: 'The dogmatic definition of the infallibility of the Sovereign Pontiff is the great remedy which God in his mercy has prepared to cure the frightful social evils of our time.'[25] The ultras also defended the temporal power of the pope. They regarded the unification of Italy as a blasphemous assault against the papacy. In 1867, Mgr Bourget took the lead in organizing a contingent of Papal Zouaves to fight for Pius IX against Garibaldi. Bishop Bourget also brought the Jesuits back to Canada in 1842, eight decades after they had been banned by the British. Bourget caused nine other orders to come to Quebec, but the Jesuits were most significant because of their avowed papalism.

Ultramontanism also meant a reactionary political theory. The French ultras were almost all royalists; after the overthrow of Napoleon III they opposed the Republic and supported the legitimist party of 'Henry V,' the Comte de Chambord. They also sympathized with royalist pretenders in Spain and Portugal. Needless to say, the ultras were hostile to liberal ideas. They followed Pius IX, who in his *Syllabus of Errors* (1864) declared that it was false to believe that 'the Roman pontiff can and should reconcile himself to and agree with progress, liberalism, and modern civilization.' In the ultra vocabulary, liberalism was a synonym for all the evils of the modern world.

Particularly obnoxious to the ultras was the separation of church and state, which they interpreted as the subordination of the former to the latter. They were afraid of the tendency in many countries to take away ecclesiastical control of marriage, education, hospitals, mental institutions, etc. The ultras counterattacked, preaching that on questions involving religion and morality the state was actually subordinate to the Church. The Church must be an active force directing her loyal sons in political thought and action.

Over many years Mgr Bourget attempted to put this theory into practice in Quebec. He repeatedly threw his influence against the Liberals, especially against the free-thinking, anti-clerical minority known as the Rouges. He did not hesitate to condemn their society, the Institut Canadien, to put its publications on the Index of Forbidden Books, and to deny the sacraments to members. His epic struggle with the Institute over the burial of Joseph Guibord was still dragging on when Riel came east after his election. Bourget had denied Catholic burial to the body of Guibord, who had refused to renounce the Institute on his deathbed. Riel's old employer Rodolphe Laflamme was contesting Bourget's decision in the civil courts; but Riel, if he had ever sympathized with Laflamme's *rougisme*, was now far removed from such ideas. Another political issue still alive when Riel came to Quebec was the so-called 'Catholic Programme.' Before the provincial election of 1871, a group of ultramontane laymen issued a manifesto which linked Catholicism to the Conservative party. Although the Catholic Programme was disavowed by Cartier and by Archbishop Taschereau of Quebec, it was openly approved by Bourget and Laflèche.The Catholic Programme was drawn up in the house of Alphonse Desjardins, publisher of *Le Nouveau Monde*. Desjardins, like several other ultras and near-ultras, had taken an active interest in Riel's case and had contributed to the fund to pay his way east. Riel often stayed at his home when he was in Montreal during 1874. The ultras helped Riel with money and friendship, as well as with ideas which were congenial to his own intense piety.

Ultramontanism in Quebec was also a philosophy of history. Ultras tended to think of French Canadians as a people protected and guided by God, with a special mission to accomplish. This feeling was given its classic formulation in 1866 by Mgr Laflèche's book *Quelques Considérations sur les rapports de la société civile avec la religion et la famille.* Laflèche wrote that human history is governed by God's providential plan, within which each nation has a special mission or destiny. 'The mission with which Providence entrusted French Canadians is basically religious in nature: it is, namely, to convert the unfortunate infidel local population to Catholicism, and to expand the Kingdom of God by developing a predominantly Catholic nationality.'[26] The French Canadians had been a missionary people ever since 1535, when Jacques Cartier had recited the Gospel of John to the Indians at Hochelaga. Cartier, Laflèche wrote, was like Abraham, the founder of a new people. Providence had governed the history of the French Canadians, just as God had used the Hebrews for His purpose. Today it was the duty of French Canada to preserve herself as French and Catholic against all attempts of the English to assimilate her population. Riel knew Laflèche personally from the days when the latter had been a missionary in the North-West; in fact, he had been one of Louis' first teachers. Even if Riel never read the book he was certainly familiar with the ideas, which became a foundation stone of the religion he wished to build.

To return to the narrative of the year 1874: Parliament had been dissolved and a general election called in the wake of the Canadian Pacific scandal. Riel was re-elected in Provencher on 13 February 1874. As soon as he heard of his victory, he went to Hull to try to arrange a meeting with Antoine-Aimé Dorion, the 'Quebec Lieutenant' in Alexander Mackenzie's new Liberal government. But Dorion would not see him.The Liberals were not any readier than the Conservatives to resolve the difficult question of an amnesty, so like their predecessors they resorted to procrastination. Riel, however, was determined to force the issue. He crossed the Ottawa River on 30 March, accompanied by an old school friend, Dr Romuald Fiset, and went to the House of Commons to sign the members' register and take the oath of office. Having achieved that much, he immediately fled back to Hull before he could be arrested.

Riel's bold move had the desired effect of bringing the amnesty question to the top of the public agenda. The Commons ordered him to appear in the House, which he could not do for fear of arrest, and then expelled him for failing to comply with the order. The House then appointed a Select Committee to hear evidence on the issue of amnesty.[27] This Committee, sitting in open session with many prominent witnesses during April and May, generated enormous publicity, as did the printing of Riel's brochure on the amnesty as well as a pamphlet written by Taché.[28] The Bishop of St Boniface finally exposed the sordid story of broken promises with which the government had been holding off Riel for four years.

However desirable this storm of publicity may have been, it jeopardized Riel's safety. He could no longer even be sure of his security in Quebec since the English inhabitants of the province were aroused. He went to St Paul, Minnesota, hoping to find peace and quiet there, and also to be nearer to the preparations for his re-election, which were commencing in Manitoba. But he stayed only a couple of weeks in Minnesota. Having been recognized on the street, and having heard that his old enemy Dr Schultz was not far away, Riel hastened back east.

He spent the summer of 1874 travelling about New York and New England. For years there had been a steady stream of French Canadian immigrants leaving Quebec in search of work; and the number increased rapidly with the industrial boom in the United States after the conclusion of the Civil War. By 1874, there was a network of 'Little Canadas' throughout New England and upper New York. Many others besides the Barnabés in Keeseville were happy to receive him. In Suncook, New Hampshire, there was Father Richer, whom Riel had known as an Oblate missionary in Manitoba. In Nashua, New Hampshire, thirty miles from Suncook, lived Father Milette, who met Riel through Richer. And in Worcester, Massachusetts, there was Father Primeau, whose cousin knew Riel's relatives in Quebec.

The large parish of Notre-Dame-des-Canadiens in Worcester became particularly important to Riel. Father Jean-Baptiste Primeau, ex-director of the Collège de Terrebonne, was a forceful, energetic man, deeply involved in political, especially nationalistic questions. Worcester was also the home of two rising young journalists, Ferdinand Gagnon and Frédéric Houde, who collaborated to publish *Le Foyer Canadien*. Under the joint leadership of Church and press, Worcester had become something of a centre for French Canadians in the American diaspora. When the officials of the St Jean-Baptiste Society in Montreal determined to extend a special invitation to Franco-Americans to come to a giant meeting on 24 June 1874, they naturally turned to Primeau, Gagnon, and Houde to organize the American delegation.

Riel did not attend that great festival, but his name was very much in evidence. The Conservatives proposed a motion of support for him; but it was opposed by the Liberals, who preferred not to embarrass their newly elected government. The Franco-Americans, particularly Frédéric Houde, who did not have to worry about Canadian party politics, spoke strongly on Riel's behalf. The matter was dropped in the end; but Riel, moved by this show of support, decided to go to Worcester to thank Houde. After spending several days as a guest of Father Primeau, Riel spoke at a public meeting at the local St Jean-Baptiste hall. He presented his side of the amnesty question to the sympathetic audience, and concluded by inviting them to come settle in Manitoba. He Houde commented afterwards in his newspaper that when Riel touched on the 'mission of the French-Canadian race, his voice, calm until then, and his hitherto phlegmatic face became singularly animated. We saw that conviction possessed him, that emotion overcame him ... .'[29]

This was the beginning of Riel's career as a public speaker in New England. He gave similar addresses in Suncook and Woonsocket, and perhaps other cities.[30] He was a powerful orator who could rouse the enthusiasm of his listeners. They were glad to sign petitions of support and contribute a few dollars, but there was little they could really do to help him. His fate lay with Mackenzie and the cabinet.

On 3 September, Riel was re-elected *in absentia* by the loyal voters of Provencher. He returned to Quebec to look for more support. While detectives shadowed him, he went to Trois-Rivières to see Mgr Laflèche, his old teacher, whose ultramontane principles he had adopted.[31] But it was the Liberals whom Riel had to influence, like it or not. Therefore he visited Mgr Larocque, Bishop of St Hyacinthe, who was not a strong ultra.[32] He also went to Quebec City, where he had an audience with the archbishop, Mgr Taschereau, who was reputed to be close to the Liberals.[33] On the way, Riel stopped in Arthabaska to see a promising young Liberal member of parliament, Wilfrid Laurier. Laurier left this encounter convinced that Riel was a 'monomaniac.'[34] Unfortunately, there is no record of what Riel did to create this unfavourable impression in Laurier's mind.

On 27 September, Riel was back in Montreal, where he said good-bye to J.-Adolphe Chapleau, a celebrated lawyer as well as an old school friend, who was leaving for Winnipeg to help defend Ambroise Lépine.[35] A year after his arrest, Lépine was going to be tried for the murder of Thomas Scott in what had become a national *cause célèbre*. Riel went to the United States, probably Keeseville, to await the outcome. On 2 November, Lépine was found guilty of murder and sentenced to death, even though the jury recommended mercy. It must have seemed the ultimate betrayal to Riel that the government, in spite of its long-standing promises of amnesty, would let matters go so far. The governor-general would later commute Lépine's sentence to two years in prison and forfeiture of political rights, but Riel could not know this at the time.

His movements are hard to trace during November, but he seems to have gone to Washington, DC, to stay with Edmond Mallet, a Franco-

American whom he had recently met. Mallet, born in Quebec, had moved to Oswego, New York, at an early age. He fought in the Civil War, was promoted to major, then went to work in the Treasury Department.[36] Although he had lost his French language and Catholic faith as a boy, he recovered his heritage as an adult and was now a rising figure among the Franco-Americans. He sympathized with the cause of the métis and looked upon Riel as a hero. Riel may have gone to Washington to see if Mallet could find him support among American politicians.

Towards the end of the month, Riel also made a quick trip out to St Paul and back, for unknown reasons. There was an air of mystery about the whole thing. Father Barnabé wrote to Riel on 14 November that in Keeseville 'everyone thinks you are in Minnesota organizing an expedition! I let them talk.'[37] What is implied by these words is certainly open to question, but they could mean that Riel had been talking of some sort of military enterprise against Manitoba, using Minnesota as a base. He unquestionably tried to arrange such a plan just a year later, so it would not be surprising if he was already thinking along these lines in November 1874.

EXILE

Shortly before Christmas, Riel left Washington to begin another round of visits with his New England friends. He was in Keeseville when the House of Commons finally settled the amnesty question in February. Those who had committed acts against the Canadian government during the North-West troubles were given amnesty, except for Louis Riel, Ambroise Lépine, and W.B. O'Donoghue. The latter received no clemency because of his raid on Manitoba in 1871. Riel and Lépine received an amnesty conditional on five years banishment from Canada or two years imprisonment. Lépine went to jail but Riel chose exile.

The government's action caused a severe moral shock in Riel. He had been struggling for years to achieve his rights as he saw them, and he had been a major figure in Canadian politics; but now the game was over. What would he do as an exile? He had no career other than politics; and as an outlaw he could not even return to Red River to live quietly with his mother and help support his younger brothers and sisters. For several months, Riel did not seem to know what to do. He went from place to place in New England, never staying anywhere very long. He even took the risk of returning to Montreal for audiences with Mgr

Bourget. It was after one of these visits that Bourget wrote him the letter which was to become, in Riel's mind, the authentication *par excellence* of his mission.

Montreal,
July 14, 1875

Dear Mr Riel,

I received your letter of July 6 yesterday and I was greatly touched, for that letter proves to me that you are animated by good motives and at the same time tormented in your mind by other inclinations or something which I do not understand, which makes you undecided in carrying out the duties imposed upon you by the obedience in which you live.

So I have the intimate conviction that you will receive in this world, and sooner than you think, the reward for all those mental and moral sacrifices you make, a thousand times more crushing than the sacrifices of material and visible life.

But God, who has always led you and assisted you until the present hour, will not abandon you in the dark hours of your life, for He has given you a mission which you must fulfil in all respects.

By the Grace of God, you will persevere in the way which has been traced out for you. This is to say, you must not withhold anything you possess. You will desire above all things to know God and to procure the greatest glory for Him. You will work unceasingly for the honour of religion, the salvation of souls, and the good of society. And you will sanctify yourself in desiring heartily the sanctification of others ... [38]

Several sentences of this letter were only a slightly modified version of things Riel had written to the bishop a week before.[39] But it did not diminish, and perhaps even enhanced the importance of the letter in Riel's eyes that Bourget was reflecting his own thoughts back to him. Riel carried this letter with him day and night, and pondered its words until he could repeat them by heart. Within a few months he began to think that the 'mission' of which Bourget spoke was not simply the mission, which every man has, to do good in the world, but a unique vocation conferred on him by God through the intermediary of the bishop's letter.

In the meantime Riel was uncertain of his next move. He talked of going to Europe, as Papineau had done during his exile; but for some reason he did not pursue that idea.[40] By mid-summer he was writing to his mother to suggest that she and the younger children join him to live in

St Joseph, but this idea was dropped, even though his mother was amenable.[41] Riel wrote on 21 October that he had meant to leave for St Joseph that week, but 'something unforeseen' had prevented him.[42]

What was unforeseen was an attempt to organize an invasion of Manitoba from an American base. Sometime during October, Riel went to Indianapolis, alone and without any introduction, to seek an interview with Oliver P. Morton, the powerful Republican senator from Indiana who was rumoured to be interested in running for president in 1876. Morton saw Riel several times, but in the end would not make a commitment to sponsor his plan. Riel later wrote to the senator: 'Your objections are sound. They are foreseen in my plan. But I am not discouraged. As I told you, I hope the divine Providence will help me.'[43]

By this time, the natural and supernatural were becoming so mixed in Riel's thinking that they were no longer separate categories. A stroke had left Morton paralyzed in both legs and Riel thought that if he could miraculously heal the senator he could gain his support. But then, thought Riel, if Morton can suddenly walk again, he will attribute his cure to natural causes and forget about my plan. The best course would be to heal just one leg as a demonstration of divine power. His other leg could be healed in due time if Morton would supply aid to the cause. Riel discussed this plan – truly a fantastic mixture of piety and business acumen – with Father Primeau, who merely laughed and told him to go ahead and try. Riel covered the curé's knees and feet with kisses of gratitude. Then he wrote to Morton on All Saints' Day, terminating the letter with the words, 'when one of your legs is healed, think of me.'[44] The senator, an atheist since youth, was not the man to be impressed by such a proposal. No miracle occurred, and Riel had to look elsewhere for help.

Riel was in Washington, DC, when he wrote this note. He had gone there to visit Edmond Mallet, who was willing to help him advance his scheme. Convinced that his failure with Senator Morton was due to his imperfect presentation of his plan in English, Riel spent most of November drafting a 'succinct, clear, and complete' version of his ideas for the invasion of Manitoba. When he was satisfied with his work, Riel took it, with Mallet's introduction, to a Congressman who had spoken favourably of him in the past. But this man, whoever he may have been, had no desire to become involved in Riel's schemes. The latter then found another patron, a man 'of good will,' who agreed to help him.[45]

Mallet succeeded in getting Riel a secret interview, under an assumed name, with President Grant.[46] A very clear picture of Riel's aims emerges from a long letter to Grant which he drafted sometime after the interview.[47] With the support of the French and English half-breeds, Riel said, as well as of the Indians, he would be able to re-establish the Provisional Government. Quebec would support him, while hundreds of French Canadians from New England would quickly come to settle in the West. Another important element in the scheme were the Irish, who would also be invited to immigrate. In return for their support, they would receive a province of their own to the west of Manitoba.

Canada would have no choice but to negotiate. The Manitoba Act, or 'treaty' as Riel preferred to think of it, would finally be implemented in good faith. Manitoba would become a quasi-independent state associated with Canada under the British crown.

What would the United States gain from such a plan? Riel promised to pursue 'a plan of action deferential to the United States,' ie, to bring Manitoba and the North-West within the American sphere of influence. If the scheme was successful it would enhance the prestige of the Republican party as well as the personal position of Grant, who might then be able to win a third term as president.

The major thing that Riel wanted from Grant, apart from permission to mount the force needed for an assault on Manitoba, was money. He wanted to issue bonds 'on a well-prepared market,' which wealthy friends of the president would be encouraged to buy at a favourable price. After the success of the military venture, and as part of the peace settlement, Canada and England would be forced to take bonds also, but at a higher price. The difference could go into the pockets of the original American investors. Riel also wanted the president's assurance that British or Canadian troops would not be allowed to cross American soil to reach Manitoba (permission had been refused in 1870); and he asked the Americans to make certain ambiguous military preparations in the West which might intimidate Canada without constituting an explicit threat.

There is no indication that Grant was attracted to Riel's plan. The métis exile had now played out all his political options. He had waited in vain for the Canadian government to grant an amnesty. He had failed to obtain an amnesty by mobilizing political pressure in Canada. And finally his flirtation with the idea of a military enterprise had come to naught. Seeing that all his political ambitions had led nowhere, Riel sought compensation in the religious realm, where greatness was still possible.

He had already been leading a life of exemplary piety. Mallet left this description of his character and behaviour during these months:

When Riel was in Washington in 1874 and 1875, he was a most dutiful Catholic. He prayed much, practised special devotions appointed by the Church to inculcate piety, and went to communion – the most tremendous religious act of Christianity – frequently. Marvellous things which I read in the lives of the saints previous to my knowing Riel, were understood by me only after I had come to know the man.

He was so far as I could judge an exemplary Catholic. His life was in keeping with his religion. His language and deportment was as chaste and modest as a virtuous young girl's. He neither drank nor smoked. He ate sparingly, generally milk, bread, cold meat, celery, etc. He was exceedingly neat in his person and dress and was [illegible] polite to the few persons he met – my wife, children, sister-in-law and a few choice friends. He would not go into society. He went to mass every morning and crept into some dark spot in some church at night to recite his evening prayers.[48]

A mystical sense of mission was now added to personal sanctification. On 6 December 1875, Riel wrote to Bourget to say that his letter of 14 July, 'in which Your Excellency announces a mission which I will have to fulfil in all respects,' was ever in his mind:

Without relying on myself, rather counting on the support of Our Lord, I accept with the greatest happiness the mission which you announce to me. I had accepted it at first. But now I accept, with gratitude and joy, all the sorrows and consolations which that mission must bring me.

Recalling the sacrament of confirmation, when he had first received the Holy Spirit, Riel again dedicated himself to the Paraclete. 'May He deign to command me, to inspire me, to lead me by the hand, now and at every moment of my life until my last breath!'[49] Riel, however, did not specify what his mission consisted of; it was probably still vague in his mind.

Two days later, on 8 December, he attended high mass in St Patrick's Church. It was an auspicious day. It was exactly the sixth anniversary of his proclamation of a Provisional Government in Red River. It was the Feast of the Immaculate Conception, and also the favourite day of the reigning pontiff, Pius IX, the idol of the ultramontanes. Pius had declared the Immaculate Conception to be an article of faith on 8 December 1854. He had issued the *Syllabus of Errors* ten years later to the day. And on 8 December 1869, while Riel was declaring his first Provisional Government, Pius opened the Vatican Council, at which the dogma of papal infallibility was proclaimed. Now at mass, while the people stood to hear the priest say the creed, Riel underwent a powerful experience of mystical illumination.

I suddenly felt in my heart a joy which took such possession of me that to hide from my neighbors the smile on my face I had to unfold my handkerchief and hold it with my hand over my mouth and cheeks. In spite of my precautions a young boy about ten years old, who was a little in front of me, saw my great joy.

After these consolations had made me rejoice about two minutes, I was immediately struck by an immense sadness of spirit. And if it had not been for the great efforts I made to restrain my sighs, my tears and cries would have made a terrible noise within the church. I prudently bore in silence the almost insupportable sadness I was experiencing in my soul. But that great pain, as great as my joy, passed away in just as short a time. And in my spirit remained this thought: 'Are the joys and pains of man short on this earth?'[50]

Riel claimed afterwards that 8 December 1875 was the commencement of his mission, of his new revelation. In his words: 'There God anointed him with his divine gifts and fruits of his Spirit, as prophet of the New World.'[51] But his friends felt that his mind had come unhinged. Riel remarked in concluding his description of that moving experience: 'Not long afterwards, only a few days, people began to treat me like a madman.'[52]

3
The Prophet in Chains

Riel's mystical ecstasy of 8 December 1875 was not an isolated event. He underwent several powerful visionary experiences which permanently changed his life.

December 14, 1875 [according to Riel], at one o'clock in the afternoon, the spirit of God comes upon him, fills his body and soul of [H]is divine light and essence; transports him to the fourth heaven and instructed him about the nations of the earth, speaking to him at least an hour and a half.[1]

Then 15 December, 'as nearly as I can recall the date, a great spirit appeared to mine; [H]e spoke to me.'[2]

Another vision which Riel has described in detail may have occurred about this time. 'While standing alone on a mountain top near Washington, DC,' Riel said,

the same spirit that appeared to Moses in the midst of clouds of flame appeared to me in the same manner. I was astonished. I was dumbfounded. It was said to me: 'Rise, Louis David Riel, you have a mission to accomplish for the benefit of humanity.' The words, spoken in Latin, were addressed to me: (First, formulate, second, respect age). I received my divine notification with uplifted arms and bowed head.[3]

Still another revelatory experience is described in a note from Riel to his friend Mallet.[4] Riel had come to visit the major, and not finding him at home, had let himself into his study. There, while working on a 'petition' (probably the letter to President Grant discussed in the preceding chapter), he saw a virgin. She appeared to him alone; then, at his request, she reappeared with her child, ie, the infant Jesus. The letter is not dated, but the symbolism of Mary and Jesus strongly suggests the Advent season.

In retrospect, Riel looked upon these experiences, particularly the one of 8 December 1875, as the inauguration of his role as a prophet. He wrote in his autobiographical notes (1885):

December 8, 1875: He [Riel] receives the Holy Spirit at the Gloria in Excelsis during high Mass at St Patrick's Church in Washington. And then God anointed him with His divine gifts and the fruits of His Spirit, as prophet of the New World.[5]

He added, with reference to the spirit who appeared to him on 15 December: 'That same spirit has directed, has assisted me in all I have done, in all I have written, in all I have undertaken since then.'[6]

These comments were made with ten years of hindsight, after Riel had long been convinced of having a special mission as 'Prophet of the New World.' It is not certain that he began to regard himself in this light immediately after the mystical experiences of December 1875. The few *contemporary* documents from this period of his life show him believing that he has a mission of some sort, but not yet calling himself a prophet, in contrast to the *retrospective* documents, which project the prophetic identity back to 8 December.

Riel wrote to Bourget on 6 December 1875 that he accepted his mission, but he did not define that mission as one of prophecy. Rather he spoke of intensified humility and obedience to the Church. He asked Bourget to inform the pope that 'a new Catholic people was arising in the world at this very time,' the métis; but he did not call them a chosen people, or in any way hint at a break with Rome. He expressed only correct and orthodox ultramontane sentiments.[7]

The same impression is created by a letter of 9 December 1875 to Riel's confessor, Father Primeau, in Worcester. Riel wrote that his mission would be accomplished through suffering 'under the seal of obedience.' He wanted to announce in Washington the message that God 'wishes to be obeyed by all the peoples of the earth,' and that this could be done only by 'submitting to the infallible voice of the holy, Catholic, Apostolic, and Roman Church.'[8]

This agrees with the testimony of Edmond Mallet, who was in contact with Riel until 16 December, that he was a 'dutiful,' indeed an 'exemplary Catholic,' who was never heard to utter anything against the teachings of the Church.[9] It seems that Riel's identity as a prophet and religious reformer only emerged gradually in the months following the formative experiences of early December. Unfortunately, the documents that would allow us to trace that emergence in detail are lacking.

But even if Riel was not yet calling himself a prophet, his religious excitement and enthusiasm were obvious to his friends. Mallet thought that Riel had lost his mind from repeated disappointments culminating in the failure of President Grant to respond to his proposals. He wished to care for his friend, but as he was not a man of means he could not afford to pay for Riel's maintenance in an asylum. Nor did Riel have any funds of his own. (There is a story that Bishop Bourget had at one point made him a present of $1000, but Riel had given it all away to a blind beggar in the American capital.)[10] Mallet, who had a wife and small children to look after as well as his job to do, could not nurse Riel personally. He wrote to Father Barnabé for help, but that priest was not in a position to act because his mother was dangerously ill.[11] On 16 December 1875, therefore, Mallet took Riel up to Worcester, Massachusetts, to stay with Father Primeau. Mallet and Riel arrived at the parish house in the morning just as Primeau was serving breakfast to Ferdinand Gagnon, editor of the local newspaper, and to Honoré Mercier, who had come to Worcester to give a benefit lecture for the poor. Mallet took the others apart to explain that Riel had undergone a crisis of insanity in Washington. Gagnon, however, thought Riel acted sensibly.[12]

Primeau wrote back to Mallet on New Year's Eve to report on their mutual friend. His news was far from encouraging. Riel was irretrievably wedded to his fixed idea. He was convinced that God was only permitting Mallet and Primeau to treat him as deranged in order to prepare them for the revelation of his true calling. 'Friday,' continued Primeau,

he asked me if he could, without disobeying me too much, begin to announce, in the city of Worcester, what he would soon have to proclaim throughout the world.

The poor child! When I told him that some of the things he wanted to do were impossible chimeras, he started to weep and said: 'But we have to do miracles – command me then ... '[13]

Primeau also reported that, exasperated by Riel's continual reproaches against him and Mallet for treating him like a lunatic, he had taken him on Christmas Eve to stay with Father Richer in Suncook, New Hampshire. They were accompanied on the journey by a man from Worcester whom Primeau had engaged to act as Riel's keeper.

The trip to Suncook was later described by Ferdinand Gagnon:

Riel's madness consisted of believing himself called to regenerate the world. He belonged to a trilogy: the Comte de Chambord, Don Carlos, Louis Riel. In his imagination he represented these three figures by three bulls: a white, that of Chambord; a black, that of Don Carlos; a red, that of Louis Riel. Sometimes the poor Riel bellowed like a bull, and it took a great effort of persuasion to make him be quiet. During the trip from Worcester to Manchester, he emitted some of these bellows: but Father Primeau had such control over him that he stopped him with a severe look.[14]

Evidently, Riel was still within Primeau's spiritual power. He did not want to disobey the priest in spite of the latter's disbelief in his mission. Primeau could still control him with no more than a glance.

Riel by this time had apparently expanded his mother's stories about his noble ancestry into a belief that he was one of the Bourbons, like the Comte de Chambord, pretender to the French throne, and Don Carlos, his counterpart in Spain. Support of royalist pretenders, particularly of the Comte de Chambord, was an important aspect of ultramontanism. He was a particularly attractive figure for a cult because of the unusual circumstances of his birth. He was the posthumous son of the Duc de Berry, who had been assassinated in 1820 in an attempt to extinguish the elder branch of the House of Bourbon. The royalists hailed the birth and dubbed the baby 'l'enfant du miracle.' He was baptized with water from the Jordan which Chateaubriand had brought back from the Holy Land. Thus support for 'Henry V' was a sacred cause to the monarchists. Spanish affairs had also recently been in the news. Don Carlos had been removed by a *coup d'état* in December 1874 in favour of Alfonso XII, who was more acceptable to the republicans. Spain was still locked in civil war at this date, and Riel would have been reading about the Carlists on the front page of the daily papers. In identifying himself with 'Henry V' and Don Carlos, Riel was saying that he, like them, was a divinely authorized ruler, unjustly kept from power by God's enemies. (Why Riel symbolized himself and the others by bulls is not apparent.)

Supervised by Father Richer and the man from Worcester, Riel stayed at Suncook for about two weeks, where he received a letter from Mgr Bourget which further confirmed his belief in his mission.[15] Bourget wrote to Riel never to depart 'from the path which divine Providence has laid out for you.' He promised that a 'time of mercy' would come for the métis, when religion would arise from its present 'state of oppression' to crown Riel's people with honour and glory. In Riel's agitated state, this promise seemed like the divine seal of approval upon his mission; and the letter's closing words – 'soyez donc béni de Dieu et des hommes' – echoed in his mind like the shouts of the crowd as Jesus entered Jerusalem: 'Blessed is he who comes in the name of the Lord.'

Bourget's words brought a moment of exaltation, but Riel was also troubled with profound feelings of failure and guilt, for which the glory of his prophetic mission was a psychological compensation. These feelings were visible in a long letter he wrote on 8 January 1876, to Bishop Taché, his former patron and protector.[16] Riel's attitude toward Taché was now markedly ambivalent. On the one hand, Riel said, he loved Taché because of all the kindnesses the bishop had performed for him and his family since his youth. But he also accused Taché of having been easily fooled by the enemies of the métis. If it had been up to him, he would have done many things differently. (Riel was referring to the conciliatory actions which Taché had often pressed upon him: to help defend Manitoba against O'Donoghue's raid, to take Macdonald's bribe to leave Canada, to give Cartier his parliamentary seat.) But, continued Riel, God was using Taché to punish him for his youthful faults. 'God has put me into your strong and generous hands to chastise me, while saving me.'

Riel interpreted his political reverses as justified punishment for his sins. 'In the autumn [of 1872],' he wrote,

I ceded my election in Provencher at your request to the Minister of Militia [Cartier]. Subsequently I had the honour to be elected three times in a row. Heaven demanded of me that I also sacrifice these three elections, one after the other, each in a different way but painfully. I tried to make these sacrifices in a Christian spirit, offering them to God to expiate the four denials which I made when I was still young against God, religion, my country, and my family.

Riel's belief that he deserved to be punished probably stemmed from his youthful renunciation of his vocation. Because of the circumstances under which he had been sent to Montreal, his decision seemed to him like a denial 'against God, religion, my country, and my family.' And indeed the rest of the letter contains Riel's rationalization for having given up his vocation in favour of doing God's work in the secular world. However, there are tantalizing hints that some greater and more secret sin was involved. Riel wrote: 'I love you because God, deigning to punish me in this world for having called myself a Jew, has chosen you ... to make me expiate my culpable defection.' This quotation was already mentioned in connection with the 'Mordecai affair'; but unfortunately the evidence on that score is too sketchy to admit any conclusion. One can only surmise that Riel was tormented by an overwhelming sense of guilt, without pretending to know all the reasons why.

Characteristically, Riel's sense of guilt was tied to an equally strong hope of redemption. He concluded the letter by vowing that he would continue to submit to his punishment because he knew it was for his ultimate benefit. 'And so that God may deign to make me succeed and triumph with Him, I hold myself obedient ... Monseigneur, in pushing me to the foot of the wall, as you have done, you have forced me to direct my gaze straight up to heaven.'

From Suncook Riel was taken to Keeseville, still accompanied by the man from Worcester acting as a guardian. It was hoped that at the Barnabé household, where Riel had spent so many happy days, he might come out of his agitated condition. But shortly after his arrival, Father Barnabé had to telegraph for help to Riel's uncle in Montreal, John Lee.[17] Lee came immediately by train, and was met by Barnabé at the station. He asked, 'What's wrong?' and he was told 'poor Riel is out of his mind [fou à lier]!' Barnabé continued that Riel would sleep neither day nor night, that he kept the house in turmoil with his crying and shouting. Lee, who spent the night in Keeseville, reported that Riel was awake the whole time bellowing like a bull.

Early next morning, 29 January, assisted by the man from Worcester, Lee took his nephew back to Canada. Riel created a disturbance on the train. When people laughed at him he said, 'Be silent' or 'Don't laugh, I am an apostle, I am a prophet!' Not wanting to conduct Riel through the crowded Bonaventure Station in downtown Montreal, his uncle had telegraphed ahead for a carriage to meet the train at the village of St Lambert. The party dismounted and resumed their journey in the carriage, crossing the frozen St Lawrence on the ice. They finally reached Lee's home in Mile End, although Louis had to be forcibly restrained from running into Bonsecours Church as they passed by.

The Lees, being people of some means, could afford to hire a trustworthy man to help them control their difficult relative. Louis was extremely excited for the first six days. He would not sleep or be silent, and 'had convulsions like an angry man.' But eventually he began to get calmer; so after four or five weeks the Lees allowed him to go to mass at the local church, St Jean-Baptiste, by himself. This, however, led to an untoward incident. After the sermon, which had been very emphatically preached, Louis arose and cried three times, very slowly, in a voice which was meant to be solemn but which was only lugubrious: 'Hear the voice of the priest!'[18] He then made no resistance as some bystanders led him out of the church and took him home. After this the Lees, fearing Riel would create a scene and betray his identity, did not let him out alone. His only excursions from the house were carriage rides, which were allowed almost every day.

On three different occasions Louis locked himself in his room, disrobed, and tore all his clothes and bed linen to shreds. He then let himself be redressed like an infant, but refused to explain why he had acted thus. On other occasions he tried to get out through the window, saying that he must go to church. When reproached for his follies he would reply: 'No, I'm not crazy! Never say I'm crazy! I have a mission to perform and I am a prophet. You should say that you don't understand. I am sent by God.'

At length, wearied of the struggle, Lee contacted Dr Emmanuel P. Lachapelle, whom he knew to be a friend of his nephew. Lachapelle had been in Riel's class at the College of Montreal. He was beginning an illustrious career that would bring him many distinctions, including the presidency of the Canadian Medical Association. Although a Liberal in politics, he had been one of Riel's confidants and supporters ever since he had come east in late 1873. Now Lachapelle arranged for him to be admitted to the St Jean-de-Dieu asylum for the insane in Longue Pointe, a suburb of Montreal. The diagnosis was 'folie des grandeurs,' or delusions of grandeur.[19]

Riel was told nothing of these preparations, and his consent for the commitment was not sought. On 6 March 1876, his uncle took him out for a carriage ride which ended at the asylum. Louis reacted stoically when he understood what was happening to him. Lee later wrote: 'I promised him to come back to see him the next day, but he seemed perfectly indifferent.' For the rest of the time he was hospitalized, Louis acted coldly towards his uncle, obviously feeling that he had been betrayed. He did not want medical treatment but recognition of his mission. What unbelievers saw as insanity was really 'continual communication with God.'[20]

In 1876, the insane asylums of Quebec were operating under the Act Respecting Private Lunatic Asylums, passed a quarter-century earlier.[21]

The statute specified that admission of a patient was supposed to take place on the application of a relative or friend plus the certification of two doctors. The physicians were not supposed to be 'partners or brothers, or father and son'; neither were they supposed to be proprietors of a lunatic asylum, nor close relatives of a proprietor. Each doctor was supposed to make a separate, personal examination of the patient not more than a week prior to admission. The criteria of certification were somewhat vague. A physician had only to certify that a person was 'a lunatic (or an insane person, or an idiot, or a person of unsound mind), and a proper person to be confined.' There were no safeguards in the admission process such as a hearing before a judge or jury.

The legal rights granted to the individual by this legislation were minimal, but it is doubtful whether even they were respected in Riel's case. Application would have been made by his uncle, John Lee, and Dr Lachapelle would have been one of the certifying physicians; but it is not known who the second doctor was, or indeed if there was one. All surviving accounts are silent on that point. For the sake of secrecy, Riel was admitted under a false name, Louis R. David. To minimize the number of those who knew what was happening, the asylum may well have dispensed with a second independent medical opinion. It may be that a second signature was obtained from a physician employed by the asylum or from a trustworthy friend. While perhaps technically legal, such an action would have contravened the spirit of the law, according to which the asylum was designed to receive patients, not seek them out.

A Kafkaesque touch was provided by the attitude and actions of Dr Henry Howard, visiting physician at St Jean-de-Dieu. He was an appointee of the provincial government; his function was to keep an independent eye on the institution. He was not an employee of the hospital, which had its own medical superintendent and staff. Before Riel was admitted, Dr Howard was consulted by John Lee and the mother superior of the nuns who ran the institution. Lee reluctantly admitted that the person he wished to commit was none other than Louis Riel. In Howard's words:

I was informed that his excitement was exhibited chiefly when political subjects were introduced, and that his friends were anxious to see him safely guarded till they could get him out of the country. His eccentricities had already produced such animosity amongst certain sections of the people, that fears were entertained for his life should he be left at liberty.

I at once cheerfully consented to the proposition to have Louis David Riel admitted into the asylum the following day under the name of Louis R. David, and said I would do all I could to have his secret kept from sisters, keepers and strangers, as if he were insane ... [22]

This was an extraordinary charade, to say the least. Dr Howard, supposedly the public guardian of the institution, agreed to admit as a patient a man he had never met, to hold him for 'protection' under a false identity, and to pretend to others that he was insane. Howard continued:

Am I ashamed of what I did? Not a bit of it. I believed him to be guilty of the murder he was accused of, and I believed every murderer to be either insane or a fool. The unfortunate man was not flying from justice; he was evading fanatics ...

In effect, Howard was setting up himself and his institution as an alternate penal system, one in which all who commit serious crimes were assumed to be of unsound mind. In spite of the fact that Riel had been granted amnesty by Parliament for the Scott affair, Howard now judged him guilty of murder, mentally defective, and in need of commitment for his own protection.

The rationale for Howard's action is to be found in his theory of mental deviations, which he published in several books and articles.[23] He distinguished between 'teratological' and 'pathological' mental deficiencies. Both were deemed to be organic. The former were congenitally present, while the latter were acquired as a result of sickness. Idiocy, imbecility, and criminality were teratological in origin, while insanity strictly defined was pathological, a disease. Both classes of defectives were equally irresponsible for their actions, and equally in need of custodial attention. Therefore Howard really had no need to examine Riel to see if he was 'sane' or not; it was enough to know that he was a 'criminal' in order to lock him up (presumably forever, since Howard was not optimistic that teratological defects could be overcome).

Thus Riel was packed away into the asylum with considerable disregard for his civil rights and the forms of legality. But it must also be admitted that he did not resist very hard. Until he was actually confined in Longue Pointe, he could have escaped from the custody of his friends; but he made no serious effort to do so. Two facts may help provide an explanation of this puzzle. First, Riel defined his mission as one of humility and obedience. He claimed to be acting under instructions received from various members of the Catholic hierarchy, especially

Bishop Bourget. Thus when he encountered resistance from his Catholic friends, particularly priests, he did not want to break with them, believing that their skepticism was only the result of misunderstanding. He preferred to stay with them, to persuade them of the validity of his mission.

Second, Riel was already a prisoner of his own cause. From the time he had come east in late 1873, and indeed even before that, he had no longer been self-supporting. He had lived from the largesse of friends, who gave him food, shelter, and often money. His friends did not begrudge their generosity, and they had a real affection for Riel; but they knew him only as Louis Riel, the heroic métis defender of the French language and the Catholic religion. When he began to transcend that identity, groping towards a new definition of himself as an inspired servant of God, they naturally wished to save him from himself. They had the means to do so because Riel, utterly without means, had already lost his independence. Ironically, he who had sacrificed everything for the métis cause as he saw it was now himself sacrificed to that cause as others saw it.

LONGUE POINTE

At the time of Riel's hospitalization, the dominant psychiatric approach was known as 'moral treatment.' It consisted of submitting the patient for a prolonged period of time to an environment of authority in which he could regain discipline and self-control.[24] At its best, this meant keeping the inmate comfortable and well fed, and relying on the passage of time to calm his troubled state of mind. At its worst, moral treatment was no better than long-term custody, often under atrocious conditions.

Institutional practices in North America were rapidly changing about the time Riel was admitted. There was a movement away from forcible restraint of inmates by mechanical devices such as crib-beds, strait jackets, and manacles; for the use of these implements to curb violence was often part of a vicious circle in which restraint provoked counter-violence. There was also a marked trend to higher standards of spaciousness, comfort, nutrition, and recreation for inmates. The prominent British psychiatrist, Dr Daniel Hack Tuke, great-grandson of William Tuke, who had pioneered in the more humane treatment of the insane in Britain, made a tour of North America in 1884. He found conditions fairly good, at least in Ontario and in the more progressive states of the American Union. But he also found unhappy exceptions, probably the worst of which was in the Province of Quebec. Publication of Dr Tuke's report provoked a major scandal in Quebec, with the result that the province's two mental hospitals, previously run by private owners, were brought under government auspices to correct the abuses.[25]

This was a decade after Riel was an inmate; but it stands to reason that the conditions Tuke found in 1884 would have existed when Riel was admitted in 1876, since the hospital administrators were the same, and nothing had intervened to change their practices. Therefore Tuke's report of what he saw at the asylum of St Jean-de-Dieu can be used with the assumption that it would have applied fairly well to Riel's stay there.

St Jean-de-Dieu was owned and operated by the Sisters of Providence. There were a few private patients, but most were publicly supported by a contractual arrangement with the provincial government. The per capita stipend was only about $100 a year, much lower than in other Canadian and American institutions. The grounds of the establishment were spacious, consisting of 600 acres on which there was a sizable farming operation. The building, which had only been opened in 1876, the year Riel was admitted, was adequate. When Dr Tuke saw it in 1884, it was sadly overcrowded, but this was probably not such a problem when Riel was there. There were comfortable single rooms on this first floor for the private and some of the more fortunate public patients. But the higher one ascended, the more depressing became the sight. The upper floors held numerous 'refractory' patients huddled together on wooden benches in barren wards. Mechanical restraint was widely used, particularly on patients prone to tear their clothes – 'a serious matter,' said Tuke, 'in an asylum conducted on the contract system!' Other individuals were confined almost continually in unfurnished, unlit cells in the basement. It was, in Dr Tuke's phrase, 'a chamber of horrors.' He wrote: 'I have visited a large number of asylums in Europe, but I have rarely, if ever, seen anything more depressing.'

Riel's stay at Longue Pointe was a story of conflict from the outset. Sister Thérèse-de-Jésus, the superior of the institution, had not really wanted to admit him. Afraid that his presence would be discovered and cause an incident, she agreed to take him only under the pseudonym of Louis R. David. This caution led to an unpleasant incident at the time of Riel's entrance. Dr Henry Howard has described what happened:

I walked directly up to him, to shake hands with him, and said, 'I am glad to see you, Mr David; my name is Dr Howard.' He started back and said, 'Why do you call me David? My name is Louis David Riel,' and thrusting his hand into the side pocket of his coat, he took from it a small prayerbook, and opening it at the fly-leaf, handed it to me, saying, 'Look at my name there, Louis D. Riel, written by my dear sister.'[26]

At once the sister who was present grabbed the book, ripped out the offending page, and said, 'You are only known here, sir, as Mr David!' A terrible struggle ensued, and Dr Howard recalled that he had never seen a man in such fury. If Riel had not been restrained, he would have attacked the nun and 'torn her in pieces.' He obviously objected to being treated so rudely, and particularly to being deprived of his name. In fact the attempted deception was not successful. Dr Howard admitted that Riel's true identity was no secret to the staff and inmates of the asylum as long as he was confined there.

Riel was unhappy at St Jean-de-Dieu, and he repeatedly implored Dr Howard to set him at liberty. His stay there was marked by numerous violent conflicts with the hospital staff, conflicts which could only end in Riel's being placed in a strait jacket or secluded in solitary confinement. His violent behaviour was aggravated by the oppressive atmosphere of the institution. In Dr Tuke's words, 'the necessity for mechanical restraint is exceptional, and ... in proportion as an asylum is really well managed the number whose movements are confined by muffs, straitwaistcoats, and handcuffs will become smaller and smaller.'[27] To a man of Riel's passionate temperament and powerful physique, the atmosphere of authority and restraint was a standing challenge to assert his independence.

Dr Howard found him one morning, only a few days after his admission, nude except for a long strait jacket. Riel explained that his suitcase had been opened during the night and his letters stolen. When he discovered the theft, he became enraged and started to make an uproar, whereupon the attendants fastened him into the jacket. Now that he had calmed down, he could laugh at his absurd position.[28] On 19 March, according to hospital records, Riel smashed everything in his room – furniture, ventilator, window. It required three strong men to overpower him.[29]

A more prolonged clash with authority was provoked by Riel's interest in the condition of the chapel at St Jean-de-Dieu. Not long after his admission, he examined the chapel and found it unsatisfactory. The sacristy, that is, the room behind the altar used for storage and as a cloak room for the priests, was in order, but the sanctuary was not perfectly clean. The altar linens were stained, and the candles were not properly cared for. According to Riel, God said to him: 'I do not see as much filth on the Jewish altars as on the Catholic. Tell those who are in charge. And if they don't improve, destroy the broken lamps.'[30] This divine commandment led Riel to invade the chapel and attempt to break everything that did not meet with his approval. As a result he was placed in solitary confinement. On 16 April 1876, it was noted in the hospital record book: 'This evening, Mr Louis Riel, insane, known by the name of Mr David, broke the glass of the chapel door, in an outburst of madness, and was taken down to the cells of the refractory patients (furieux).'[31]

One may discern a double motive in these attacks on the chapel. Riel's concern for the physical condition of the chapel was a symbol of his mission to reform the entire Church. The resistance he met from the hospital staff represented the opposition accorded to the prophet by a sinful world. God said to Riel: 'Here the stage is small, but tomorrow it will be great.'[32] His symbolic cleansing of the chapel was a preparation for the general purification of the Church which he would soon undertake. In addition to the symbolic meaning, Riel's attacks on the chapel were a part of his struggle with the hospital authorities. Dr Howard related that he found Riel in a strait jacket one day after one of these incidents. Riel began to smile, and said he was doing these things to see how the mother superior would treat him if he acted like a gentleman.[33] Dr Howard advised him to act like a gentleman all the time, but Riel was too recent a newcomer to the asylum to have lost all his rebelliousness. As long as he was at Longue Pointe, he continued to probe the limits of authority.

His campaign against the chapel was extremely important to him. When Father Albert Lacombe, the famous missionary to the Blackfoot, happened to be in Montreal a few weeks later, he visited Riel and found his conduct quite normal until the subject of the chapel was mentioned. Father Lacombe asked Riel why he had behaved so wildly; and as the latter replied, 'his features contorted, his face changed, his eyes suddenly looked as if they were seeing something.' Riel then launched into his explanation about the lamentable state of the sanctuary as compared to the sacristy; and this, as far as Father Lacombe was concerned, was the end of reasonable conversation.[34]

Conflict over the chapel led to a hunger strike. After being seized by the orderlies and put into confinement, Riel did not eat for four days and nights. Whenever he was offered food, Riel would reply: 'Let me into the chapel where my mission makes me master. Let the sister superior herself come to me to ask forgiveness and kneel before me.' But these tactics did not work; Riel was still barred from the chapel. God finally said to him, 'The struggle is too much for you. I'm going to give you help.' Riel then called the chaplain and asked for permission to consecrate bread and wine. Rather shrewdly the chaplain replied, 'If that's the way you want to eat, go ahead,' whereupon Riel broke his fast by repeatedly consecrating bread and wine and then consuming it. However, God told him to cease this practice because skeptics were saying that it was just a subterfuge to take some nourishment.[35]

These struggles over eating and over access to the chapel cannot be dated precisely, but they seem to have occurred in March and April. In May a new subject of conflict appeared – clothing. Riel began to destroy his clothing and display himself nude as he had done at the home of his aunt and uncle. Destruction of clothing, which meant a financial loss to the hospital, was a blow against the authority of the institution. It was also, together with nudity, a symbolic statement. It represented the execution of Bishop Bourget's injunction to retain nothing of what belonged to him. On one occasion, Riel took off all his clothes and tore them to shreds when the sisters refused to allow him to give them to the poor. As a further symbol of his complete devotion to God, he tied a string to each wrist, showing that he would be led by his divine Father just as French children used to be taught to walk with strings on their wrists.[36] Nudity also symbolized innocence as well as the eschatological theme of coming redemption. These last two ideas were a development of well-known traditions of Judaism and Christianity. Adam and Eve put on clothes only after losing their innocence through original sin. In the thought of the Apostle Paul, Christ, who brings salvation to men, is called the new Adam. Riel, who wanted to announce salvation to the present age, combined these themes in the symbolism of eschatological nudity:

When man divests himself of himself, it will not be twenty-four hours before I [God] complete in him the work of redemption and bring him into my presence, as were Adam and Eve before their sin, in the enjoyment of the delights of innocence. ... He who is good should show himself entirely nude, for he is beautiful. He who is disobedient should hide himself, for he is ugly. ... The day is coming when men will arise naked from the breast of the earth.[37]

One reason why the sisters were determined to keep Riel under such strict control was their fear that his presence would be discovered by the

Orangemen of Montreal. Riel himself also had apprehensions on this score. Dr Howard claims to have found him in his room one morning around the middle of May in a state of mortal terror. Riel said that the bars had been removed from his window during the night to encourage him to escape. 'If I escaped last night through that window, I would have been murdered. Say nothing about it. I won't speak of it to anyone; but for God's sake try and get me away.'[38] Whether or not this story is true (and it seems very improbable), Riel's departure took place on 19 May. He was transferred to the only other asylum in Quebec, located at Beauport, a suburb of Quebec lying between the city and Montmorency Falls.

The transfer was more or less clandestine. Dr Alphonse Deschamps, brother of one of Riel's schoolmates, appeared at Longue Pointe bearing the following note: 'I, the undersigned, a practising physician of the city of Montreal, certify that I am leaving on a short trip and that I am taking Mr L.R. David with me to restore his health.'[39] It is not clear whether the sisters in charge of Longue Pointe knew at this point that Riel was leaving for good. His name was kept on their books until 15 January 1877, when he was officially registered as discharged.[40] The net result was a falsification of the records but at this distance, and in the absence of the original documents, one cannot say who was responsible. Further improprieties were committed at Beauport, where use of the alias 'David' was continued and supplemented by yet another false name, 'Larochelle.' Again Riel was apparently committed on the strength of one doctor's signature, that of Dr Lachapelle.[41]

These furtive proceedings were possible because of sympathy in high places. The provincial secretary, responsible for the Quebec asylums, was J.-Adolphe Chapleau, the friend of Riel's who had helped defend Ambroise Lépine at his trial in 1874. Chapleau himself, accompanied by Riel's old friend and staunch defender in Parliament J.-O. Mousseau, as well as Dr Lachapelle and Dr Deschamps, assisted in putting Riel aboard the steamer that was to carry him down river to Quebec. John Lee, who witnessed the scene from a distance, reported that it was a pitiful sight.[42] Riel did not want to board the boat; he shouted and struggled with his friends. Recalling the incident, Riel later said: 'I made myself go limp, and they were hard put to hold me up. I looked at old Mousseau, his face covered with sweat, and I laughed up my sleeve.'[43]

It cannot be determined exactly why Riel was removed from one asylum to the other. Dr Lachapelle later said that he had Riel moved because he was not getting the right sort of care at Longue Pointe.[44] Dr

Howard, on the other hand, claimed to have engineered the move to protect Riel's safety after the incident of the window bars.[45] There may be truth in both of these explanations. The nuns' anxiety about Riel encouraged them to be authoritarian in their treatment of him, which in turn provoked him to acts of violent resistance. Dr Lachapelle, perhaps also worried about discovery and certainly seeing that Riel would remain stubborn in this atmosphere, thus arranged for the removal to Beauport. In the provincial capital, less riven by racial strife, greater security might make possible a more relaxed environment.

BEAUPORT

The asylum of St Michel-Archange at Beauport had been founded in 1845 as a private, profit-making enterprise. When Riel entered, the proprietors were the medical superintendents, Drs François Roy and J.-E. Landry. The day-to-day business of the institution was handled by a non-medical manager, Clément Vincelette, whose wife functioned as matron. The chaplain was Father J.-B.-Z. Bolduc, pastor of the nearby church of St Roch and also an important administrator in the archdiocese of Quebec.

Conditions at Beauport were similar to those at Longue Pointe. There were some cheerful and pleasant rooms, but a larger number of repugnant cells and dormitories. Various means of mechanical restraint were commonly used. Public patients were supported by the provincial government at the rate of $11.00 per month, more than at Beauport but still not very much, considering that the work of the asylum had to be done by paid employees, not nuns who had taken a vow of poverty. The tight budget at Beauport meant that attendants were few in number and poorly paid. Orderlies received less than $200.00 a year, female attendants less than $100.00. Dr Tuke observed that hiring more numerous and a 'higher class' of attendants would have greatly reduced the necessity of keeping order by means of mechanical restraining devices.[46]

At Beauport, incidentally, Riel was still within an ultramontane environment. Most of Quebec City, under the leadership of Archbishop Taschereau and Laval University, tended to be Liberal, but there was a small group of ultramontanes who founded an association called Le Cercle Catholique in 1877. Beauport asylum was one of the main centres of this club: Dr Landry and Dr Roy were charter members, while the president of the Circle was Clément Vincelette. Other members were the prominent journalists Jules-Paul Tardivel of *La Vérité* and Israël Tarte of *Le Canadien*.

When Riel was admitted to St Michel-Archange, Dr Lachapelle filled out a medical history, consisting of twenty-seven questions and answers, which has been preserved in the archives of the hospital.[47] It is an important source of information about Riel's behaviour and about the way he was treated. The document retained Riel's fictional identity. His name was given as Louis R. David, his race as French-Canadian instead of métis, and his place of residence as Montreal. He was described as a 'gentleman without profession' who had 'no visible means of support' – a designation which was not entirely inaccurate but hardly did justice to his political career.

Lachapelle reported that this was the patient's first bout of madness, that it had begun in October 1875, and that at the present time it was worsening rather than improving. There were no physical symptoms to mention, and indeed the psychological symptoms were barely noticeable except for a tendency to become uncontrollable ('furieux'), a tendency which was aggravated by the visits of friends and acquaintances. Lachapelle summarized Riel's problem in the following crisp sentence: 'In religious matters he thinks himself a prophet.'

Lachapelle affirmed that his patient was not suicidal, and had never harmed another person, although he had uttered threats against some people. Riel had no unusual or distasteful personal habits except for occasionally tearing his clothes and destroying dishes, furniture, etc. He had no serious physical disease, had never received an injurious blow to the head, and did not use strong drink, tobacco, or opium. Lachapelle attributed Riel's madness not to physical causes but to 'frustrated ambition' ('ambition déçue'), one of the standard diagnoses of the day. The doctor added that one could not but be struck by the 'effrontery' of Riel's plans, and by his 'superstitious piety.' Confinement for two months at St-Jean-de-Dieu had not erased these characteristics, so perhaps a change of surroundings would be beneficial.

We are less well informed about Riel's behaviour at Beauport than at Longue Pointe, because the documents which have survived deal more with his thoughts than with his actions. Dr Daniel Clark, who talked in 1885 with Dr Roy, said that Riel spent several months at Beauport in the refractory ward.[48] This may well be true, although, as stated earlier, Dr Clark is not a very reliable witness. One letter survives which suggests that Riel may have spent some time in manacles for resisting a medical order to take away his New Testament, on the grounds that it contributed to his insanity.[49]

No letters from Riel to Bourget written after 29 May 1876 have been found. Probably the correspondence was continued; but since Bourget retired as Bishop of Montreal in May 1876, being elevated to the honorary title of Archbishop of Martianapolis, Riel's letters were not preserved in the diocesan archives. The one surviving letter from Beauport suggests that on his arrival there Riel found himself in conflict with the staff just as he had at Longue Pointe. He sent some loose sheets to Bourget, one of which contains this notation:

Beauport! Yesterday, May 21, 1876, the Prophet of the Lord could not celebrate the Eucharist within your walls. Beauport! Yesterday, the Prophet of the Lord tried all day to obtain from your people the means of saying Mass. You gave him wine, but that wine is not wine for Mass.[50]

On 30 July, Riel was still attempting to exercise the powers of a priest, indeed of a bishop or pope. He wrote to the chaplain, who, we may infer, had barred him from attending the chapel, probably for creating a disturbance:

I forbade you orally this morning, and I forbid you this afternoon in writing, to say or sing the holy mass. ... I have the right to command you in the name of the Holy Spirit, because the divine spirit has consecrated me sovereign pontiff, His prophet and priest-king, by descending upon me; and because the bishop of Montreal, bishop of apostolic, Catholic, and Roman ordination, has endowed me with total jurisdiction in pronouncing over me the following words: 'Therefore be blessed by God and men.'
Louis 'David' Riel.
By the grace of Jesus Christ
Prophet, Infallible Pontiff, and Priest-King.[51]

This grandiose manifesto is the last clear sign of a clash with the hospital authorities, although Riel may have become involved in an imbroglio in August connected with a move from one part of the hospital to the other.[52] He must have gradually settled into a calmer state. He was not happy, for he still felt unjustly confined; indeed his uncle, who came to Beauport three times, found him even more melancholy than at Longue Pointe. But apparently he ceased to kick against the goad, after which he was kindly treated. An employee reportedly said afterward that he saw Riel every day for two years, and he was 'never treated as a patient, but had perfect freedom about the institution.'[53] This seems plausible: when Dr Tuke visited Beauport in 1884, he found it very much like Longue Pointe in having comfortable facilities and a degree of liberty for co-operative patients, combined with extremely repressive handling of difficult inmates. The key was Riel himself. He had learned by experience that he had no choice but submission. Had he been prepared to admit this in St Jean-de-Dieu, doubtless his stay there would not have been so tempestuous.

Of course, life in an asylum is not idyllic, even under the best of conditions. Riel was still deprived of freedom of movement. Contrary to what has sometimes been written, it seems unlikely that he was allowed to travel about the province by himself, although he was taken for occasional outings.[54] There were also unpalatable circumstances within the asylum to contend with. Riel wrote to the manager on one occasion to report that an orderly had committed sodomy with a patient. The letter suggests that the staff was divided by internal power struggles, which could not have made life any easier for the inmates.[55]

As a co-operative patient, Riel was allowed to attend the sessions of the Cercle Catholique, to hear the speakers they invited, and to participate in the political and religious discussions. He became quite friendly with many of the members, especially Clément Vincelette and his family. Apart from this diversion, Riel seems to have occupied himself chiefly with reading and writing. He spent much time drafting the main ideas of his new religion, polishing them so carefully that it seems he intended to publish them. These extensive writings, which will be discussed in the next chapter, show him utterly convinced of his own ideas. If he had reached a period of stability in his behaviour, he had not repudiated his prophetic mission. To those in charge, that must have meant he was still insane, albeit easier to control.

Riel also returned to his habit of writing verses. If he had composed much poetry since leaving Montreal in 1866, very little has survived. But poems are frequently included among Riel's papers after 1876. One piece of particular interest in this context gives Riel's own view of his encounter with the medical profession. He accuses the 'physicians of the body' of ignoring the needs of the soul. They chatter a great deal about physiology, but know nothing of 'psychology' (in the etymological sense of 'science of the soul'). They have confined him in a lunatic asylum to demonstrate their power over men and their adherence to their own 'proud systems.' But Riel will not give in; he will place his 'entire confidence' in Jesus.[56]

An important event during the long months of confinement was the visit of Bishop Taché in November or December 1876.[57] Taché, who was in the Province of Quebec on other business, took the opportunity to visit his unhappy protégé. After their reunion, Riel sent Taché a letter liberally interspersed with passages of poetry.[58] He was trying to reinstate himself in the bishop's good graces after the hard things he had said in his letter of 8 January 1876, when he had called Taché God's instrument to punish him in this world. Now he proclaimed his loyalty to Taché and his desire to be counted as one of his children. Riel also asked Taché to have him released from the asylum: 'Be my liberator. I want to reach the United States.' But Taché approved of Riel's confinement and did not, as far as we know, try to have him released. In his view, the hero of the métis was now 'dead mentally.'[59]

Although Taché did not obtain Louis' release, he did procure an important consolation for him by arranging for correspondence to begin between him and his family. Louis appears not to have written to his family after early 1876. For months they did not know where he was, and it was only in July of that year that they learned of his enforced hospitalization.[60] Even then, correspondence did not resume. It may be that Riel did not wish to write to his family. It may also be that he was prevented. Mental patients in those days did not have the right to communicate with the outside world, which is now generally accorded them. As Riel said in a letter to Bourget, 'I write neither when I want nor as I want nor what I want.'[61]

Once Taché returned to St Boniface, he informed Riel's relatives that he would act as an intermediary for mail. He would forward letters to Father Bolduc, chaplain of the asylum, who in turn would pass them on to Riel. Riel's mother and his sister Sara wrote to him in January 1877, he responded, and regular contact resumed. One might think these letters would be of great personal interest; but in fact they are curiously dull and flat, filled with trivialities about the weather, the health of friends and relatives, and little else. Probably both Louis and his family had been warned that each must not distress the other with emotional outbursts or with references to Louis' mental state. Yet we know from other correspondence that Sara was so concerned about her brother that the nuns at Ile-à-la-Crosse feared she might also be losing her mind.[62]

Riel's family began to speak of an improvement in his condition in February 1877.[63] Their letters thereafter often mention that they have heard he is better, and that he is recovering his health. What did this 'cure' consist of? An insight is furnished by these comments of Father Bolduc, culled from his letters to Taché.

25 Nov. 1876
It would be difficult to find a man more foolish and stubborn.
17 Feb. 1877
Our dear Riel is not too sick, he is beginning to forget his role as prophet. He hardly prophesies any more ...
27 Aug. 1877
Riel is a little better in his mental aberrations. He isn't pope any longer. He went to communion yesterday.[64]

Theological and medical categories are entirely fused in Bolduc's reports. Riel is no longer quite so 'sick' because he prophesies less. His reception of communion is offered as a sign of mental health just as a physician might report that his patient's appetite was restored. But even if Riel externally seemed to be less of a prophet, we know from his writings that he still maintained his unorthodox beliefs, in fact he was elaborating them on paper in considerable detail.

Riel's recovery meant little more than external conformity. He learned how to keep his prophetic enthusiasm under control without actually giving up his beliefs. He became able to dissociate thought from action, so that he could believe in himself without rushing into rash actions which would only defeat his purpose. He learned to segregate the world of his revelations from the mundane world of everyday activities and relationships. When first hospitalized, he could speak or write of nothing save his mission; he was in a state of perpetual excitement. At Beauport he learned how to make his mission part of himself without letting it dominate everything else.

At times Riel spoke as if he had actually been sick, and had now recovered his sanity, implying that all his cherished beliefs were only delusions produced by an overwrought mind. His two main statements on the subject were made to a Quebec doctor at the time of his discharge from Beauport, 23 January 1878:

I had come to believe myself a prophet or something similar. ... However, one day, tired of remonstrances and objections, I asked myself if perhaps I was wrong and everyone else was right. From that moment light dawned in my mind.

Today I feel better, I even laugh at the proud hallucinations of my brain. My mind is clear; but when one speaks of the métis, of those poor people pursued by Orange fanaticism. ... Oh! then my blood boils, my head swirls, and ... it is better that I talk about something else.[65]

and:

I remember well enough what went on in my poor head during the months when it was thought proper to lock me up. I will still need calm for a long time. I will go to the United States to till the soil, unknown, far from Canadian affairs, far from all excitement. And if later the sacred cause of the métis reclaims my services, could I, their compatriot, refuse them my life, my blood?[66]

These ambiguous utterances are not easy to interpret. Riel openly rejects his beliefs as delusions, and yet at the same time he admits that they still have a certain power over him. If he can keep his mind off the subject of the métis, he is all right; but when he thinks of them, his 'blood boils' and his 'heard swirls.' Furthermore, Riel's subsequent history makes it clear that he was having visions and receiving revelations within a few weeks of his discharge from Beauport. If he ever did repudiate his prophetic beliefs, it was not very deeply and not for very long.

Riel's cure meant that he had learned how to conduct himself externally, not that he had undergone a deep internal transformation. He was still a prophet, but temporarily incognito. Maybe that is what Dr Roy meant when he testified at Riel's trial that his famous patient had been cured 'more or less' at Beauport.[67]

4
The New Religion

Riel's initial impulse was to renovate the Catholic Church from within.[1] Through his sufferings, through his absolute obedience to the hierarchy, he would contribute to the universal triumph of the Church. But he became more radical when his Catholic friends turned a deaf ear to his message and interpreted his enthusiasm as insanity. He began to think that his mission was to break with Rome, to establish on the soil of the New World a successor to the Catholic Church, which had lost its spiritual vitality. The new Church would have a distinct organization, theology, and moral code. In short, Riel aspired to found a new religion.

He never settled on an official name for his new church. He used several titles, the most grandiose of which was 'église catholique, apostolique et vitale des Montagnes Lumineuses.'[2] Other formulations were similar, with perhaps a word or two changed; but the adjective 'vitale' was always present. This is rather curious, for the normal French word for 'living' would be 'vivante.' Why did Riel prefer 'vitale'? Because the holy place of his new church was to be his family's home of St Vital. Riel's name for his religion was a pun which stated, in half-hidden form, his own importance in the new scheme of things. Beyond that, the list of adjectives 'catholique, apostolique, et vitale des Montagnes Lumineuses' recalls the famous four attributes of the Roman Church: 'one, holy, catholic, and apostolic.' Riel's imitation of these terms shows that his creation was not intended to be a mere sect, but the universal church inheriting the spiritual primacy of Roman Catholic tradition.

This project is well documented, since Riel used his enforced leisure in the asylums of Longue Pointe and Beauport to commit his thoughts to paper. Fortunately, enough of these manuscripts have been preserved to yield a reasonably complete portrait of his new religion.[3]

The central concept in Riel's thinking was that of mission, derived from his belief in Providence. The existence of Providence implies that each man has a mission, inasmuch as his life is part of a divine plan. In addition, Riel thought that he had been endowed with a divine mission in a very special way. Bishop Bourget's words, that God 'has given you a mission which you must fulfil in all respects,' meant that he had been consecrated to the service of the Holy Spirit.[4]

Riel's view of his mission is summarized in the fantastic signature which he sometimes used in Beauport: 'Louis "David" Riel: Prophet, Priest-King, Infallible Pontiff.' This extreme self-glorification was compensation for the many reverses of his career. It was also correlated with an equally extreme self-abasement. Over and over, Riel repeated that he was the worst of sinners, that he had succumbed to 'liberalism,' that in himself he was nothing, that only God's grace had elevated him. Sinner and pontiff were the opposite poles of a relationship which was the religious counterpart of failure and success. Riel was objectively a failure at this point in his career. But in the world of religious exaltation he could become a success. His sufferings would redeem him. He could achieve the power which had been denied him in secular life. Prophet, priest, king, pope – all were symbols of the divine power which would intervene to compensate Riel and his people for their sufferings, to punish their enemies and reward their friends.

Let us look at the significance of these titles:

David

In the last year of his life, Riel recalled that the name David had been given to him by Joseph Dubuc in October 1873, when he was hiding in the woods of St Norbert to avoid arrest.[5] Although this may well be true, the first contemporary documented reference to the name David is found in slightly different circumstances. Riel was elected member of parliament for Provencher while he was in hiding, and preparations were made to send him east. Dubuc wrote to him: 'In hotels and on steamboats you will be more or less obliged to give a name. And it would not be prudent to use your own. So take some name ... A very ordinary name like Pierre David or Jean Dubois has been suggested.'[6] It is not known whether Riel traveled east under the alias of David, but he definitely used it on occasion in Quebec.[7] However, there is no indication that he attached any mystical significance to it.

When John Lee and Dr Lachapelle committed him to Longue Pointe asylum on 6 March 1876, they employed the pseudonym 'Louis R. David' to avoid detection. Riel, in contrast, insisted that his name was 'Louis David Riel' – the first recorded instance in which he used 'David' as a middle name rather than an alias. He obviously found it significant that his friends were using the alias of David to conceal his identity. He wrote to Bourget that God had told him:

It is your enemies whom I have used to make you resemble David [by compelling him to flee for his life] and your so-called friends whom I am using to make you have the name of David [by using a false name at the hospital].[8]

Riel later wrote to Taché that he had particularly asked for the help of the 'Holy King David' during the troubles in Red River. He had promised David that if the latter would defend him, he would one day definitely place himself under his patronage by taking his name. Now he asked Taché:

Deign to bless me in Jesus and Mary, and confirm my second Baptismal name, the name of a great servant of God, that I may have the grace of signing Louis 'David' Riel.[9]

In fact, Riel had been using this signature at least since his transfer to Beauport, and continued to so do, whether or not he ever received Taché's permission. He normally put 'David' in quotation marks to emphasize the supernatural meaning of the name.

Riel saw numerous resemblances between himself and David. Both had experienced unexpected youthful success against formidable odds. Both had been forced to flee from the power of government. Both had been taken by others to be insane: David, when he sought safety at the court of the Philistines; Riel, when he stayed with his friends. And both were poets; Riel's verses would be the psalms of the modern era.

Riel also thought of an ingenious genealogical similarity between David and himself. He was seven-eighths French Canadian and one-eighth Indian, his father's grandmother having been a Chipewayan woman. David was seven-eighths Hebrew and one-eighth Gentile (his great-grandmother was Ruth, the Moabitess).[10] Furthermore, as discussed later in this chapter, Riel believed that the Indians of North America were of Jewish descent. Thus he could write that his genealogy was a mirror image of David's:

By the Indian blood which flows in your veins, you are Jewish. And through your paternal great-grandmother you belong to the Jewish nation as much as the first David belonged to the Gentiles, through his paternal great-grandmother. And as the first David belonged to the Jewish nation through all his other ancestors, so you belong to the Gentiles through all your other ancestors. You are the David of the Christian era, of whom the former David was only the symbol.[11]

David was an appropriate model for Riel because he had been most of the things that Riel wanted to be. He had been prophet, priest, and king. Since the Hebrews made no distinction between church and state, David was a supreme religious and political leader at the same time. Riel, in his exaggerated ultramontanism, likewise wanted to unite religious and secular life under his own leadership. The true meaning of his identity as David was not only that he was prophet, priest, and king, but that he was all of these at once.

Prophet

Riel called himself the 'Prophet of the New World.' All previous prophets had lived in the Old World; now for the first time the voice of God resounded in America.[12] Let us look more carefully at what a prophet is. Prophecy has become confused with prognostication, but the two are conceptually distinct. A prophet is one who speaks from the living inspiration of God. The Hebrew word for prophet, *nabi'*, means 'one who is chosen.' The Greek *prophētēs* means 'spokesman.' The prophet may incidentally foretell the future, but his main function is to reveal God's will to mankind. The prophet, following Max Weber's classic analysis, should be carefully distinguished from the priest.[13] A priest is an official, a functionary, who owes his position to the organization which he serves. A prophet is extra-institutional; his authority rests upon divine charisma, manifested in his holy life, his visions and revelations, his ability to work miracles.

Riel laid great stress on his role as spokesman. 'I am,' he said, 'in direct communication with my creator,' which meant that he was continually receiving revelations in the form of visions and voices.[14] It was his prophetic mission to transmit these truths to men. In an ingenious metaphor, he illustrated his position by calling himself the telephone of God (the telephone, invented in 1876, was just being introduced into Quebec):

> Quand je vous parle, c'est la voix de Dieu qui sonne
> Et tout ce que je dis vous est essentiel.
> Je suis le joyeux téléphone
> Qui vous transmet les chants et les discours du ciel.[15]

Was Riel in fact subject to paranormal experiences of a visionary character? He certainly claimed to be, and his pages are filled with circumstantial accounts of these revelations. But the descriptions which seem most genuine are those of experiences, like that of 8 December 1875, which were powerful and moving, but not visionary. Riel did not claim to see or hear anything on that occasion; he merely described the feelings which surged through him. When he actually describes his alleged visions, the accounts are so contrived as to be scarcely believable. Their elaborate symbolism seems to come from conscious reflection, not visionary spontaneity.

Priest

Interestingly, Riel craved official confirmation of his status. He claimed the charismatic authority of divine inspiration, yet he also desired human, institutional authorization. He was not entirely comfortable in the lonely role of prophet. His attitude is understandable in view of his background. Authority in the Catholic Church is vested in the priesthood, and this was especially true in the ultramontane version of Catholicism. Mgr Bourget saw the Church almost as an army in which the faithful were private soldiers while the priesthood made up the officer caste. Obviously fascinated by this authoritarian brand of Christianity, Riel sought the right to command, which he could do only as a priest.

He had once aspired to an ecclesiastical career; now he became a priest in a novel way. On 20 April 1876, he wrote to Mgr Bourget that he kept the bishop's letters with him day and night and meditated continually on their words. He now understood what Bourget had meant when he wrote to him: 'Soyez donc béni de Dieu et des hommes' ('Be blessed by God and men').

I see that I am elevated by your words; for in reality how could I be blessed by God and men if I could not give men, in God's name, what is necessary to them, that is, salvation? But how could I give salvation to men, in the name of our God, if I could not absolve them of their sins and give them the nourishment of the body and blood of Jesus Christ? ... You have endowed me with the priesthood.[16]

Riel was now a priest, not by the normal process of ordination, but by a special infusion of grace mediated through the Bishop of Montreal. He was a priest 'of universal jurisdiction,' ordained to bring salvation throughout the world. As we have seen, he attempted to consecrate bread and wine, as a priest would do, both at Longue Pointe and at Beauport.

King

It was revealed to Riel that he, as 'the David of the Christian era,' would found a new kingdom for the Jews on the soil of Poland, with the aid of the Bourbon pretender, the Comte de Chambord:

You will re-establish the people which is dear to me. ... A third of the Hebrew people is going to be converted now. Through the triumphant and victorious Henry V, you will give Poland to the House of Jacob, so that on its soil I may once again gaze upon the throne of David.[17]

Riel would be 'the messiah of human glory whom the people of Jacob expected to find in the incarnate Word.'[18] The Jews had rejected Jesus because His Kingdom had been spiritual rather than temporal. The new David would give them the temporal kingdom they had desired, while also converting them to the truth of Christianity. Note that Riel did not claim to be a messiah in the Christian sense of a divine redeemer. He called himself 'the messiah of human glory' to distinguish his role from the messianic function of Christ. He would play the lesser but still exalted role of 'King of the Jews' which Jesus had disdained. Riel also called himself the 'spiritual and temporal king of all nations without exception' but did not explain how this was related to his being the earthly messiah of the Jews.[19] Presumably he had in mind some notion of a new world order, such as he elaborated in his cell in Regina a decade later.

Infallible Pontiff

Riel was attracted by the grandeur of the pope's position, particularly the doctrine of infallibility, recently declared at the Vatican Council. On 18 July 1870, the Council voted to acknowledge that the pontiff could not err when speaking *ex cathedra* in matters of faith and morals. The Quebec ultramontanes had been strongly in favour of this proclamation. Now Riel, whose career had been ruined by his fatal mistake in the affair of Thomas Scott, yearned to have that infallibility for himself. He wrote in verses dedicated, ironically, to the chaplain at Beauport:

> Le Rédempteur me consume
> Du feu de sa charité.
> J'ai les marteaux et l'enclume
> De l'Infaillibilité.[20]

It is not altogether clear what Riel meant by calling himself a pontiff. His views seem to have gone through several stages not obviously demarcated from one another.

On 20 April 1876, he wrote to Bourget that he had received the 'supreme pontificate' through his blessing. But this did not mean that the Roman papacy had lost its authority. Riel was to announce to Pius IX, the reigning pope, that his pontificate was 'of forty years like that of Moses.' Since Pius IX had come to the papacy in 1846, this meant he would reign for another ten years until the Roman papacy would 'find its salvation in the New World.'[21] On 1 May, Riel wrote again to Bourget to confirm his loyalty to the pope. He asked Bourget to transport him magically and secretly to the Vatican so that he could comfort Pius IX by telling him about his mission.[22] On 15 May, Riel reported that God had told him, 'You are also the Pope.' But again he emphasized his devotion to Rome. 'You,' God had told him, 'will help the Pontiff of the seven hills to govern the human race.'[23]

Thus Riel spoke of himself as a pope at Longue Pointe, but did not draw the conclusion that he was the only pontiff and that the Roman papacy had lost its legitimacy. He seems to have seen himself as part of a double papacy, exercising authority in the New World while coming to the aid of the pope in the Old World. This arrangement would persist at least for the lifetime of Pius IX; there is no indication about what might happen afterwards.

In July 1876, Riel went a step further. He denounced the city of Rome for having made a prisoner of the pope after the Italian conquest of Rome in 1870. Speaking as the voice of God, Riel said: 'I am taking away the immortal Pontiff. I am taking away my solemnities from you.'[24] Rome would be destroyed even more thoroughly than Jerusalem. There would be a volcanic eruption covering everything for thirty-three miles around the city.

In another passage Riel pictures himself as leaving the city of Rome. He predicts devastation for the cathedral of St Peter:

Prophets and just men prayed in the temple of Solomon. And yet it was destroyed without regard for its magnificence.

The faithful and loving Nehemiah built a second temple. And the incarnate Word sanctified it with His real presence, His sacrifice, His prayers, and His teachings. No temple was more honoured, but it was destroyed without regard to its glory.

Beautiful basilica [St Peter's]! Jesus Christ also visited you. You were His Holy See. And you are the most admirable and the most honoured of the Cathedrals of the World. You have died; but your sudden death will preach the nothingness of all terrestrial things.[25]

Riel's ire is directed only against Rome, not personally against Pius IX. But in the report of a vision of 12 March 1877, Pius IX is pictured as an unscrupulous compromiser, occupied with 'la politique du monde.' His back is turned on the North-West, which is to say that he does not respect Riel's new revelation. When Riel realizes the pope's true character, his heart is emptied of the 'profound veneration' which he has always had for him. He denounces the pope, tells him that his pontificate has been terminated.[26] But Riel does not claim the papacy for himself. He now attributes it to Bishop Bourget. 'The bishop is at Mount Royal. Yes, the bishop of universal jurisdiction is at Mount Royal; he has been there since December 8, 1875.'[27]

Riel's final disillusionment with Pius IX may have been caused by contemporary developments in the old feud between ultramontanes and liberals in Quebec. Matters came to a head in 1877 when the ultramontanes, led by bishops Bourget and Laflèche, tried to create a clerically dominated voting bloc in Quebec politics. Archbishop Taschereau of Quebec City, whose sympathies were more with the Liberals, objected to village curés' threatening to withhold the sacraments from Catholics who voted Liberal. The whole question of clerical influence in politics was referred to Rome for adjudication; and an apostolic delegate, the Irish Bishop Conroy of Ardagh, was sent to investigate the dispute. The ultramontanes were defeated in the end. At the urging of Bishop Conroy, the Quebec bishops agreed to refrain from using spiritual threats to influence voting. The ultras were more than a little disillusioned by the failure of the Holy See to stand behind them. Bishop Laflèche's newspaper, *Le Journal de Trois-Rivières*, commented sourly: 'The year 1877 could be designated as the special epoch of concessions to liberalism and of cowardice, the epoch of the triumph of Catholic liberalism.'[28] Riel, following these events from his captivity in Beauport, may have decided that the Roman papacy was finished, that the Paraclete had left Rome and Pius IX to take up his abode in Montreal, the Rome of the New World.

Be that as it may, the evolution of Riel's view of the papacy was something of a paradox. He began by calling himself an 'infallible pontiff' possessing the 'supreme pontificate,' yet he wanted to remain loyal to Rome. He ended by repudiating Rome and Pius IX; but by then he felt that Bishop Bourget was the true pope, and he no longer claimed that distinction for himself.

CHOSEN PEOPLE

The transfer of the papacy to Montreal was only a step towards its ultimate settlement in St Vital, Riel's home town in Manitoba. The French Canadians had a temporary role to play in the economy of salvation, but the métis would finally emerge as God's chosen people. Riel's notion that the métis had a special mission to perform was built upon common French-Canadian views of the destiny of their nation. They thought of themselves as a Catholic and agricultural enclave on a Protestant and industrial continent, called to co-operate in God's work of spreading the true faith in America.[29] The ultras encouraged this feeling, particularly Bishop Laflèche in his book *Quelques Considérations sur les rapports de la société civile avec la religion et la famille* (1866). Riel adopted these notions while extending them. His fundamental idea was that the métis would continue, expand, and perfect the evangelical mission of New France in America.

Riel integrated this concept into an overall view of Catholic history. France is sometimes called the 'eldest daughter of the Catholic Church' because the Franks were the first major Germanic tribe to be converted to Catholicism after the collapse of the Roman Empire. Riel repeatedly referred to France as 'the eldest daughter,' with the implication that she had always had a special status in the Church. New France carried on the work of the mother country by spreading the gospel in the American wilderness. And now the métis would inherit the mission of New France. In Riel's words:

The French-Canadian nation has received from God the wonderful mission of continuing the great works of France on this side of the ocean. ... When the French-Canadian nation will have done its work and will be afflicted with the infirmities of old age, its mission must pass to other hands. ... We are working to make the French-Canadian Métis people sufficiently great to be worthy to receive the heritage of Lower Canada ... [30]

The mission of France lasted until the Revolution of 1789 infected that country with 'liberalism.' Indeed, the whole continent of Europe was affected. One consequence of the Revolution was the unification of Italy by liberal politicians like Cavour. The Papal States and Rome itself were lost to the pope, a sign that the Roman papacy had come to its end. As of 8 December 1875, the commencement of Riel's mission, the papacy had been spiritually transferred to Bishop Bourget in Montreal.[31]

French Canada was about to reach the highest stage of her mission. Until now she had been in a preparatory stage of suffering. God had allowed her subjection to Protestant England in punishment for her sins. But deliverance was at hand.[32] New France would reach the height of her glory when the papacy was transferred to Montreal.

Like France before her, New France would ultimately turn from her duty. In another four and a half centuries, men of liberal principles would gain power in Quebec. They would persecute the Church and force her to flee. Refuge would be waiting among the métis. 'The spirit of the sovereign pontificate will mount upon the chariot of Elias and flee to Manitoba.'[33] St Vital would be the final home of the papacy; from there the last pope would greet Christ returning in the Second Advent.[34]

If the métis had inherited a special mission on their fathers' side through French Canada, their ancestry on their mothers' side was also significant. When Riel was staying with his uncle, John Lee, in February 1876, it was revealed to him that the North American Indians were actually descendants of the Hebrews.[35] He subsequently communicated this revelation to Bourget with an extraordinary wealth of detail.[36]

About the time that the infant Moses had been exposed to the waters of the Nile, an Egyptian ship lost its way on the Atlantic. Forty-four persons were on board: twenty-seven Egyptians and seventeen Hebrews. The latter, hoping to escape from slavery in the land of Egypt, had persuaded the ship's captain to take them to Asia, on condition that they serve as slaves during the passage. The Hebrews consisted of three families, headed by Ihami of the tribe of Zabulon; Agaréon, also of Zabulon; and Oïorug of the tribe of Reuben. The Egyptians numbered twenty-two men and five women.

The ship went off course and wandered on the high seas for a year and a half until Agaréon thought of sacrificing bread and wine to the God of his fathers. He prayed as he made his sacrifice: 'O God of Abraham, of Isaac, and of Jacob! Do not take from my children the land which you promised to give to the seed of Abraham. Bring them to shore and save us all.' While Agaréon spoke, his four-year-old daughter played beside him with her little dog. She suddenly said, 'Father! You're always looking back towards the land of the Egyptians. But it's not there.' The girl pointed to the setting sun and cried: 'Let's go towards the light.' Soon they began to see islands; and nineteen days after Agaréon had sacrificed to God they landed on the Yucatan peninsula.

Although the Egyptians had nothing but contempt for the Hebrews, they were afraid to harm them because of the way God had heard Agaréon's prayer. So they contented themselves with driving the Hebrews off to the north, keeping some of their daughters to supplement their own scanty number of women. The Egyptians became the ancestors of the great empire-building Indians of South and Central America, while the Jews were the progenitors of the North American Indians.[37]

This tale had an important place in Riel's system of ideas because it provided a link between the first chosen people and the last. It was a symbolic justification of the special role that the métis would play in the economy of salvation. Such myths have been created in many millenarian creeds. They are a symbolic genealogy, a way of lending the grandeur of a vanished people to a nation whose own present is anything but grand. The Rastafarians of Jamaica claim that Ethiopia is their true homeland, since Ethiopia was the one black country not conquered by white men. The Black Muslims of the United States claim to be not really Negroes but lost descendants of the original Black Nation of Asia. Such myths impart dignity through denial of the present degraded identity in favour of a hidden but glorious ancestry.

MOSAIC LAW

Riel's admiration for the Hebrews went even farther than claiming them as ancestors. He also proposed to adopt their moral code, the Mosaic

Law. He did not plan to take over all aspects of the Law; his criterion was the Law as interpreted in the light of the gospels. Here again Riel was treading a well-worn path. Imitation of the first chosen people has been a very common feature of millenarian religious revivals.

Riel had two different reasons for his desire to follow the Mosaic Law. One was its intrinsic worth. Riel wrote that the Mosaic Law was 'conservative,' a bulwark against 'liberalism.'[38] In his special vocabulary, that meant he admired the all-embracing subordination to divine will demanded by adherence to the Law, which regulates all aspects of human behaviour. Extrapolating the ultramontane point of view that there was nothing outside the purview of religion, he approved of the totalitarian claim of the Law upon man's will. His second reason was based on precedent. He argued that Jesus and his earliest followers had obeyed the Law and lived as faithful Jews. The decision made by the apostles not to require Gentile converts to follow the Law was only a tactical necessity. 'They thought that the Gentiles would be more difficult to convert if, along with the gospel, they were also obliged to embrace the Mosaic prescriptions.'[39] So the apostles reduced the Law to nothing more than the ten commandments. God was not particularly pleased about this, but He allowed it as a way of evangelizing the world. Now that that task was accomplished, man would have to return to the Mosaic code, or at least to certain key provisions of it.

One was circumcision. 'It was ordained for Abraham and all his posterity. The Lord did not want Moses to remain without circumcision. Jesus Christ himself obeyed that law. Why have we put it aside?'[40] (Circumcision in Riel's day was not a standard medical procedure, performed on almost all male infants, as it now is in North America.)

Riel also spoke of reviving the Saturday Sabbath. He argued that the only important liturgical change from the Old Law to the New was the substitution of Christ as the symbolic victim for the animals which previously had been sacrificed as literal victims. This change did not necessitate a shift from Saturday to Sunday as the day of rest and worship. 'The day that the body of the Lord passed in the repose of the tomb is the same day that Christians were meant and are still supposed to observe as the Lord's Day.'[41]

Reform of the family was another of Riel's preoccupations. He did not so much wish to revive the Law of Moses as to invent new provisions vaguely inspired by it. His three reforms of marriage can be discussed under the headings of incest, polygamy, and a married clergy. He wrote that under certain conditions marriage between brother and sister would be permissible or even desirable. The first case he discussed was the following:

Our Lord Jesus Christ permits that if, after the death of the father of the family, an unmarried son takes care of his mother and his mother's children, as he should do for the love of God and of his family; and if, in order to remain more able to carry out this great duty, being poor, he neglects to marry, Our Lord permits, I say, that the son request the hand of one of his sisters and that his mother give or promise the son the hand of one of her daughters...[42]

Significantly, this passage is almost an exact description of Riel's own position after the death of his father. He was not yet twenty when his father died, and there were eight younger children. Although Louis did not immediately undertake their care, he did eventually come back to Red River to be head of the family. It seems more than a coincidence that Riel's first revelation about incest would have applied above all to himself. One can hardly help inquiring about personal motives, especially since incest is forbidden in the Mosaic Law, which he ostensibly wished to revive.

If Riel nourished an incestuous passion towards one of his sisters, the obvious candidate would be Sara, later Sister Marguerite-Marie. She and Louis were unusually close in spirit. However, they were widely separated almost all their lives. Louis left for Montreal shortly before his fourteenth birthday; Sara was then about ten. When he returned a decade later, she had already been a professed nun for two years. She left Red River for good in 1871, going as a missionary sister to Ile-à-la-Crosse, her father's birthplace. She remained there until her death and never saw Louis or any of her immediate family again. If Louis did have incestuous desires towards Sara, they must have remained purely in the realm of imagination.

Unfortunately, almost all of Louis' letters to Sara have been destroyed. In the few that remain from him to her, and in the more extensive correspondence from Sara to him, there is nothing incestuous, although a great deal showing love and sympathy between them.[43] More positive evidence can be found in Louis' love affair with Evelina Barnabé, to whom he became secretly engaged in 1878, when he went to stay in Keeseville after being discharged from Beauport. In his poetry to her, Riel liked to address Evelina as 'ma sœur'; she in turn used to sign her letters to him 'votre petite sœur.' This confusion of roles of sister and fiancée is interesting, although in itself hardly conclusive. But it highlights a poem Riel wrote to Evelina containing these lines, which touch directly on the theme of incest:

> Et tout à vénérer que soit le sanctuaire
> De la famille, hélas, il se trouve souillé
> Plus souvent qu'on voudrait, même entre sœur et frère.

> Excusez la parole claire
> Car je ne vous tiens pas un discours embrouillé
> Et si jamais Dieu veut que vous devenez mère,
> Evelina, souvenez-vous
> Que le fils du David, Ammon, commit l'inceste
> Avec sa sœur Thamara. Et le divin courroux
> S'alluma pour punir ce désordre funeste.[44]

This is certainly an unusual subject to include in a poem to one's fiancée. It becomes even more interesting in view of the reference to the family of David. Was the poem a coded warning to Evelina about Louis' incestuous desire for his sister? Unfortunately the evidence ends here; and, as with many questions about Riel's innermost thoughts, we are left wondering.

Riel wished also to institute polygamy, that is, the marriage of one man to several wives (he was not willing to reverse the privilege). 'God wants polygamy; it is one of the greatest barriers against liberalism among men and women.' An ordinary man would be allowed to have up to five wives, while certain individuals like a king or a governor-general could have more, depending on rank.

Kings who practise the religion of the sovereign pontiff of Ville-Marie in Lower Canada can have as many as fifteen wives. ... The heir apparent of the crown can have eight wives. A governor-general of several provinces can have seven wives. A lieutenant-governor of a single province can have six wives.[45]

Riel adduced several reasons in defence of polygamy, apart from the obvious one of imitation of the Hebrews. Polygamy would allow more women to marry and would enable the women to give each other support in child raising. Furthermore, polygamy would 'teach women once again that the only way for them to be pleasing to God and their husbands, and to enjoy unbroken honour in the world, is to sincerely practise the virtues of modesty, thriftiness, and kindness,' which in essence means that women should be put back in their proper station of subservience.

Riel's theory of polygamy seems to be a fantasy of repressed sexuality. He had long wished to marry but had been prevented by circumstances; and there was simply no approved sexual alternative for a loyal Catholic. Now his doctrine of plural marriage emerged like the gluttonous daydreams of a starving man. As in his discussion of incest, Riel's statements on polygamy were laced with indirect references to his own life. He attacked the custom of the father's determining whom his daughter shall marry, and defended the freedom of the woman to choose her own husband. 'When a young person of either sex, having reached the age of consent, has arranged a suitable match and desires to marry, the parents are bound in conscience to favour the marriage.'[47] This may seem difficult to reconcile with the institution of polygamy, which ordinarily makes the father almost an absolute monarch over his wives and children; but Riel was moved less by abstract considerations of logical consistency than by his own painful memories. He could not forget how his own projected marriage had been stymied by his fiancée's parents. Now his anger and shame spilled out in a long attack on St Paul, who had supported the father's control over the marital prospects of his daughters.[48] Riel castigated Paul as a 'liberal,' an enemy of marriage, and the destroyer of the Mosaic Law.

Priests would also be permitted to marry in Riel's new church, as long as they took nuns to be their wives. In his new dispensation, Riel could have his cake and eat it too: he could become the priest he had always wanted to be, yet he could satisfy his desire to marry. Once again the novel teaching seems to be related more to Riel's inner world than to his perception of outer realities.

APOCALYPSE AND HISTORY

Riel's marriage doctrine was connected to a theology of history. 'Abraham, Isaac, and Jacob,' he wrote, 'are each in the Holy Spirit the symbol of the three great epochs of the Kingdom of God.'[49] Abraham, who had several wives, personifies 'the Jewish priesthood or Jewish church.'[50] Isaac, on the other hand, had only one wife; and he ended his days in sorrow, tricked by the collusion between his wife and his younger son Jacob. Isaac represents the Roman Catholic Church, and his sad end symbolizes the corruption in which the Roman papacy, having outlived its usefulness, now drags out its days. Jacob, who had many wives and was blessed with many sons, symbolizes 'the French-Canadian Métis priesthood of St Vital.'[51] History reaches a third age with the restoration of polygamy.

This theology of history resembles that of the mediaeval chiliast Joachim of Fiore (c1145-1202).[52] Joachim taught that history moved through three great ages – of the Father, the Son, and the Holy Spirit. These three periods corresponded to the Old Law, or Judaism; the New Law, or Christianity; and the final stage still to come, which would be the perfection of Christ's message, just as His gospel had been the culmination of Judaism. Joachim thought that his own time fell at the end of the second and thus at the beginning of the third age. The coming Age of the Holy Spirit would be the highest state of human spiritual experience, a millennial realm of glory unlike anything ever seen on earth.

There is no evidence that Riel drew upon Joachim or upon any other writers who stand in the long Joachimite tradition. However, his views are structurally similar to the Joachimite model. Riel's third epoch, the age of Jacob or of the French-Canadian Church, is parallel to Joachim's age of the Holy Spirit. Each, in its own system, is the culminating historical period following the Old Law and the New Law; each begins in the present when evil is at its height due to the decay of the Roman papacy; each is millennial in character.

One of the most interesting elements of Riel's futuristic scenario is that he claimed to know exactly how long it would be until the papacy would be forced from Montreal to take up its even more glorious home in St Vital. Exactly 457 years would elapse, counting from the year 1876, the fall of Rome, meaning that the transfer would take place in 2333 AD. Afterwards the papacy would remain at St Vital another 1876 years, at the end of which time Christ would return to earth in the Second Coming. These numbers have an explanation which casts an important light upon Riel's thinking.

According to the conventional chronology of Old Testament history, Ezra, a Babylonian Jew, arrived in Jerusalem in 457 BC, bearing a letter from King Artaxerxes of Persia which gave him religious authority over those practising Judaism in the area. The Jews had begun to return from the Babylonian captivity almost a century before, and the second temple was completed in 515, but it was Ezra who purified their religious practices. The year 457 BC, therefore, may be taken as a symbolic date of the rebirth of Judaism. A Christian point of view might regard the time between 457 BC and the birth of Jesus as a period of preparation for the New Law.

LOUIS RIEL'S VIEW OF HISTORY

Mission of Ezra	Birth of Christ	Riel's mission begins; transfer of papacy to Ville-Marie	Transfer of papacy to St Vital	Second Coming
457 BC	0	1875/76 AD	2333 AD	4209 AD

457 years	1876 years	457 years	1876 years
Jewish preparation	Roman fulfilment	French-Canadian preparation	Métis fulfilment

2333 years	2333 years
Cycle 1 Religion in the Old World	Cycle 2 Religion in the New World

Riel probably had something similar in mind when he declared that the papacy of Ville-Marie would last 457 years. He was, in effect, saying that it was a time of preparation for the higher stage of religion, which would have its focus at St Vital. That period, the culmination of human religion before the Second Coming, would last 1876 years, like the reign of the Roman papacy. Riel's mystical numbers thus divide history into two cycles, each of 457 plus 1876 equals 2333 years. First comes the Judaic preparation followed by the Roman fulfilment, then the French-Canadian preparation followed by the métis fulfilment. This great process is bisected by Riel's life, or more precisely by the inauguration of the mission which was given to him on 8 December 1875, and which he definitively announced to Bourget on 1 May 1876.[53] From this point, there extends on either side of him a space of 2333 years, backward to the reformation of Ezra, forward to the Parousia. Riel himself is the midpoint of history.

The simple structure underlying these complexities is illustrated by the diagram above.

The number 2333 was more than the accidental sum of 1876 and 457; it was significant in its own right. In one of his visions, Riel fixed his gaze upon the chair on which the pope was seated.

As the Lord wanted, I measured the length of the chair. It was 23 feet, three inches, and three lines long. The feet are centuries; the inches are epochs of ten years; and the lines are years.[54]

The addition of these quantities yields a sum of 2333 years. In a letter to Bourget, Riel introduced still another symbolic period of time, 'fifteen months and a week' in length:

When Daniel in his exile said, still seventy weeks, he saw looming before him the beauties of the first dawn and the rising of the sun. Monseigneur, your blessing makes me say in my exile, still fifteen months and a week. For I see shining before my joyous eyes the beauties of the second dawn and the splendours of the great day.[55]

The reference to Daniel provides the key for unlocking the meaning of both the 2333 years and the 'fifteen months and a week.' The Book of Daniel is a storehouse of mystical numbers which has been repeatedly ransacked by prophets seeking information about the chronology of coming events. Riel, too, found inspiration there. Shortly before his death, he told Dr Augustus Jukes, the NWMP surgeon at Regina, 'I am the Daniel of the Christian era.'[56] This was a metaphor to describe the danger of his position, fearing not lions but the hangman; but perhaps Riel also meant it in a more literal way. By interpreting the sacred numbers in the Book of Daniel, he had discovered the secret of the history of the Christian era. As Daniel was to the Old World, he was to the New.

Daniel, however, speaks not of 'fifteen months and a week' but of 'seventy weeks,' commencing with the decree to refortify Jerusalem (457 BC):

Seventy weeks are marked out for your people and your holy city; then rebellion shall be stopped, sin brought to an end, iniquity expiated, everlasting right ushered in, vision and prophecy sealed, and the Most Holy Place anointed. Know then and understand: from the time that the word went forth that Jerusalem should be restored and rebuilt ... (Daniel 9:24-5)

In interpreting this cryptic passage, commentators of the allegorical school have assumed that one day in a mystical number equals one year of earthly time, so that seventy weeks would symbolize a period of 490 years. If this period begins at 457 BC, it ends at 33 AD. Hence Daniel's text must be a prophecy of the Redemption of mankind effected through the Crucifixion and Resurrection. The 'seventy weeks' of exile are the time between the revival of Judaism and the beginning of Christianity.

Riel reduced the seventy weeks to fifteen months and a week or approximately sixty-six weeks. He acknowledged the validity of Daniel's seventy weeks as a preparation for the 'first dawn,' but posited the slightly shorter period of waiting from himself to 'the second dawn.' How many years are symbolized by fifteen months and a week? In a later text, Riel specifically says that it represents 457 years.[57] (The calculation, which is not obvious, requires setting all months equal to thirty days. Then $15 \times 30 + 7 = 457$.) Hence the 'second dawn' is the transfer of the papacy from Montreal to St Vital, and Riel's exile represents the period of preparation, or the papacy of Ville-Marie.

What of the 2333 years? This number is not found in Daniel, but one very close to it is. Daniel 8:13-14 reads:

The one said, 'For how long will the period of this vision last? How long will the regular offering be suppressed, how long will impiety cause desolation, and both the Holy Place and the fairest of all lands be given over to be trodden down?' The answer came, 'For two thousand three hundred evenings and mornings; then the Holy Place shall emerge victorious.'

Assume, as allegorical commentators usually do, that an 'evening and morning' is the same as a day. Assume furthermore, that this period of 2300 days, symbolizing as many years, should begin at 457 BC, like the 490 years or seventy weeks. Then, by adding 33 years (which he had to subtract from the 490 to get 457), Riel would obtain 2333 years which, beginning in 457 BC, would end in 1876 AD, the year of his own emergence as a prophet. By making these minor alterations in the Book of Daniel, Riel could claim that his own mission was foretold, that he was a legitimate prophet relying on sacred scripture.

It is possible that Riel's numerology was inspired by the Millerite movement which had swept the United States a generation before, when William Miller had foretold the Parousia for the years 1843/44. His reasoning had also been based on the sacred numbers of the Book of Daniel, especially the seventy weeks and the 2300 mornings and evenings. His solution, like Riel's, was to let both periods begin at 457 BC.[58] Since he did not tamper with the number 2300, that period ran out in 1843 (or 1844, allowing for a certain margin of error), which Miller took to be the year of Christ's return to earth. The Millerites caused a great excitement all over New England; and even though the Son of Man did not appear as predicted, a viable church, the Seventh Day Adventists, grew out of the movement. Riel may well have learned about Miller during his many visits to the United States. If so, he probably was struck by the fact that the main year of the Millerite excitement, 1844, was the year of his own birth. Be that as it may, Riel's numerology was similar in principle to the apocalyptic calculations in vogue among American Protestants.

Another motif which Riel borrowed from Daniel was that of the four empires. The Book of Daniel was written during the Maccabaean uprising against Antiochus IV, the monarch of Syria. The prophecies within the book were meant to give comfort to the hard-pressed Jews by predicting their heavenly deliverance. In one passage, Nebuchadnezzar calls Daniel to interpret a dream in which the king has seen the four metals of gold, silver, bronze, and iron. Daniel declares that they represent four kingdoms, of which Nebuchadnezzar's Chaldean empire was the first. The fourth empire, the Macedonian, will be unstable, because the iron is mixed with clay. God will destroy it, and then establish a fifth monarchy, 'a kingdom which shall never be destroyed ... it shall itself endure forever' (2:44). In a parallel passage, Daniel is reported to see in a vision a succession of four dreadful beasts, followed by the Son of Man coming on the clouds of heaven. Again, the implication is that four earthly kingdoms will be followed by a realm of divine rule. To the Jewish rebels, these promises meant that God would assist their revolution by sending a messiah to establish an enduring kingdom. It would be the fifth and last, following the four secular empires of the Chaldeans, Medes, Persians, and Macedonians (Seleucids).

These texts have passed into the prophetic tradition of Judaism and Christianity, but their interpretation has to be repeatedly updated to take into account the vagaries of world politics. Later prophets have interpreted the fourth empire as Rome, or the Holy Roman Empire of the German Nation, or some other state enjoying temporary sway. But the structure of the prophecy never varies; it always predicts that the power of the state is about to be destroyed, to be replaced by an age of theocratic bliss. Riel followed the stereotype. 'The four great empires of Mahomet, of Photius, of Luther, and of the English colossus have appeared before my eyes like the four sparks of light you might see from four fireflies lost in the night.'[59] If Britain's empire was the fourth, it must be the last human kingdom. The 'fifth empire' would be the spiritual and temporal reign of the papacy, first of Ville-Marie and then of St Vital.

Riel couched his prophecies in apocalyptic imagery, and his writings are full of vivid predictions of disaster.

I saw the spirit of Jesus Christ our Lord shatter all the British possessions; and of all the vast maritime empire of England, there was only one sail left in the port of London. ... I saw the capital of Scotland plunge into the ocean and disappear. ... London and Liverpool will sink to the bottom of the water.[60]

The time had come for the entire world to be purified. In Spain the 'Liberal phalange' of Alfonso XII would be destroyed. The Confederacy of the southern United States would once again be ravaged for having adhered to slavery. Washington, DC, would be humbled. 'Great capital! With one kick of my heel I will make your hills bend like the back of a bull when he struggles to his feet, aroused from sleep by a kick from the herdsman.'[61] Everywhere God would reward the good and punish the bad.

Muddy waters of the Mississippi, I will travel your banks from the falls all the way to the Gulf. To those who have done penance, and who have practised charity after having offended Me, I will show mercy. But I will make my justice strike its blow on the banks of the Mississippi, so all will remember that I am the God of strength.[62]

Riel let the voice of God speak through him in a sadistic metaphor of divine power:

In My hands the earth is no bigger than an egg. If I wanted to lose it, I would only have to let it fall in space. But I do not want to abandon it. I will take care of it, I will hold it. For the time being, I only want to shake it. For by shaking the egg near My ear I can tell by the noise what it's going to do ...[63]

When God shook the earth, the fires below would be let loose in volcanic eruptions. Rome would be buried more than Pompeii and Herculaneum, so deeply that no one would ever dig it up. But the faithful would be spared.

O my spouse! [ie, the Church of the New World] You, you have nothing to fear. ... Daughter of the New World! Do not fear the volcanoes, not even the most terrible eruptions. It is I who do all. I amuse myself with the points of My crown and pierce the shell of the egg.[64]

As already noted, Riel called himself the messiah of the Jews. This was a millenarian symbol, because the conversion of the Jews is generally a part of the Christian scenario of the Last Things. Riel was a forerunner of Christ returning in power and glory. He applied to himself the predictions of the Book of the Apocalypse. He became the knight on the white horse (6:1-2).

The Apocalypse is a trustworthy guide which I have never understood. But now I can explain its parables and its divine numbers. The Lord Jesus Christ tells me:

Louis, you are Louis: you are the knight to whom I give my white horse of the Apocalypse.

The Lord Jesus Christ tells me: David, you are David: you will chant the psalms of my glory till the end. Your throne is established for ever.

The Lord Jesus Christ tells me: Riel, you are Riel. I will give you strength of body and soul against the spiritual and temporal enemies of my catholic, apostolic, and vital church of the Shining Mountains.[65]

Riel's new religion was essentially a millenarian Christian revival. The doctrinal and ethical novelties like incest and polygamy were supported by traditional apocalyptic symbols drawn from biblical sources such as the books of Daniel or Revelation. Like all millenarians, Riel took the Lord's Prayer seriously: 'Thy Kingdom come ...'

LIBERALISM AND THEOCRACY

Riel's political ideas were an exaggerated form of ultramontane thought, in which the fundamental concepts of liberalism and theocracy were extended to their ultimate limits. Liberalism became synonymous with evil itself. To be liberal was 'to turn one's back on God, to flee the duties of lasting virtue for the love of ease, of self-indulgence, and of sensual pleasures.'[66] Anyone who opposed Riel was automatically a liberal. While at Longue Pointe he received this message from God:

This hospital is in fact the image of the entire world. Sister Thérèse is the image of the House of Austria. Dr Howard is the image, not exactly of Bismarck, but of Protestant Prussia (Bismarck is the result of human perversity today). [Riel was writing at the time of the *Kulturkampf*.] Dr Lachapelle is the image of the blackest liberalism; it is he who represents Bismarck. The sisters represent the nations of the world. And you ... are not only the prophet that I send, but you also are the pope, the priest-king. Expect your rescue not from men but from Me alone.[67]

Riel, in his own mind, was not a madman detained in an asylum; he was the spiritual rejuvenator of the world, incarcerated by the powers of liberalism.

Liberalism meant a life of individual self-indulgence, whereas Riel's new order would be a community of godly persons living under the united régime of church and state, directed by a 'priest-king.' His program was frankly theocratic, as is typical of millenarian thinkers. This point needs to be emphasized, for Canadians have often assumed that because Riel was a radical and a revolutionary, he was a defender of human freedom. He sometimes used the vocabulary of natural rights and liberty to state his case against the Canadian government, which he accused of despotic actions in the North-West. However, when Riel spoke of freedom, he referred more to the liberty of the métis as a people rather than to individual freedom in the liberal sense. His ultimate hopes for the reorganization of mankind under clerico-theocratic rule were the antithesis of liberalism. Consider the implications of these statements on the powers of the priesthood:

For eighteen hundred years, the true priesthood has had, properly speaking, nothing but means of persuasion to convert the world. ... [But now] Jesus Christ wants to perfect the government of His Church and to make His apostles able to exercise charitable coercion on men ...[68]

From 'persuasion' to 'charitable coercion': Riel's theocratic intentions could hardly be clearer. As 'the Elias who will re-establish all,'[69] he was prepared to merge church and state in a true kingdom of the saints. Today's left-wing radicals may wish to claim him as a spiritual ancestor because he struck out against the 'system,' but his own political philosophy was so far to the right that it had no place on the Canadian political spectrum, even in its own day.

EVALUATION

Riel defined himself above all as a prophet, God's voice of remonstrance to a sinful world; and a prophet must reach his fellow men if he is to carry out his mission successfully. By that criterion, Riel's prophetic outburst was a decided failure. No one except himself took him seriously. His ideas and behaviour seemed so bizarre to others that he was placed in confinement and not released until he ceased to play the role of prophet, at least in public.

It is not surprising that the new religion earned no immediate sympathy from others. Extreme ideas like incest and polygamy were bound to deflect attention from anything else Riel wished to say. Even more important, the religion was highly self-centred. Many of Riel's ideas seem to have been generated more by his internal needs than by an objective view of external reality. His religion was a refuge from a hostile world with which he could no longer contend in a conventional way. His prophecies were an elaborate device for awarding himself the rewards of success and honour which had eluded him in politics.

This urge for self-glorification was not something temporary or peripheral in Riel's nature. It was a permanent part of his character and was at all times a powerful impulse behind his religious innovations. But it was capable of modification, of expanding and contracting according to circumstances. And precisely the situation of involuntary commitment to a lunatic asylum seems to have aggravated Riel's need for glory. If no one else would take him seriously, he could at least bestow upon himself title after title, honour after honour. Thus his religion developed in isolation, greatly encouraging his natural tendency to vanity.

Things were quite different in 1885, however. Riel then had a sympathetic audience, his own people, the métis. They could share in his glory; for if he was God's prophet, they were the chosen people. These conditions meant a profound change in Riel's religion. What he taught in 1885 was recognizably similar to what he had said in 1876, but the extremism and self-glorification were now much attenuated. There was no mention of incest and polygamy nor of Riel's more pretentious titles such as 'priest-king' and 'infallible pontiff.'

Thus Riel learned from the débâcle of his first attempt to be a religious founder that a prophet cannot succeed without a willing audience. He ultimately demonstrated the ability in religion, as he had already done in politics, not only to speak but to make himself heard, to lead by offering his followers a message they could accept.

5
Waiting

Louis Riel was discharged from the asylum of Beauport on 23 January 1878. Accompanied by J.-A. Langlais, a member of the Cercle Catholique of Quebec City, he made his way to the New York state line.[1] He crossed and went to Keeseville to stay with the Barnabé family.

Riel, there can be no doubt, was a chastened man. He wrote to Bishop Taché:

Thank God I have passed my worst time of sufferings. ... I bless God for having humiliated me; and for having made me understand so well what human glory is, how quickly it passes, and how empty it is for him who, having attracted the attention of men a little, suddenly feels the hand of God weigh upon him.[2]

Having come to see the will of God in his humiliation, Riel was no longer bitter against those who had laughed at his ideas and confined him in an asylum. He exchanged friendly letters with Lachapelle and the Vincelette family, with Bishop Bourget and Father Primeau.

Yet he had not quite given up his mystical faith in his own mission. He still experienced occasional visions and revelations, and he still saw the hand of God in earthly events. He was struck with the coincidence when he learned that Senator Oliver Morton had died on 1 November 1877, exactly two years to the day after Riel had written to him offering to heal his paralyzed legs. Surely this was a sign from above. In January 1878 Riel composed a little prayer which he never forgot: 'My God, if You wish, if You have so decided in Your eternal plans, resurrect "Olivier Pie Mort-Tonne" [ie, "dead thunder"] just as he was; and then heal him so he will help us in the United States.' In March of that year, when he was visiting friends in Glenn's Falls, New York, he had a vision about the same subject. He saw the American eagle smile at him in the direction of the North-West, and a voice said: 'Olivier Pie Mort-Tonne is free to leave Rome.'[3] It seems that Riel somehow identified Morton, whose middle initial he wrote as 'Pie,' with Pope Pius IX ('Pie' in French), who died 7 February 1878. These revelations suggest that Riel was hoping for miraculous help from God, in the form of American support, to establish his new religion in the North-West.

But even if he was secretly thinking about such things, he wanted to stay out of public life. He wanted to sell the land he owned in Red River and use the proceeds to buy a farm in Nebraska, where he would lead a quiet pastoral life, far from the turmoil of Canadian politics. This idea had occurred to Riel during his confinement at Beauport, where he had written a poem about it, 'Le Chant d'un cultivateur.' He pictured himself living poor but honest in the countryside, surrounded by his loving wife and children, enjoying 'la paix qui rend heureux.'[4] This idyllic vision appealed not only to Riel, but to his friends, who hoped that an agricultural life would keep him from overexciting himself about public affairs.

Probably no man was ever less suited to be an unknown farmer than Louis Riel, but in any case the scheme could not be tried for lack of money. He sent a power of attorney to his mother so she could sell his property, but she had to report that the Winnipeg real estate market was extremely depressed.[5] Unsure what to do, Riel remained in Keeseville. He rented three acres of land which he cultivated himself, as a symbolic head start on his plan to become a farmer. He wrote to his mother on Easter Sunday that he was still desperately eager to establish himself after his long years of wandering and struggle.[6] As the months passed, another factor arose to strengthen this determination: Louis and Evelina fell in love and began to think of marriage.

Evelina's love introduced further complications into Riel's life. He could not ask for the hand of Father Barnabé's sister until he could support her in reasonable comfort. The situation resembled that of his youthful romance with Marie-Julie Guernon, except that this time his prospective in-laws, instead of being opposed to him, were warmly favourable. But he still had to find a way to make a living. In late September Louis went to New York City, ostensibly to seek suitable employment, but also to sound the political waters. Although the evidence is fragmentary, it appears that he was considering some sort of political movement or even armed invasion of the Canadian West.

Years later, when Riel surrendered after the North-West Rebellion, a Fenian spokesman in New York said:

Riel came to this city secretly at the time that Melody and Condon, the released revolutionists, arrived here. He proposed to the Irish leaders a plan by which they should co-operate in a Manitoban rebellion. ... All that was needed was money, and he asked us to supply that. He promised to found a great northwestern republic in the event of a victorious outcome of the proposed war.[7]

On 14 September 1878, the *New York Times* had carried a front-page story that the two Fenians Melody and Condon were about to be released from their English prison and would come directly to New York. Riel was in New York within two weeks.[8] He was present when the Fenians welcomed Melody and Condon at Sweeney's Hotel and according to one who witnessed the scene, 'was dressed like a dandy and spent his money freely.' He spoke of a plan 'which he said would result in freeing two races [ie, métis and Irish]. He offered to bring about an armed revolution in the Saskatchewan Valley if the Fenians would furnish money ...'[9] But unfortunately for Riel, the Irish only laughed at his offer. There is no way to know whether these details, furnished to the press by Fenians in 1885, are entirely correct. In particular, one may doubt whether Riel's plans were centred on the Saskatchewan Valley; this sounds rather like a garbled recollection coloured by the current events of the North-West Rebellion.

Letters written to Riel by friends about this time have something of a conspiratorial air. They speak of the search for employment, but of something else as well. Father Barnabé wrote on 7 October that 'it seems extremely difficult to me to get from these egotistical men, devoid of patriotism, money which they want to use for their own advancement.'[10] A week later he wrote:

Well, there is another delay in your work on the N.W. It's true that the element which appeared necessary to you is not blessed by God. ... But the time seems favourable. England is getting involved in war.[11]

Evelina wrote in a similar vein. About the middle of October, she sent Louis a letter which said:

Your amnesty is probably going to be granted this month, according to *Le Nouveau Monde*. What do you think of that? I'm only too sure that you won't want that to happen, it would make your plans fail.[12]

This last sentence suggests that Riel was involved in a political intrigue which might depend for its success on his position as an exiled patriot.

Further evidence comes from a letter by Father T. Glenn, an American priest and friend of Barnabé, who had visited New York City in the early part of October. Afterwards he wrote to Riel that one of his letters to him had disappeared in the mail, and concluded that 'we should be very cautious in our communications.'[13] One would not advise caution in corresponding, and would not worry about letters going astray, unless the contents were likely to be embarrassing if passed on to the wrong people.

Although Riel may have dabbled in conspiracy, he was also genuinely seeking work.[14] He stayed in New York until mid-November, when he returned to Keeseville without having found suitable employment. For some reason, he was not enthusiastic about journalism or law, the two careers other than politics for which he was most obviously fitted.[15]

He stayed only a couple of weeks in Keeseville, then he left for St. Paul, Minnesota.[16] His aim was to involve himself in the establishment of Catholic colonies in the West. The most prominent figure in this movement was Bishop John Ireland of St Paul, whose Catholic Colonization Bureau had been founded in 1876. Bishop Ireland acted in effect as a land agent for the railways. In the five years after 1876 he succeeded in founding ten Catholic villages in western Minnesota. The settlers came directly from Europe, or else from the immigrant populations living in squalid conditions in the industrial cities of the eastern United States. It was hoped that an agricultural life would help the Catholic immigrants retain their faith. Living in small villages under the guidance of their priests, they would be isolated from the pernicious influences of the cities.[17]

Father Barnabé was enthusiastic about this project and the idea naturally appealed to Riel as well. He had already tried to persuade the New England French to move to Manitoba. Now he was attracted by the prospect of working with Bishop Ireland, who seemed like a promising patron for him. Educated in France, the bishop still spoke the language fluently. Barnabé seems to have met him, perhaps through the Oblate establishment at Plattsburgh, and Riel may well have made his acquaintance on one of his many visits to St Paul.[18]

Riel succeeded in getting an interview with Bishop Ireland in St Paul during the Christmas season of 1878; but nothing came of it as Ireland kept him at arm's length, perhaps fearing that such a man would embroil his program in political controversy. The bishop was also unmoved when Barnabé sent him a letter recommending Riel and offering to come to his diocese to help with the work of colonization, to aid the French Canadians 'to preserve their faith by becoming farmers.'[19] Riel lingered in St Paul for part of January, hoping for a sign from the bishop; but finally he gave up and travelled on to Pembina where he could stay with old friends and receive visitors from Manitoba.

One of many who came to see him was Joseph Dubuc, a college friend who now held the parliamentary seat of Provencher. On 20 January 1879, on his way back to Ottawa, Dubuc spent the day in Pembina with Riel and several of his former métis supporters. There was much talk of politics, in which Riel expressed himself in vague generalities. Dubuc noticed that Riel often returned to the subject of his hospitalization, saying things like, 'I was in an asylum in the company of madmen; what does one care about the words of a poor lunatic?' Dubuc, hoping to draw him out, replied: 'That's not what your people think,' adding that all the métis believed either that the government had put Riel in an asylum to persecute him or that he himself had feigned madness. After some hesitation, Riel stated that the latter alternative was true. He had pretended to go insane so that he would no longer seem capable of leading his people. Then the government might stop persecuting the métis, who were no threat without his leadership.[20]

As Dubuc realized, the story was a fabrication. There is not the slightest evidence in all of Riel's writings to suggest that he simulated madness in order to be confined. But now that he was among his own people again, he did not wish them to think that his sanity had ever been in doubt.

INDIAN CONFEDERACY

Riel particularly wanted to re-establish his reputation as a leader of men because he had conceived another plan of action. He was dreaming of a great confederacy of half-breeds and Indian tribes which, using the Montana Territory as a base, would invade western Canada and establish an independent native republic. This daring idea resembled what Riel had brought to President Grant in the waning days of 1875, and to the New York Fenians in 1878, except that now the métis would be assisted not by the Irish nor by American investors, but by their own cousins, the Indians.

There were abundant possibilities for intrigue on both sides of the border. First, there was the problem of the Sioux led by Sitting Bull. After having annihilated Custer's detachment at the battle of the Little Big Horn in the summer of 1876, the Sioux had sought refuge in Canada. There were now several thousand well-armed and aggressive warriors encamped around Wood Mountain. They were a continual source of irritation to Canadian Indians, whom they kept from the buffalo remaining in the Cypress Hills region; and they also frequently crossed back into Montana to hunt or raid. The Canadian government did not want them, yet had no way to force their return to the United States except by a policy of slow starvation.

Canada had tried to regulate matters with its own Indians by a series of seven treaties. The Cree and the Blackfoot had been settled on reservations, although a few Cree chiefs, of whom the most important was Big Bear, were still leading a nomadic life with their bands. But the Canadian scene was not as tranquil as it seemed, for the government had not made sufficient preparations for feeding the Indians in time of famine. The Blackfoot experienced grim starvation in the summer of 1878 when prairie fires kept the buffalo away from their hunting grounds. In 1879 the problem became general as the buffalo simple disappeared from the Canadian plains. The Blackfoot, the non-treaty Cree, and the refugee Sioux had no choice but to cross the border into Montana, where a substantial herd still remained.

The Montana Indians had all been consigned to reservations. The Crows were south of the Yellowstone. Various groups of Assiniboines, Yankton Sioux, and Gros Ventres were strung out along the Missouri and Milk rivers in northern Montana. There was a large contingent of Blackfoot, Bloods, and Piegans in the foothills of the Rockies. And in the uplands to the west of the front range of the Rockies was a reservation for the Flatheads, Pend d'Oreilles, and Kootenais.

These reservations were large and widely separated, but the tribes, except for the mountain Indians, were all dependent on the same herd of buffalo which roamed across reservations and public lands without discrimination. The various tribes could not help coming into frequent conflict with one another. As Riel must have seen from his vantage point in Pembina, this touchy situation would become even more delicate when the Canadian Indians would be forced south of the line in the winter of 1879-80. The tensions would be great, but so would be the opportunity if an enterprising leader could weld these nations together. They could form an alliance so powerful that no one, certainly not the few hundred Mounted Police, could stand against it.

It was the old dream of native unity which had been pursued by Indian leaders like Tecumseh and Pontiac, but Riel thought he had one additional advantage over them: the Services of the large métis population which roamed Montana and the Canadian North-West, following the buffalo and trading with the Indians. They were in contact with all tribes and had relatives in many. Riel envisioned them as the central, cohesive element in a native confederacy.

There was already a foundation to build upon. After the Red River insurrection of 1869-70, Gabriel Dumont had forged a series of alliances between the métis and various Indian tribes.[21] Several prominent chiefs were also interested in native unity. Sitting Bull and Crowfoot had met twice in 1877 and 1878 to pledge lasting peace between their tribes.[22] Big Bear, hoping that a united approach to Ottawa would result in renegotiation of the treaties, had made overtures to the other tribes wintering in the Cypress Hills in 1878-9.[23] But none of these discussions had gone as far as the idea of a military campaign to set up a native republic; that was Riel's distinctive contribution.

The first documentary evidence of his intentions is found in a poem he composed 26 December 1878. The poem expressed Riel's joy to be in Minnesota, so close to Manitoba. But his homeland, now languishing under Canadian domination, was in need of salvation. He would go to the country of the high Missouri, and summon the wildest Indian tribes to rescue their cousins, the métis:

S'il plaît à Dieu, je vais dans un immense effort
T'apporter le recours des nations sauvages
Que le Missouri voit courir sur ses rivages
L'homme de foi constant est toujours le plus fort
Je veux aller quérir des nations cruelles
Que les métis verront arriver sur les ailes
Du vent du Nord.[24]

At this juncture, however, Riel's thinking was still tentative. The remainder of the poem suggests that perhaps such plans were not in harmony with divine Providence. Maybe God still wanted him to become a simple farmer, or maybe he would die without ever having the opportunity to drive the Canadians from Manitoba.

However, he felt confident enough to send the poem to Evelina. She encouraged him in language that was surprisingly pugnacious for a gently reared, convent educated sister of a priest: 'I learned [from your letter] that your aim in going out west was not only to recover your health but also to create an Indian movement. If it please God that you succeed, don't hold back from massacres until no more of that infamous race [Orangemen] remains in your country.'[25]

Louis and Evelina were in frequent communication that spring, and he continued to send her details about his plan. Unfortunately, his letters are lost, but we can discover some of his thinking in her replies. She referred to Riel's 'movement' and hoped 'that the Indians will be ready to agree with all your plans.' She was glad that 'Mr Lépine is going with you.' She herself would like to be with Riel, 'to fight by your side,' to help 'overthrow the English'; but she was afraid that she lacked the necessary courage to take part in what was going to happen. One would want 'the bravery of the heroine Joan of Arc' to be there.[26]

These few allusions are the only record we have of Riel's preparation for the Indian uprising. Ambroise Lépine came to see him at the end of April, and presumably they talked about the future.[27] But Riel does not seem to have been entirely committed; he remained in Pembina until mid-August, which does not betoken a man who has made up his mind what to do.

While he waited in Pembina, Riel whiled away the hours writing poetry. One of his productions was a long and bitterly sarcastic attack on Sir John A. Macdonald, in which Riel revived his old dream of an alliance between the French Canadians and the Irish of the United States:

Les nombreux rejetons de l'Irlande indomptable
Ne sont pas, sans dessein, dans les Etats-Unis.
Le jour qu'ils se mettront sous un chef acceptable
Et qu'ils voudront marcher dans des chemins bénis,
Les Canadiens-français et les Métis sincères
Marcheront avec eux comme avec de bons frères.[28]

It is uncertain whether this reference to the Irish was only an idle daydream or an integral part of Riel's plan for the Indian confederacy. Perhaps he thought an Indian invasion of western Canada would touch off a Fenian attack in the East.

Riel left Pembina around the middle of August. A trip of twenty-eight days by ox cart took him to Wood Mountain, where he wrote back to his mother: 'I was rocked in my cart as I haven't been rocked for a long time. I assure you, chère Maman, I am glad to see the prairie. It gives me strength, it heals me.'[29] His presence in Canada was illegal, and he would not have run the risk without some reason. His purpose was to establish contact with Sitting Bull. He had picked a good time because Superintendent James Walsh of the NWMP, who normally kept a close watch on the Sioux, was absent for reasons of health. There is no record of any discussions which may have taken place, but it seems that Riel left without an agreement, after having asked friendly métis to keep him posted on the actions of the Sioux.[30]

Crossing into Montana, Riel joined a small group of buffalo-hunting métis, about thirty lodges. He wrote to his mother on 12 October that although there were many half-breeds and Indians following the buffalo, they were getting enough to eat. Riel was tasting buffalo for the first time in years, and it agreed with him. 'Buffalo meat is good medicine,' he wrote; 'I feel stronger.'[31]

His presence in Montana aroused the suspicions of Indian Commissioner Edgar Dewdney, who happened to be travelling through the Territory. On 10 November, Dewdney, who was then in Fort Benton, noted in his diary that Riel was in the area trading buffalo robes and purchasing ammunition. Dewdney feared he was up to mischief.[32]

The métis were now in the country north of the Missouri River, which was part of the Wolf Point and Fort Belknap Indian agencies. Assiniboines and Yankton Sioux lived on the former, Gros Ventres and others, mostly Assiniboines, on the latter. It was necessary for the half-breeds to secure permission to winter on the reservations. On 15 November, the Indian agent at Wolf Point reported that he had been approached on this score by Riel.

The Half Breeds are also in force on the Milk River. They also have been very importunate in regard to staying in this country, and latterly one Riel (the leader of the trouble in Manitoba in 1869), has acted as their ambassador. He is staying with them, with what object I am unable to say. He can wield the Half Breeds at will, and also probably the Crees.[33]

This agent, and his counterpart at Fort Belknap, were both opposed to allowing the métis and Canadian Indians on their reserves because it encouraged illegal trading while also making it difficult for their own Indians to follow the buffalo. But the Indian agents did not possess effective authority. If the métis and British Indians were to be moved, they would have to be escorted by the military. The commander of the nearest garrison at Fort Assiniboine was anxious to let sleeping dogs lie; so with the concurrence of his superiors in St Paul and Chicago, he told the interlopers they could winter along the Big Bend of the Milk River but would have to move in the spring. He even provided some work for the métis chopping wood around the fort.[34]

Riel presumably acted as spokesman in dealing with the military, but his movements in this period are not well documented. He passed through the town of Fort Benton in mid-December, at which time Lépine, who was living at Cypress Mountain, was reported to be near Fort Assiniboine.[35] On 28 December, Riel, again at Fort Assiniboine, wrote to his family that he was wintering with about 150 métis families on the Big Bend of the Milk River, and that he had been elected 'chef du camp.'[36] The métis camp was surrounded not only by American Indians but by tribes from the Canadian side – Sioux, Blackfoot, and Cree – who had followed the buffalo into Montana. It was an ideal situation for carrying on negotiations.

Our chief sources of information on Riel's activities over the winter are Jean L'Heureux, a French-Canadian interpreter who traveled with Crowfoot, the renowned Blackfoot chief; and Superintendent Walsh of the Wood Mountain NWMP post.[37] Since both wrote down their impressions of that winter some years after the event, neither account can be considered reliable in every detail, but the general picture they provide is consistent with contemporary letters from L'Heureux as well as NWMP intelligence reports.[38]

Walsh arrived at Wood Mountain shortly after Riel's departure in late September or early October 1879. He soon learned that Riel had been in the area and was now across the border in Montana. He also heard rumours that Riel had secured the adherence of the Wolf Point Assiniboines to his plan. Walsh at once rode into Montana to find the camp of Red Stone, the Assiniboine chief. On Walsh's request, Red Stone produced an article of agreement signed by him and Riel in red ink or blood. The document set forth that the country belonged to 'the Indians and their brothers the Half-Breeds' and that Riel 'was the true and rightful chief.' If the Indian tribes would unite under his leadership, he would recover their land, with the political support of his white friends in eastern Canada and the United States. Walsh stayed overnight in the camp and persuaded Red Stone to withdraw from the conspiracy. When Walsh demanded that the Assiniboine chief surrender the incriminating document, Red Stone refused, saying he had given his word to Riel not to let the paper out of his hands, but he agreed to burn it and send word to Riel that he was withdrawing from the confederation.

Walsh later claimed that he did not pass on his intelligence reports to his superiors because he thought he could handle things himself. He knew that the Sioux, the strongest fighting force among the natives, were the key to any military operation. So before the Sioux left to winter in Montana, he extracted pledges of fidelity from Sitting Bull and the other important chiefs. He also discontinued the sale of arms and ammunition at Wood Mountain, and rounded up weapons in the possession of traders.[39]

In the meantime Crowfoot's followers among the tribes of the Blackfoot League, having received their fall treaty money, were instructed by Indian Commissioner Dewdney to spend the winter south of the 49th parallel. In December, Crowfoot settled near Riel's camp on the Milk River. According to the interpreter L'Heureux, métis began to visit the Blackfoot almost immediately after their arrival. Riel himself arrived within a few days, accompanied by four advisers. He met with L'Heureux and invited him to attend an important assembly of the métis about fifteen miles away. At the meeting L'Heureux learned that Riel was planning a general uprising of Indians and half-breeds. He prominently displayed letters from his friends in the East, claiming that his cause had support in Ottawa. Riel's strategy was to use the horse-stealing that went on incessantly among all tribes as a pretext to attack the NWMP. Wood Mountain would be taken first, then Fort Walsh, Macleod, and Battleford, the capital of the North-West. The objective was to declare a provisional government and sign a treaty with Ottawa. To prepare for a June invasion, all the tribes should congregate on the last day of May at the Tiger Hills on the Milk River.

Riel asked L'Heureux to persuade Crowfoot to join the Confederation, but instead the interpreter successfully urged the chief to move further south to the country along the banks of the Missouri. Riel's emissaries came to the new camp to trade and persuade; but although they excited some of the younger warriors, it does not seem that they seriously tempted the Blackfoot chiefs to join.

Riel also made attempts to win over the Crees. According to L'Heureux, he took the parchment treaty papers of Little Pine, a Cree chief who had signed Treaty No. 6 in 1876, and trampled them underfoot, declaring that it was folly to keep faith with such lies.[40] He also met with Big Bear during the winter, but was not able to gain his adherence to the pact.[41]

The leaders of the Sioux were similarly reticent. Late in January, Sitting Bull came down to the Big Bend for a meeting with the métis, but there were no tangible consequences.[42] It must have become clear to Riel by February that his great confederation would not become a reality. The métis broke camp in mid-March, when the exceptionally severe winter had begun to soften a bit. Riel sent a letter to Colonel Black, commandant at Fort Assiniboine, thanking him for his kind treatment of the half-breeds. 'Having no other way,' said Riel, 'to acknowledge efficiently such a favour, [the] Métis have exerted themselves during the whole winter to pacify the Sioux; Sitting Bull himself and all his friends.'[43] This statement was disingenuous at best: Riel's plan for the Sioux had been to reinstate them in the good graces of the American government while unleashing them against the Canadian North-West. But the time for such dreams was over, and the métis dispersed, a few returning to Canada, most following the buffalo south across the Missouri and into the Judith Basin. Although rumours of a great Indian uprising continued to fly across the prairies, the danger, if there ever was one, was past.

Why did Riel's movement fail so utterly? Both L'Heureux and Walsh took credit for thwarting his plans. L'Heureux had informed the Canadian and American authorities of the movement in the middle of winter. Walsh had dispatched messengers to the American Indians on whose lands the métis were wintering, to encourage them to protest to their Indian agents and to try to have the foreigners removed. Both L'Heureux and Walsh seemed to attribute the breakup of the métis camp to harassment by American officials, caused in turn by their own efforts. But the reports of the Indian agents in this period show only a certain unease about the presence of the métis and British Indians, not awareness of a conspiracy. Nor is there any record of unusual harassment of the camp by the military. The army from the beginning had taken the position that the British half-breeds and Indians could winter on the reservation but would have to move as soon as possible; and that is exactly what happened.

There is no sign that Riel's movement ever had much genuine support from any quarter among the Indians. Riel was revered by his own people because of the role he had played in 1869-70 and his subsequent devotion to the cause of the métis, but to the Indians he was an unknown

quantity. Most probably they, at least astute chiefs like Sitting Bull, Big
Bear, and Crowfoot, regarded him with some suspicion, divining that
the Indians were human raw material for his own projects.

Information about the religious dimensions of Riel's proposed confederacy comes from a short essay entitled 'The Future of the French-Canadian Métis Chiefs in the United States.'[44] Although undated, its subject
matter and internal allusions place it in the winter of 1879-80. It begins
with the sentence 'Louis is the only one who can lead the Blackfoot,
Crows, Gros-Ventres, Pendant d'Oreilles [sic], Flatheads, etc.,' and continues with a series of elaborate puns on the French names of these
tribes:

The Blackfoot [Pieds-Noirs] are not what you think. For the tribe of this name
has red feet, red from the cold, from walking on thorns and spikes of cactus.
They walk barefoot. Their feet are red with blood.

The [true] 'blackfeet' are those who walk in the darkness of injustice; who follow the path of desires contrary to God's; and who throw themselves down the
way of passions most contrary to love of neighbour. The 'blackfeet' are easy to
recognize, for they are proud of the blackness of their feet. The feet are so black
that they even shine.

The point is that the Indians are not what their name seems to imply.
Their name indicates a quality of sinfulness; but the Blackfoot are not
really 'blackfeet,' because they have not turned away from God's will.
The other puns all run along the same lines.

The text demonstrates that Riel's efforts towards forming an Indian
confederation had a religious significance. The Indian tribes were symbols of the forces of goodness throughout the world, presently in bondage to the powers of evil, but destined to triumph under his leadership.
However, this aspect of the movement seems to have been private to
Riel. There is no evidence that he made any public religious claims at
this time. He did not call himself a prophet, denounce Rome, or try to
establish a new church, as he was to do in 1885.

CONTINUED DISAPPOINTMENTS

Riel turned to less sweeping projects after the collapse of his native confederation. One pressing necessity was to do something about the status
of the métis in Montana. They had become a brawling, hard-drinking
gang, a far cry from the fun-loving but respectable métis Riel had

known in Red River. Like the Oblate missionaries, Riel saw moral degeneration as a consequence of a nomadic existence; so he determined to settle the métis in one spot in Montana. On 20 August 1880, he presented himself at Fort Keough on the Yellowstone River with a petition to the renowned Indian fighter, Colonel Nelson A. Miles. The petition, drawn up 6 August at a camp on the Musselshell River, was signed by about a hundred men, who, with their families, made up a substantial proportion of the total number of métis in Montana. It requested that a tract of land, similar to an Indian reservation, be set aside for the métis, and that money be appropriated for schools and agricultural implements. For their part, the petitioners promised to be law-abiding citizens, to exclude liquor from their reservation, and to provide their good offices as mediators between white men and Indians. Riel suggested in a covering letter that a couple of counties taken from the Crow reservation south of the Yellowstone might be appropriate, or perhaps land between that river and the Musselshell, which was actually nearer the buffalo range.

Miles thought the idea a good one but had no authority to make a land grant. He passed the petition upward for consideration by his military superiors, who in turn transmitted it to the secretary of the interior. The proposal was rejected after consultation with the Indian agent of the Crow reservation in Montana, who pointed out that the métis were British subjects, that they had a bad reputation for whiskey trading, and that his own Indians would be loath to share their land.[45]

Although the United States government had no legal or moral obligation to the wandering métis, it seems a pity that their request could not be granted. They might have become a stable community under Riel's leadership in Montana. As it was, they continued to wander, the object of contempt from white men and of suspicion from the local Indians.

Riel wandered with them, supporting himself as a petty trader. He had established a working relation with Thomas O'Hanlon, a good-natured Irish Catholic who was the agent for T.C. Power and Co. at Carroll on the Missouri River, the jumping-off point for the wild country of central Montana where the métis followed the last buffalo.[46] Riel procured trade goods from O'Hanlon, probably on credit, which he then peddled to métis and Indian hunters in return for buffalo hides. It was undoubtedly a meagre living.

Riel's movements are rather difficult to trace after August 1880. In September he was in Fort Benton, buying supplies for the winter trading season.[47] The winter of 1880-81 was spent at Flat Willow Creek, a tributary of the Musselshell, where the métis, having secured the permission of the commander of Fort Maginnis, made a large camp.[48] There Riel became a sub-agent for James Willard Schultz, an independent trader.[49]

At times Riel was still dogged by his old reputation. A recruit for the NWMP who made a trip through Montana in 1881 recalled that on 29 May he saw Riel board the paddlewheel steamer at Carroll to go up to Benton, but 'among our crowd were a number of Orangemen who ... had a very hostile appearance which Riel did not like ...' Riel got off the boat ten miles downstream, before trouble could develop.[50]

For a period of almost two years beginning in mid-1880, Riel sent no letters home to his family in Manitoba. They wrote repeatedly to him, but he failed to reply.[51] The situation recalls his long silence after leaving Montreal in 1866. The one happy occurrence in these months was his romance with Marguerite Monet, or Bellehumeur, as the family was commonly known. Marguerite was the young, illiterate daughter of a métis hunter living near Carroll. Riel must have courted her over the winter of 1880-1. A common-law wedding took place 28 April 1881, which was then blessed by a Jesuit missionary in Carroll on 9 March 1882.[52] With the permission of the priest, Louis went through the ceremony as Louis 'David' Riel, and inscribed his adopted name on the wedding certificate. Their first child, Jean, was born exactly two months later.

Marriage gave his life a new measure of stability. He began to write again to his relatives in Manitoba after his son's birth. Delighted to be in touch once more, they sent family news to Louis and warm letters of welcome to Marguerite. But marriage also meant additional problems. Continually short of money, Riel was plagued with worries about how to support his wife and children.

He began to play a role in the public affairs of Montana during 1882. Always opposed to the excessive consumption of alcohol which was the curse of the métis and Indians, he determined to stamp out the whiskey traffic. He claimed to be able to prove that a métis named Simon Pepin, working for the C.A. Broadwater Co. (the rival of T.C. Power, with whom Riel was associated), had illegally sold whiskey to the Indians. Riel's search for a sympathetic lawman finally led him to US Marshall Alexander Botkin of Helena. Encouraged by Botkin, Riel launched a lawsuit against Pepin, which came to trial in the spring of 1883. The case was thrown out because sales to Indians were not proved, and sales to half-breeds were not against the law. In this judicial débâcle, Riel lost what little money he had.

This enterprise inevitably involved him in Montana politics. Colonel Broadwater was a Democratic stalwart, Marshall Botkin was a Republican who was planning to run for Congress in the election of November 1882 against the Democratic incumbent, Martin Maginnis. Riel became an ardent Botkin supporter and worked hard to deliver the métis vote to the Republicans. His activities made him an obvious target for the charges and counter-charges of vote fraud that flew about after the election. Riel was not yet an American citizen, and the nationality of most of the half-breeds was open to question. In May 1883, Sheriff J.J. Healey of Fort Benton, a Democrat, found Riel near Sun River and arrested him on a warrant for complicity in vote frauds.[53] Riel was not long in jail, and the charges against him were ultimately dismissed, although the case was not finally disposed of until April 1884. The arrest, indictment, and accompanying publicity can only have strengthened his habit of viewing himself as a lonely fighter for good against formidable forces of evil.

While becoming involved in local politics, Riel was also sinking deeper roots in the United States. He became an American citizen on 16 March 1883. He used his messianic name Louis 'David' Riel, as at his marriage.[54] He also took up more permanent employment than the life of a small trader. He accepted a position with the Jesuits as school teacher at St Peter's mission near the Sun River. Strategically located between Helena and Fort Benton, St Peter's was an important mission from which several out-stations were served. The school in which Riel was to be the instructor for about two dozen Indian boys was housed in a substantial stone building. The Ursuline nuns were expected to come in the following year to open a girls school. All in all, St Peter's was the centre of missionary Catholicism in Montana.

Riel, however, could not have been wholly content with his situation. Teaching Indian children to read and write did not hold out much excitement to a man who had run a government for more than half a year, who had three times been elected to Parliament, and who had three times tried to organize an invasion of western Canada. And there was the perpetual problem of money. With his unsold lands and the debts accumulated by his lawsuit against the liquor traffic Riel was a poor man.

GUILT AND HOPE

An abundance of manuscripts affords considerable insight into Riel's inner life during these years. Very little of the material can be dated precisely, so we cannot follow his thinking step by step, but we can pick out certain recurrent themes. Prominent among these was Riel's feeling of guilt. To be an impecunious breadwinner for a wife and small children contributed to his oppressive sense of failure. Sometime after his second child was born, he wrote these verses, which touch the reader's heart in spite of their artlessness:

Mû par une indiscrète flamme
J'ai follement pris une femme
Avant que de pouvoir la faire subsister.
Mon extrême indigence a dû la contrister.
...
Et je suis démoralisé.
Mon deuil est grand: je suis brisé.

Poverty was not all that troubled Riel's marriage, if we may believe these additional lines, which speak of sexual impotence:

J'ai prostitué ma jeunesse.
Dans la débauche j'ai presqu'été sans égal.
Et jeune encore je suis déjà dans la viellesse.
Je ne puis pas remplir mon devoir conjugal.
Mon épouse est plongée, hélas, dans la tristesse.[55]

Riel's impotence could hardly have been continual, since he fathered three children by Marguerite in less than four years. His condition is less important than his reaction to it. He attributed his impotence to his youthful sinfulness: 'I was almost without equal in debauchery.' This unlikely assertion bears eloquent testimony to Riel's pervasive sense of guilt.

Other poems written in these years also contain truly extraordinary manifestations of guilt. Repeatedly Riel accuses himself of almost every conceivable moral failing – gluttony, drunkenness, waste, onanism. He characterizes himself as a 'fallen man,' sunk in an 'abyss' of sin. He has squandered both his physical and his moral health. He has not taken advantage of the opportunity for convalescence which he received by staying with the Barnabés in 1878. He is the epitome of sinfulness, whom only God's mercy can save.[56]

The other side of this burden of guilt was Riel's penchant for self-glorification, evident in the following verses about his fantasy of descent from the royal family of France:

Ma mère est de race guerrière.
Elle vient du pur sang français.
Son nom de la gimodière
Est illustre, je le sais.

Ma mère est du sang de Louis Onze
La chose est facile à trouver.[57]

Such dreams provided solace in dark moments. Sometimes consolation also came in visionary experiences. On 1 March 1883, when Riel was on the bank of the Missouri, he saw his departed father

pale and as if he feared for me. Seeing him, I went straight to him and he came straight to me, although we met each other in the middle of a crowd of people. Before reaching him, I threw myself at his knees to receive his blessing. And I saw him stretch his arm towards me. ... And I saw that he blessed me, as if to complete and make doubly strong and lasting the blessing which, for her part, Sister Saint-Thérèse had passed on to me.[58]

He had first received his father's blessing via Sister Saint-Thérèse in 1873, when he was deeply perturbed about the abandonment of his religious vocation. He had intepreted that blessing as heavenly approval of his decision not to enter the service of the Church. It had also probably symbolized paternal forgiveness for his 'fall.' Now, at a low point in his career, he conjured up his father for forgiveness, reassurance, and encouragement to keep on with his mission.

He also sought to resolve his worries by writing a book which would explain the mystery of man's success and failure. Incomplete drafts, consisting of a series of numbered paragraphs, contain both philosophical and religious themes.[59] Philosophically, Riel began from the assumption that the universe is composed of 'essences,' which seem to be vaguely electrical in character. God is the source of all 'active essences,' and is Himself the supremely active essence, while man is made of 'passive essences.' Man's passivity needs to be complemented by God's activity; man cannot live and grow without God's help. God withdrew much of His support from mankind after the sin of Adam and Eve, but He still offers enough of His essences to sustain life. The child receives a store at birth sufficient to carry him through life – sufficient, that is, except for man's propensity to sin. Men squander their active essences through sin, above all through excess. The result is both physical and moral degeneration leading to death and damnation.

The general idea is similar to that of the medical orthodoxy of the day, which held that the body had only so much vital force, which was wasted by over-indulgence in such acts as sexual intercourse or masturbation. Such moralism wrapped up in scientistic jargon was attractive to Riel, who was plagued throughout his adult life both by poor health and by feelings of moral guilt. His theory linked the two phenomena, making his fragile health seem the consequence of his sinfulness.

Once man 'sets his foot upon the path of excess,' his only hope is that God's grace will restore his active essences. Here Riel permitted himself a characteristic flight of fanciful hope. God's power was unlimited; His essences could restore not only health, but life itself. Riel tried in this way to provide a reasoned explanation for the feeling he had had since January 1879, that God was going to raise Senator Oliver Morton from the grave to help him establish a new order in the North-West.

In a short sequence of numbered paragraphs he concisely summarized his proposals for religious reform: that 'Ville-Marie in Lower Canada should take the place of Rome; that New France, as a sacerdotal country, should be substituted for the Papal States; and that Bishop Ignace Bourget should be regarded as sovereign pontiff of the New World.' Riel reflected egotistically: 'God has given me a genius greater than that of Mahomet and I can found a religion and empires more famous than his, even if I wanted to work like him, without putting myself under the discipline of divine authorization.' 'But,' he continued in an effort at humility, 'that glory does not tempt me.' He would subordinate his initiative to the divine will. If his new doctrine was true, it would be spread by 'the miraculous co-operation of God.' And if that heavenly assistance did not come, Riel said, he would admit he was in error. He would remain submissive to the Roman Church, which, in spite of its faults, would remain the only true church, 'until it shall please God Himself to establish a better one.'

This text shows an important development in Riel's thinking: the notion of 'the miraculous co-operation of God.' Riel now seems to have concluded that God would provide a direct, miraculous demonstration to the world of the validity of his new religion (perhaps through the resurrection of Oliver Morton). It was not incumbent upon Riel to convert the world by his own persuasion. He could remain a loyal member of the Catholic Church in communion with Rome until God Himself would give the sign. He might try to prepare for that day by writing a book such as this, but he was also prepared to submit his manuscript to Bishop Taché for pre-publication censorship. Riel imagined himself going to Taché and saying: 'Monseigneur, here is what I have written. I wanted to publish it without speaking to anyone, but I thought I would come show it to Your Grace first.'[60]

Since his discharge from Beauport, Riel had externally lived as an orthodox Catholic while internally holding to his belief in his mission. His idea that God would miraculously exculpate him before the world rationalized that paradox and allowed him to live in obedience while anticipating deliverance. Quite possibly he had had this idea for several years, but this is the first time he wrote it down. It was to appear again and again throughout the rest of his life.

During these years, Riel occasionally confided his secret thoughts to others. James Willard Schultz, the independent trader for whom Riel was sub-agent from 1880 to 1882, recalled that Riel once told him:

Do you know, these people of mine are just as were the children of Israel, a persecuted race deprived of their heritage. But I will wrest justice for them from the tyrant. I will be unto them a second David.[61]

Riel unfolded his hopes in still greater detail to his political ally, Marshall Botkin. He outlined his dream of gathering all the half-breeds from the United States and Canada to build a nation in the Canadian North-West. Its government would be republican in form but theocratic in substance. Rome would be repudiated, and Riel's version of Catholicism would be established as the state religion. In Botkin's words: 'No doubt need be entertained as to his choice of the man who was to be leader of this unique experiment.'[62]

Some rough notes found in Riel's papers may be related to this scheme. He wrote that immigration from the Catholic countries of Europe like Ireland, Italy, Poland, and Bavaria, would be promoted, and that the immigrants would be encouraged to intermarry with the Indians. 'Thus the entire Indian race of North America would give way to a new race: a race of métis of different fatherlands.' These new métis nations, living alongside the French-Canadian métis, would be under the tutelage of the United States. They would learn 'the art of government from Washington, just as the European nations learned from Rome how to command and to obey.' There might even be room for certain non-Catholic nations in this federation. All would be held together by a system of political and religious councils of an ecumenical type. The result would be 'a religious system [ordre] of universal harmony,' whose purpose would be 'the unceasing reform' of the members of every denomination.[63]

Riel disclosed his thoughts to the Jesuit missionaries, at least to a degree. When he went to confession to Father Frederick Eberschweiler in Fort Benton around the beginning of 1884, the priest assigned him as penance to write to Bishop Bourget to enquire what he had meant years before when he had written to Riel: 'You have a mission which you must fulfil in all respects.' Riel showed Father Eberschweiler the letters, and tried to explain them; but the Jesuit was unimpressed, and insisted that Riel write for clarification.

Riel did not want to follow these instructions. It seems that Archbishop Bourget had already written to him previously, denying that he had ever meant to confer a special mission on him. At least that appears to be implied in this diary entry made by Riel 1 June 1884:

The Archbishop Ignace Bourget is a great saint. He is almost a thousand times more holy than Saint Ignatius Loyola, and yet he [Bourget] has acted like Saint Peter. After having said and written to me, 'God has given you a mission which you will have to fulfil in all respects,' he retreated, by writing to me several years later that *he had never believed and that he still did not believe in the mission which I was convinced I had received from heaven.*[64] [Riel's emphasis]

Riel's vainglorious comparison of himself to Christ and Bourget to St Peter cannot conceal the threat of Bourget's lack of confidence in him. If he should write again, and receive still another negative reply, his entire existence as a prophet would be jeoparidized.

Nonetheless, following his policy of obedience, he sat down to write to the archbishop. He made several drafts, groping for the right words.[65] In one version he poured out his worries about his present situation:

My wife and children and I have no home. We live with others. We have neither bed or pillows. We sleep on straw.

I ardently desire to procure the glory of God as much as possible. And yet I am considered an eccentric. People scorn me, they laugh at me, they speak of me only to shrug their shoulders. ... The newspapers vilify me. I was put in jail. ... And for the sum of my actions, people treat me as a public nuisance.[66]

The other drafts display more self-confidence. He explained to Bishop Bourget why he was writing, and made it clear that it was Eberschweiler's idea, not his. He also pointed out that he had received from God, as a result of Bourget's intervention, 'grace, help, and inspiration' of which the bishop could not be aware. He listed a series of private revelations, culminating in the visionary experiences of early 1879 when he saw the American eagle smile towards the North-West and when he began to pray for the resurrection of Oliver Morton.

Riel insisted on the authenticity of his mission, but interpreted it in the same way as in the philosophical-religious synthesis described above. That is, he was the messenger of the news that Bishop Bourget was the pope now that the Holy Spirit had left Rome for the New World, but he was not calling for an immediate, public break with Rome. It was not for a mere man to declare that Rome had lost favour with God. 'To separate from Rome, we must wait for Jesus Christ Himself to give the command.'[67]

Riel worked on these drafts (it is not known if a letter was ever sent) in February 1884. It is possible to reconstruct the ups and downs of his inner life fairly well from this time onwards. Easter Week of 1884 must have been a period of exaltation, for he received two encouraging revelations.[68] The Holy Spirit told him on 7 April: 'You must march out in front.' Two days later he mystically heard the Latin words, *statue cum fiducia,* which may be translated, 'Believe with confidence.' The import of these revelations was not clear, but they were heartening.

The following month, however, brought Riel to the nadir. On the night of 15 May he had a vivid and terrifying dream of Purgatory, which was followed on subsequent nights by further dreams and revelations. He heard voices telling him to detach himself from all worldly things. Another voice intoned: 'Riel, thirty years of Purgatory.'[69] Shaken by these experiences, he wrote down a series of daily 'prophecies' from 16 May to 24 May.[70] Some contain advice to mortify his flesh by the practice of asceticism, to ward off the pains of Purgatory. For example:

At my table, I will only have what is strictly necessary – water or milk to drink, no dessert, no syrup.

I do not even want to sit comfortably. I want to punish myself, mortify myself in everything. (21 May)

Examples could be multiplied, all showing a preoccupation with peni-
tence in preparation for 'a happy death.'

Other 'prophecies' suggest that Riel was even beginning to doubt his
mission, seeing in it signs of pride. 'O my God, it is You who are waiting
for me. And I was doing the opposite by waiting for You.' These words
may mean that Riel was now reproaching himself for waiting for God's
miracle rather than actively devoting himself to his soul's salvation. 'I
put aside opinions and disputes about the personal worth of the different
races of men.' Was Riel beginning to wonder whether his cherished
métis were really the new chosen people? And again:

I love to work for the welfare of the souls of others! But I am afraid that this
work might distract me, and that through my weakness I might expose myself
to the prisons of purgatory. ... What I want is to never again have any will of my
own. ... And I do not want to act on my own again. ... Who am I? Who am I to
try to direct events?[71]

His mood suddenly changed in early June. On the first of the month he
entered in his diary the comparison, quoted earlier, of himself to Christ
and Bishop Bourget to St Peter – a strong affirmation of his mission. On
2 June he awoke feeling the power of God, saying 'Now I am saved.' The
next day he was no longer in such dread of Purgatory: 'God wants you to
immediately enter the joys of eternal life as soon as you die.' And he remembered what Father Jean-Baptiste Primeau had once told him: 'Riel,
you will succeed when everyone thinks you are lost.' Now he felt that
success might be his. God would help him, the 'chief of Manitoba,' to recover the property that was due him in Canada. He would then use 'the
goods of this life' to advance God's cause in the world.[72] How different
from 24 May, when he had written: 'I no longer aspire towards the
influence which accompanies wealth or fortune.'

How can this sudden ebullience be explained? Had Riel somehow
been forewarned that Gabriel Dumont, Moïse Ouellette, Michel Dumas,
and James Isbister were riding across the prairie to invite him to come
to the Saskatchewan Valley? Possibly, but there is no proof. Riel was at
mass when the delegation arrived at St Peter's on 4 June. Afterwards, he
came out to speak to them, and they issued their fateful invitation. Riel
declined to commit himself immediately, but his tentative answer was
optimistic: 'There are four of you, and you have arrived on the fourth of
June. That is a Providential coincidence. If I agree, I will tell you
tomorrow.'[73] He made a written reply the next day, announcing his will-
ingness to come for three months, with the intention of returning to St

Peter's in September. He expressed skepticism about how much good his intervention would do with the Canadian authorities. He added that he had his own claims to press. He had never received the land grant of 240 acres to which he should have been entitled by the Manitoba Act.[74] The issue of scrip had been delayed several years after 1870, by which time he was out of the province.

A few days later Riel and his family, accompanied by the delegation, set out for the north. They met Father Eberschweiler near Fort Benton. Somewhat reluctantly, for he did not want to embolden Riel, the priest invited them to come to the church. There he donned his surplice and blessed the little entourage. While he made the sign of the cross, Riel prayed: 'My God, bless me according to the intentions of Your Providence, which we love even when they are beyond our measure.'[75] It was a significant moment for Riel; for, interpreting his mission as an extension of Roman Catholicism, he treasured any signs of approbation from the clergy.

Many years later, Father Eberschweiler recalled that he had said to Riel: 'Supposing you win every battle, but in each engagement you lose fifty men – then you will ultimately be defeated.' Riel retorted, 'Father Eberschweiler, you are a good man, but you have not been obliged to endure the many injustices which the Indians to the north of you have suffered. I tell you finally, I intend to go through with the revolt.' Riel added a little later: 'Father Eberschweiler, I see a gallows on top of that hill and I am swinging from it.'[76] As it stands, the dialogue is improbable. No one was yet speaking of an armed revolt. The old priest's memory had certainly been affected by subsequent events when he recounted the story decades afterwards. But the anecdote probably has this much truth in it, that when Riel left Montana he was in a mood of determination and expectation. He hoped that God might be ready to grant a significant improvement in his own fortunes as well as those of the métis.

6
The Prophet in Arms

The North-West Rebellion was as much a religious movement as a political uprising; Riel was, in Machiavelli's immortal phrase, 'a prophet in arms.' I will touch only lightly on the political and military aspects of the Rebellion, which have been well treated by numerous authors, and will concentrate on the religious side of events, which has not yet been thoroughly explored.

PRELUDE

The invitation to Riel from the inhabitants of the Saskatchewan valley was the result of discontent affecting all classes of the population: métis, English half-breeds, whites, and Indians. For decades, métis buffalo hunters had made winter camps in the protected river valleys of the North-West. Some of these gradually grew into permanent settlements. From the early 1860s métis were living along the South Saskatchewan River in the vicinity of Fort Carlton. Their leader was first Isidore Dumont, then his more famous son Gabriel. Their first parish of St Laurent was established in 1872 by the Oblate missionary Father Alexis André. In 1873 they adopted a simple form of local government, over which Gabriel Dumont presided until 1875, when the Canadian administration made itself felt.[1] Their numbers were increased, particularly after 1880, by emigration from Manitoba. The métis of that province were being swamped by a flood of English settlers, and many chose to withdraw further to the west.

At first the métis of the Saskatchewan Valley supported themselves in their traditional ways: the buffalo hunt, cartage for the Hudson's Bay Company, and petty farming. But the fur trade was in long-term decline, and after 1878 there were no more buffalo on the Canadian prairie. The transportation business of the métis faced severe competition from steamboat and railroad. Thus they were thrown back upon agriculture, which had never been more than a supplement to their economy.[2]

This new dependence on agriculture made the land claims of the métis even more pressing. As part of the Manitoba Act, each half-breed residing in Manitoba as of 15 July 1870, was supposed to have received an issue of 240 acres, more if he had children. But the half-breeds resident in the North-West had been allocated nothing, even though the Dominion Lands Act of 1878 had allowed a distribution of land in the North-West, at the discretion of the Cabinet. Furthermore, many Manitoba métis had, for one reason or another, not gotten their scrip. Both groups now demanded another issue of land in the North-West. Their voices were strengthened by other métis who had received the original scrip, disposed of it to speculators, and now wished to try again. Further complaints, as in Red River fifteen years before, revolved around the survey. The half-breeds who had arrived before any surveying was done had squatted on river lots, which did not fit into the rectangular survey used by the Ministry of the Interior. Then there was the problem of the sections reserved for the Hudson's Bay Company and the Canadian Pacific Railway. What of the métis who had unwittingly squatted on these lands? There were other grievances, too, less fundamental but still significant, such as the claim to cut wood without taxation. Finally, the government had been rather slow in issuing official title to property. Some métis who had been there for years still did not have patents, even on uncontested lots.

The métis had repeatedly petitioned Ottawa for redress of their grievances. They had also persuaded church dignitaries such as Bishop Grandin and Archbishop Taché to intercede for them, but to no avail. The federal government simply was not responsive. Sir John A. Macdonald, Minister of the Interior until succeeded by Senator David Macpherson in 1883, had other things on his mind; while the latter, plagued by poor health and approaching retirement age, was an ineffective minister.

If the métis had difficulties, the plight of the Indians was desperate. The passing of the buffalo had destroyed their whole way of life. Unprepared to take up farming, they were reduced to perpetual poverty, with life sustained only by government rations. These were cut after the crash of 1883, as the government attempted to save money. This move accelerated the movement among the Indians to seek renegotiation of their treaties. Among the Crees, the agitation was led by Big Bear, who had only agreed to Treaty No. 6 in 1883 and had never settled on his reserve. As the invitation to Riel was being prepared in the spring of 1884, Big Bear and Poundmaker were making plans for a joint Thirst Dance in June on the Battle River reserve. The intention was to weld the Cree bands into one effective force to achieve a better negotiating position against the federal government. The Indian agitation proceeded on its own lines, without direct connection to parallel movements among the whites and half-breeds. However, the threat of an Indian outbreak certainly lent a sense of urgency to the efforts of the other groups.

The dissatisfaction of the white settlers was chiefly economic. For one thing, nature was against them. 1881 inaugurated a long series of bad weather and poor harvests. The international economy was also unfavourable. The crash of 1883 depressed grain prices so low that sales were hardly worthwhile, while protective tariffs kept up the cost of imported and manufactured articles. The farmers blamed much of their misfortune on the railway monopoly and high freight rates (they were perhaps particularly bitter against the CPR because the decision to take the southern route had destroyed the incipient land boom in their area). They wanted regulation of the railways and of the grain companies, as well as a railway link to Hudson Bay. But there was also a political dimension to their protest. Some settlers, especially those of Liberal sympathies, did not like their territorial status, which meant rule by an appointed governor and a territorial council, responsible to the Conservative government in Ottawa rather than to the local population.

Over the winter of 1883/84, a Settler's Union was formed at Prince Albert to agitate for reform. The secretary was William Henry Jackson, a highly partisan young Liberal. Jackson was instructed to seek the support of the métis, who had been engaged in their own discussions, for a joint approach to Ottawa. It is not entirely clear who first thought of bringing in Louis Riel to help prepare a petition, but the idea won enthusiastic assent at a joint meeting at the Lindsay school-house on 6 May. Métis and English half-breeds, and at least some of the white settlers, agreed to send a delegation to Montana to appeal to Riel.

AGITATION

Riel and the delegation arrived at Fish Creek on 2 July, where they were given a tumultuous welcome by a crowd of métis. After proceeding to Batoche, Riel stayed with Moïse Ouellette, then with Charles Nolin, one of the chief agitators among the métis. On the 8th, he spoke to the métis at Nolin's house, on the 11th he addressed an audience of English half-breeds and settlers at the Lindsay school, and on the 19th he went to Prince Albert to speak to a large crowd. His words and bearing were moderate. He spoke strictly of a peaceful and constitutional movement to send a petition to Ottawa.

He was encouraged by the warm reception he received. After the Prince Albert meeting, he wrote that the will of God had given events a 'peculiar, unexpected, surprising turn.' A little while ago he had been 'a humble schoolmaster' on the banks of the Missouri, and now he was 'among the most popular public figures of Saskatchewan.' God had done 'great things' for him. But he still planned to return to Montana in September.[3]

After the meetings, Riel settled down to work on a petition of grievances. He was to co-operate with William Jackson, from the English side, to create a document that would have wide approval. It was intended to present the petition personally to the Minister of Public Works, Sir Hector Langevin, who was supposed to visit the area that month. But Sir Hector, liking neither the impending confrontation nor the cart trip north from Regina, cancelled his journey. Thereafter the agitators returned to the original strategy of preparing a document to go to Ottawa. Riel did not press as hard as one might have expected. He was even reproached by certain English settlers for being too slow.[4]

Surviving documents show that Riel's intentions went considerably beyond what any of the local people, either French or English, had thought of. The métis had chiefly been concerned about individual title to land, squatters rights, the issue of scrip consequent upon the Manitoba Act, and related questions. Riel, while accepting all of this, also wished to advance a half-breed claim of aboriginal title to the soil of the North-West. This would have to be extinguished through grants of land to the half-breeds as individuals, through reservation of land for their descendants, and through cash payment for land surrendered to Canada.[5]

In the end, Riel could not make his views prevail. He did not sign the joint petition which was finally completed and sent to the government on 16 December.[6] This document said nothing of the half-breeds' aboriginal title. It did, however, exhaustively enumerate the particular grievances of the métis with respect to their individual land claims. It also contained the major points dear to the white settlers: abolition of the protective tariff, a rail outlet to Hudson Bay, responsible government coupled with provincial status, and local control of natural resources. As a concession to Riel, it narrated his version of the entry of Manitoba into Confederation and the subsequent disputes between Ottawa and the métis but no clear demand was made in this connection. The petition was a forthright statement of grievances, but it was moderate in tone. It did not read like the prelude to a revolution.

Although the major focus of Riel's activity was political in these months, he did not neglect religion. He began to disclose his secret doctrine to a small number of close associates. About a month after his arrival, he showed Charles Nolin one of his letters from Bishop Bourget, as well as a book which he had supposedly written seven years ago with buffalo blood. Riel sometimes referred to this book as 'The Prophecies of St Bridget.'[7] Although Nolin thought the reference was to Bridget of Ireland, Riel probably had in mind Bridget of Sweden (1303-73), author of the *Celestial Book of Revelations*. Mediaeval and Renaissance oracles – Bridget, Hildegard of Bingen, Nostradamus, etc. – were widely reprinted in ultramontane circles along with the revelations of contemporary prophets like Bernadette of Lourdes. Collectors of such lore believed that these apocalyptic predictions would come true in the present age, as a prelude to the Second Advent. Riel's reference to St Bridget makes it seem that he had seen some of this literature.

By the light of the evening fire, Riel disclosed the essentials of his doctrine to Nolin and Maxime Lépine. He was a prophet whose every word was inspired. Even the rumbling of his stomach, he said one night, was the sound of the Holy Spirit at work in his body.[8] There would soon be a great war in which he would defeat England and divide the territory of Canada. Quebec would be given to the Prussians as punishment for her sins, Ontario would go to the Irish, and the North-West would be partitioned among immigrants of several European nationalities. Rome was corrupt and the Holy Spirit was now in Bishop Bourget. Riel himself was a descendant of St Louis, King of France. He was the sacred king, foretold by the prophets, who would restore order in the world by destroying the forces of evil. His friends Nolin and Lépine would be his lieutenants, marching to battle with crosses on their breasts.[9]

It is impossible to say whether these recollections of Nolin and Lépine accurately represent what Riel told them. Their testimony was given many months after the event, when they had a strong motive to depict Riel in the most radical way possible.

The only contemporary written evidence about Riel's religious views in these months is a notebook of prayers, which contains a few salient entries. They show him holding the theory which he had adopted in

Montana, that the Roman papacy would retain its authority until God Himself gave a dramatic sign to the world to confirm that Bishop Bourget was the new pope. Riel prayed repeatedly for the Catholic Church and the Catholic clergy without questioning their legitimacy. He prayed for religious unity between Europe and America: 'O eternal Christ, make the Holy See be visibly united to Your altar in the New World; let it be, so to speak, the facade, or rather, let it be the greatest, the most elevated, and the most certain step leading up to the tabernacle of the living God.' But while praying to 'keep myself in harmony with Your Holy See, O Christ!' he also implied that the location of the papacy could change, by asking Christ to 'locate Your Holy See so that it is always among very fervent people.'[10] Around 1 November 1884, the anniversary of the death of Senator Morton of Indiana, Riel jotted down the prayer he had once composed for his resurrection: 'My God! If you wish, if You have so decided in Your eternal plans, resurrect Oliver P. Morton as he was and then heal him, so that he may aid us in the United States.'[11] Would this resurrection be the anticipated sign to openly acknowledge the papacy of Mgr Bourget?

Riel was thus in an uneasy tension between heresy and orthodoxy. He defined himself as a loyal Catholic and continued to participate in all the rites of the Church; but if his views became known in full to the local missionaries, they would have to regard him as a heretic. It seems that Riel did gradually disclose many of his unorthodox ideas to them – perhaps intentionally, perhaps in moments of passion.

When he first arrived at Batoche, Riel went at once to the church of St Laurent to meet Father Fourmond, the curé. 'I left,' he said, 'with the blessing of the Reverend Fathers of St Peter's in Montana; now that I am here, I come most humbly to request the blessing of the Reverend Fathers of St Laurent. I do not wish to undertake anything except under the direction of the clergy and according to their advice.'[12] This was the first time Fourmond had met Riel. The rather naïve priest was 'enchanted by his conversation and his fine spirit'; he admired 'the faith which suffused all his words, the gentleness of his expression and speech.'

When Riel met Father André in July he made a good impression on that priest, who was far more astute than Father Fourmond.[13] But when Riel spoke to the people on 10 August at St Antoine-de-Padua church, he seemed to be unhappy that he was not receiving stronger and more open backing from the clergy. His relations with André became strained the following week. They had a private meeting at Batoche in which

Riel swore that he had no hidden plans, but André thought his ideas seemed 'rather revolutionary.'[14] Riel and Maxime Lépine came to Prince Albert on 17 August where they had a blazing row with André. Riel revealed a substantial part of his thinking in the heat of argument. He declared that the métis were a distinct people and that French Canadians who moved to the North-West should identify with them, dropping their old nationality. When contradicted by André on this score, Riel swore that God would remove from his path all the troublesome priests who would not acknowledge his 'special and divine mission.' He added that the word of priests was not necessarily law, either in politics or religion.[15] After this discussion, André concluded that Riel was a 'true fanatic,' who professed 'heretical and revolutionary ideas.'

At this time, the cancellation of Sir Hector Langevin's visit had not yet been announced. Riel's plan was for a large public ceremony at which the grievances of the métis would be articulated. He also intended to make a speech stressing that the métis were a separate nationality, the offspring of New France just as the French Canadians were the offspring of Old France. Some French Canadians thought the métis were inferior, but this was no more justified than the opinion of the English that the French were an inferior race.[16]

Langevin's visit did not take place, but Riel found an even better opportunity to publicize his view that the métis were a genuine nationality. Early in September, Vital Grandin, Bishop of St Albert, came to Batoche to administer the sacrament of confirmation. Riel demanded a meeting with the bishop to discuss the local grievances. He accused Grandin of trying to control the métis through his priests. He as much as said that the clergy were servile tools of the government. That evening Grandin wrote to his acquaintance Lawrence Clarke, chief factor of the Hudson Bay Company at Prince Albert, that Riel appeared to be 'consumed with pride and vanity.'[17] He could not be contradicted without losing his temper. He was arousing the métis with talk of submission to '*justified* authority' and of '*enlightened* obedience to the priests.' Grandin was disturbed about where it all might lead. Riel had become a 'little god' to the métis, who might follow him in any venture, no matter how rash.

After several speeches at a great public meeting on 5 September, Riel closed discussion by proposing that, in recognition of the status of the métis as a distinct people, the bishop should grant them a patron saint and a special national festival, so they would be like the French Canadians with their feast of St Jean-Baptiste. Riel advanced before the bishop, joining hands with a Frenchman and a French Canadian to demonstrate the kinship and unity of all the children of France. When Mgr Grandin approved the plan, Riel suggested St Joseph as a national patron; and Grandin allowed them to take 24 July as a national holiday.[18]

Riel's proposal had symbolic dimensions which can only be appreciated in the light of his entire doctrine, which of course was not known to the others who were present. If John the Baptist was the precursor of Christ, St Joseph was His earthly father and also bore the title 'Patron of the Universal Church.' 24 July came exactly a month after 24 June. The implication was that the métis were not only a people distinct from the French Canadians, but had a mission which was higher than theirs had been.[19]

Since 24 July had already passed, Mgr Grandin gave the métis permission to inaugurate their new feast day with a special celebration on 24 September. A crowd of hundreds assembled on the appointed day at St Antoine-de-Padua. Father Moulin, the pastor, insisted on preaching the sermon, even though he had been away and was not acquainted with events. He must have pricked the national pride of the métis when he began to preach about John the Baptist, assuming that the patron of the métis could be none other than the saint of the French Canadians. Father Touze, standing at his side, whispered to him that he was in error, and Moulin quickly deserted John the Baptist to embrace St Joseph.

Riel spoke for three-quarters of an hour after mass. Having already gained his symbolic victory, he did not go too far. His talk emphasized how much the missionaries had done for the métis and stressed the duty of obedience which Catholics owed their priests.[20]

Riel kept up a display of ostentatious piety which helped to establish him in the eyes of the métis as a spiritual leader. Although he had no money of his own, and was compelled to live from charity, he distributed the money that was given to him, either to the poor or to the priests for masses to be said. A wedding in November gave him a chance to indulge his dramatic flair. He prevailed upon the father of the bride to leave the place of honour vacant, in commemoration of Jesus at the wedding feast of Cana. He then prayed all night on his knees in the loft while the guests danced to the music of the fiddles.[21]

While in public he maintained his extraordinary piety and devotion to the Church, Riel's relations with the missionaries were worsening. He was exasperated by their unwillingness to lend him the sort of support he had enjoyed from Ritchot and Dugas in 1869-70. He unleashed a tirade against Father Vegreville the day after the wedding feast. 'There should be,' he declaimed, no one called bishop, priest, father; all should be called servants of God. All the priests, bishops, and archbishops should march with us; we will know how to bring them into line. I am nothing; I come from a grain of dust, and I shall return to dust, but *I have a task to accomplish by reason of a divine vocation.* The priests and bishops see only money and comfort. They must become poor and support themselves by the work of their hands as did the apostles ... [22]

Father Vegreville was itching to retort, but he kept silent because Riel was surrounded by a group of loyal admirers.

Riel came to Prince Albert on 3 December and had another terrible quarrel with André. Soon after, he went to St Laurent, where the missionaries of the district were gathered for their monthly retreat. When Riel vigorously attacked them, André declared that the Oblates would treat him as an enemy from now on and openly oppose him among the métis. At that Riel burst into tears, fell to his knees, and begged for forgiveness. The priests led him into the chapel, where he promised before the tabernacle never to lead a revolt against the civil authorities. After this melodramatic scene, the fathers seriously debated whether Riel should be barred from the sacraments as a heretic. They decided against such drastic action, on the grounds, as Fourmond put it, that his extravagant words and wrathful outbursts were due to 'the spiritual ordeals and misfortunes of his past, which were enough ... to put his unstable mind into a state akin to madness, where he was not really responsible for what he said.'[23]

BLACKMAIL?

When Riel agreed to return to Canada, he made it clear that he intended to press his own claim for land scrip under the Manitoba Act. He also hinted that he might have broader demands; he wrote that the Canadian government 'will readily find out that they owe me something else.'[24]

When Bishop Grandin paid his visit in September, he was accompanied by Amédée Forget, clerk of the North-West Council. Forget suggested to Octave Regnier, the local schoolteacher, that perhaps Riel would like to be a member of the Council, with a salary of $1000 a year. According to their subsequent account, Charles Nolin and Maxime Lépine exclaimed when they heard this: 'So that's it!' They warned Riel not to accept, and he said, 'Do you think I'd dirty my name by going to a place like that?'[25] Yet Riel also saw Forget privately, and the latter left convinced that an arrangement might be possible. He passed the word to Governor Dewdney, who later in the month wrote to the prime minister suggesting the whole affair could be resolved by making Nolin an Indian agent and putting Lépine and Riel on the Territorial Council.[26]

Early in December, Riel began to speak to his confidants Nolin and Lépine about his 'desire to have money.' He said that he wanted $10,000 or $15,000, that he did not know how to obtain it, but that the Canadian government owed him an indemnity of $100,000.[27] Riel explained at his trial why he thought the government owed him money. It was compensation for his services to Canada, such as governing the Red River colony until the arrival of Wolseley's troops, helping Governor Archibald repel O'Donoghue's raid in 1871, and allowing George Cartier to be elected in his place in 1872.[28] The $100,000 was apparently a round number not supported by detailed calculations. The $35,000 which Riel was shortly to propose as an appropriate compromise, or at least a first instalment, was the amount which, according to Riel, Sir John Macdonald had offered him in October 1873 to leave the country.[29] This offer is not authenticated by any documentary source, although there is no doubt that the prime minister did pay Riel several thousand dollars in February 1872 to get him to leave then.

Nolin advised Riel to approach the government through the clergy. On 12 December, Riel requested Father André to intercede for him. André agreed to set up a meeting with D.H. MacDowall, elected representative of the District of Lorne to the Territorial Council.[30] André and MacDowall came to St Laurent, where a meeting took place 23 December. Riel told MacDowall that the government owed him $100,000, but he would acept $35,000 as a first instalment. He would leave the country as soon as the money was paid.

It is not known exactly what else Riel promised. According to André's trial testimony, Riel said twice: 'If I am satisfied, the half-breeds will be.'[31] It is not clear whether this meant merely that Riel's followers would be mollified if their chief received his personal due, or whether he was promising to persuade the métis to do the government's will.

André and MacDowall seem to have put the stronger interpretation on the ambiguous words. MacDowall reported the meeting to Governor Dewdney and estimated that $3000 'would cart the whole Riel family across the boundary.'[32] Father André wrote in the same vein, that if the government would part with a few thousand dollars Riel would make his followers 'agree to any conditions.'[33] Subsequently MacDowall wrote once more and André twice more to urge this plan upon the governor.[34] Dewdney thought it was at least worth considering, but he could do nothing by himself, so he forwarded their letters to the prime minister. Macdonald firmly vetoed the idea by return mail: 'How would it look to be obliged to confess we could not govern the country and were obliged to bribe a man to go away?'[35]

It is uncertain what Riel intended to do with his money if he received it. At various points, he said that he would go to the United States, or to Quebec, or 'wherever the Government wished to send him.'[36] According to Nolin, he also supposedly said:

that if he got the money he would go to the United States and start a paper and raise the other nationalities in the States. He said before the grass is that high in this country you will see foreign armies in this country. He said I will commence by destroying Manitoba, and then I will come and destroy the North-West and take possession of the North-West.[37]

But there is no other evidence that Riel at this time was seriously considering an invasion of Canada from the United States. Nolin's statement is doubly suspect: at the time of their conversation, Riel was trying to appear militant, to prevent Nolin from discrediting him among the métis; and at the trial Nolin was also trying to make Riel appear as militant as possible, to put all the blame for the Rebellion upon him. But is it not implausible that Riel would have used the money to found a newspaper, possibly in co-operation with William Jackson, as is mentioned in another report by Nolin.[38]

Riel never tried to deny this attempt to obtain money from the government, but he maintained that it was collection of a legitimate debt, not extortion. André and MacDowall, Dewdney and Macdonald seem to have regarded it more or less as blackmail – not in a legal sense, since Riel did not threaten damage to anyone's person, property, or reputation, but in a moral sense. The sort of evidence that would allow a clear judgment about Riel's intentions is not available to us today.

INSURGENCY

Little happened until 27 January. On that day Riel and Gabriel Dumont approached Nolin to demand that he withdraw his tender to construct a telegraph line between Edmonton and Duck Lake, as a sign of dissatisfaction with the government. Nolin said he would do so if Riel would represent the North-West in the House of Commons and give up his plan of returning to the United States. Riel allegedly agreed.[39]

On 4 February, the prime minister, with some prodding by MacDowall, telegraphed to Dewdney that a commission would be appointed to enquire into the land claims of the half-breeds. Dewdney notified the métis by passing the telegram to Nolin, apparently a deliberate slight of Dumont and Riel, the real leaders. Riel was enraged when Nolin showed him the telegram on 8 February. The action promised would be slow, it would deal with only part of the métis grievances, and, most important, there was no reference to Riel's personal claims. According to Nolin, Riel cried that 'it was 400 years that the English had been robbing, and that it was time to put a stop to it.'[40] According to Fourmond, Riel exclaimed: 'Ottawa will have my answer in forty days!'[41] The provisional government was in fact declared on 19 March, the fortieth day afterwards.

There is no sign, however, that Riel turned immediately in a radical direction. In the middle of the month he took part in a Forty Hours devotion at St Laurent. Father Fourmond allowed him, much to the chagrin of Father André, to read an act of consecration in front of the people before the sacrament exposed on the altar. Using his messianic name 'David,' Riel dedicated himself and his people to the Sacred Heart. He asked God to accept the métis as His favourite nation ('peuple de prédilection'). He prayed for their Protestant neighbours, that there might be one flock and one shepherd in the North-West. And he was careful to emphasize the duty of obedience to the Church.[42] Although one can recognize several themes dear to Riel in this prayer, it gives no sign of an impending revolution or break with the Church.

But Riel was growing in inner strength and self-confidence around this time. His health had been poor earlier in the winter. He had adopted a unique diet consisting of vegetables, milk, and cooked blood, and had filled his diary with prayers for health. He began to feel much better in January, 'as if [he] had never been in poor health.' He wrote in extravagant terms:

Oh, how well I feel! I recognize, O my God, that I am Your spouse, the holy Church of the elect. My beauty extends afar like the light which the rising sun casts before itself upon the sea. My glory embraces the world ...

This feeling of well-being brought self-confidence to the point of absurd vanity. Riel characterized himself in his diary as 'unusually wise and farsighted,' with an intelligence 'far above any other.' He also felt less concern about the fear of purgatory, which had plagued him since his terrifying dreams of May 1884. In eight and a half months, he wrote, he had already expiated half of the thirty years of purgatory with which he had been threatened.[43]

Riel began to act late in February. On the 24th he called a meeting of the métis at which he announced that he would leave Canada. It was obvious, he said, that the government did not want to negotiate with him, so he was more of a hindrance than a help to his people in obtaining their rights. His partisans, distributed throughout the audience (perhaps by design), made a terrific uproar and shouted for Riel to stay. Riel asked: 'But the consequences?' 'We will accept them,' the métis answered. Father Fourmond, guileless as ever, arose to praise Riel's patriotism.[44] Riel received a 'consoling' revelation the same day. The Holy Spirit told him: 'In three or four years you will have your lands.'[45] After mass on Sunday, 1 March, he spoke at the door of St Laurent. He would make a show of force, he said, since peaceful means had not swayed the government. 'I have only to lift my finger and you will see a countless multitude of nations rush here, who are only awaiting my signal.'[46]

He seems to have given the impression in this speech that he expected military support; but a diary entry from about this time shows a different emphasis. He wrote of bringing from the United States the 'religious Irish,' the 'pious Bavarians,' the 'faithful Poles,' the 'wise Italians,' the 'sincere Belgians,' the 'intelligent Canadiens,' the 'intrepid and good French,' and the 'hardworking and docile Scandinavians' to become 'the most respectable and holy settlers' in Manitoba and the North-West. There is nothing of military support here, although definitely an apocalyptic mood. At the end of the passage, Riel wrote in a bold hand and emphatically underlined: 'Thy Kingdom come.'[47]

Riel and several métis met with Fathers André, Fourmond, and Touze at St Laurent on the evening of 2 March. Excitedly, Riel demanded that André support the immediate formation of a provisional government, as he had sponsored Gabriel Dumont's local government a dozen years earlier.[48] The next day there was a meeting at Halcro between sixty métis, who came armed, and a number of English half-breeds and whites. Riel spoke belligerently, although he did not clearly enunciate a policy of rebellion, perhaps sensing that he was receiving little support from the English. The biggest sensation at the meeting was caused by Willie Jackson, who announced he was going to resign as secretary of the Settler's Union. He intended to prepare himself to become a Catholic.[49] Riel had another stormy interview with Father André on 4 March. He no longer bothered to mask his intentions. When André contradicted him, he swore he would go to the United States and return with thousands of men, that blood would flow, and that the responsibility would be André's for not having supported him.[50]

The next day Riel held a secret meeting with ten of the most militant métis, including Gabriel Dumont and several of his relatives. He drew up a revoluntionary oath to which they affixed their mark.

We, the undersigned, pledge ourselves deliberately and voluntarily to do everything we can to

1 save our souls by trying day and night to live a holy life everywhere and in all respects.
2 save our country from a wicked government.

Invoking God and the saints, the conspirators also pledged 'to raise our families in a holy way' and to take for their banner 'the commandments of God and the Church and the inspiring cross of Jesus Christ our Lord.'[51]

Riel and Dumont then went to Nolin to demand his adherence. Nolin, who wanted no part in any violence, made a counter-proposal. He suggested a novena, that is, nine days of prayer during which a decision could be made. (The idea of a novena was in the air because Nolin's wife, who had long been ill, seemed to be cured after a novena to Our Lady of Lourdes which was held 16-25 December 1884. This recovery had been accepted by the métis and their priests as a genuine miracle.)[52] Riel at first opposed Nolin's idea, but acquiesced the next day, perhaps after realizing that the novena could be timed to end on 19 March, the feast of St Joseph, the new patron of the métis.

Father Fourmond was enthusiastic about the idea. Attendance was good at the daily ceremonies, but he would have done well to notice that Riel did not come except on Sunday, when his presence at mass was mandatory. Fourmond preached energetically on the duty of obedience to the civil authorities and threatened to refuse the sacraments to any who rebelled, but Riel was not impressed, only irritated. After mass he reproached the priest for meddling in politics.[53] On 17 March Fourmond, sanguine as ever, wrote to Bishop Grandin: 'We are not too worried about the people of St Laurent.'[54] The insurrection began the next day.

By 18 March, Riel and Dumont had gathered a large crowd of men under the pretext of coming to St Laurent to celebrate the feast of St Joseph and the baptism of Jackson, scheduled for that day. The men were told to bring their guns to fire off a volley of joy. John Willoughby, a doctor from Saskatoon, encountered Riel that day with sixty or seventy armed men. Riel explained that the time had come to take arms to assert their rights. He claimed to have a proclamation ready for publication at Pembina which would bring help from the Indians, as well as the United States. He sketched out a plan to divide the North-West into seven portions, one each for the Irish, Bavarians, etc. Orangism would be eradicated from the North-West. When Willoughby replied that there was a difference between Orangism and Protestantism, Riel excitedly agreed. He said that the Christian religion was like a great tree. Christ was the trunk and the various denominations were the branches. The Roman Catholic Church was the 'strongest branch,' but not the only one.[55] This conversation reveals a growing ecumenical spirit in Riel, which had first become noticeable in Montana. His new religion would include Catholics and Protestants alike in a unified church of the New World.

The métis moved into open rebellion 18 March, incited by the rumour that 500 Mounted Police were advancing against them. The truth behind the rumour was that the commander of the police, alarmed by reports of sedition, had ordered a column of 100 men north to reinforce Fort Carlton. Riel and Dumont confiscated a supply of arms and ammunition at George Kerr's store, and also took several hostages to use in bargaining with the Canadian government. The rebels then went to hold a meeting at the church of St Anthony of Padua. When Father Moulin objected, Riel brushed him aside, saying to the crowd that his protests made him a 'Protestant.' Riel made a speech outside the church, declaiming: 'Rome has fallen.'[56]

Inside, a remarkable scene ensued, if the following report can be believed. Riel stood near the altar and said that when he had first come to this church he had stood at the back with his head bowed. Each time afterwards he had moved a little further towards the front. 'Where am I today? At the altar. Who has brought me here? The Good Lord. Who speaks through my mouth when I speak to you? It's God.' Then, Riel said, he would actually touch the altar if anyone wished him to. Silence. 'Well,' said Riel, 'no one says anything, I'll touch it another time.' After this Riel urged the men to imitate the scene at the entry of Jesus into Jerusalem. While he sang, his followers danced around him emitting cries of joy. He imparted the Holy Spirit to his men by breathing strongly upon them. He repeated that the pope was no longer their master. Declaring that the priests had too many books for true religion, he showed his little pocket notebook, saying 'That's my book and we don't need any others.'[57] Riel marched his army down to St Laurent in the evening, where he addressed Fathers Fourmond and Paquette:

The Provisional Government is constituted; we already have five prisoners. The 'old Roman' is set aside. I have a new pope in the person of Mgr Bourget. You will be the first priests of the new religion, and from now on you have to obey me.[58]

Fourmond was inclined to resist at first, but it occurred to him that it might quiet the mob if he proposed to baptize Willie Jackson, even though it was 10:00 PM and the ceremony was supposed to take place the next day, the final day of the novena. In Fourmond's words:

Riel, suddenly having become as calm as if we had only been exchanging pleasantries, thanked me for the favour and especially for letting him act as godfather, in spite of everything. Thus Jackson was baptized and edified everyone by his pious demeanour during the baptism.[59]

The godfather signed the parish register with his prophetic name, Louis 'David' Riel.

A provisional government was selected at a mass meeting 19 March. Riel nominated Gabriel Dumont as 'Adjutant-General'; Dumont then selected the other members of the council or 'Exovedate.' Riel did not take an office, as befitted a prophet whose authority stemmed not from man but from God.

REBELLION

The subsequent political and military history of the Rebellion, which is well known, may be briefly summarized. The rebels demanded the surrender of the police garrison at Fort Carlton, commanded by Superintendent Crozier. At the same time, they unsuccessfully sought the adherence of the nearby English half-breeds to their movement. There was a bloody clash on 26 March at Duck Lake between the métis and a column of a hundred men commanded by Crozier. The police were forced to retire at the cost of twelve men dead; the rebels lost five.

The métis did not press their advantage. They allowed the police to retreat and join up with the reinforcements which had arrived from the south. This combined force retired to Prince Albert, where it sat out the rest of the Rebellion. Fort Carlton was accidentally burned by the police themselves in their hasty departure.

Temporarily master of the area, Riel sent numerous letters asking for support from other métis communities in the North-West. These yielded only meagre results. He and Dumont also attempted to rouse the Indians. A few came to Batoche, while two bands of Cree went on the warpath. Big Bear's Crees massacred eight white men at Frog Lake on 2 April, while Poundmaker's band attacked Battleford. The Indians, it seems, were moved more by the successful example of the métis than by their direct urging. There was never any effective co-ordination between the Indian and métis forces. The rebels also discussed aid from the United States; but Riel, in spite of his earlier talk about American support, refused to do anything in that direction.

While the métis waited at Batoche, the Canadian government put its expeditionary force into the field. General Frederick Middleton led a column of 800 men from Qu'Appelle towards Batoche. Dumont wanted to carry out a campaign of guerrilla harassment against the advancing Canadians, but Riel forbade it. Finally Dumont, determined to act, ambushed Middleton at Fish Creek, about ten miles south of Batoche. The advance of the Canadians was temporarily checked, as they lost ten dead and forty-five wounded, against four dead and three wounded for the métis.

But the outcome was not seriously in doubt. After four days of fighting from 9 to 12 May, the rebels of Batoche were crushed. No one knows exactly how many men they had under arms, but the total was certainly less than three hundred métis and Indians together. Not all had rifles, and ammunition was in short supply. Against that Middleton could muster 800 well-armed men, backed by cannon and a Gatling gun loaned by the United States. The Canadian army lost only half a dozen men in the battle of Batoche. The métis lost a dozen, plus an undetermined number of Indians.

Riel's strategy in the Rebellion has always been something of a puzzle. He seems to have been imprisoned in the memory of 1869-70. He declared a provisional government and took hostages with the intention of forcing Ottawa to negotiate, as in the first rebellion. After surrender he always maintained that negotiations had been his true objective, which is corroborated by his diary. On 29 April, 1885, he asked God to help him quickly make a good treaty with Canada, to resolve the grievances of the métis and Indians, and to gain 'the indemnity which is my due, not a small indemnity, but an indemnity which will be just and equitable before [God] and men!'[60]

His actions indicate that he was not really eager to fight in spite of his bellicose pronouncements about a 'war of extermination.'[61] He restrained Dumont from pursuing the temporary advantage gained at Duck Lake, and from conducting guerrilla warfare against Middleton. He preferred to wait at Batoche, hoping against hope that the Canadians would come in small, divided forces with which the métis could deal. This is hard to understand; for, given his experience in the East, he must have realized the capacity of Canada to deliver an overwhelming blow. As George Woodcock has shown in his biography of Gabriel Dumont, a strategy of quick action and mobile warfare had at least some chance of success. A series of early victories, such as the capture of Prince Albert, might have touched off a universal rising of Indians and half-breeds. Then Ottawa might indeed have negotiated, rather than face a protracted war.[62]

Riel sealed his doom by declaring war and shrinking from the consequences. He wanted to repeat his success of Red River, which had been obtained virtually without fighting. But he does not seem to have realized how different that situation was. Then the title of Canada to Rupert's Land was not yet solidly established, but now there was not the slightest doubt about Canadian sovereignty in the North-West. Then Canada had been cut off from her western lands by an impassable wilderness of rock and water, but now an army could be deployed within weeks by means of the Canadian Pacific Railroad.

One explanation of Riel's misjudgments lies in the religious aspects of the Rebellion. As we have seen, religion and politics were inextricably mingled in the events leading up to formation of the provisional government, and this continued throughout the Rebellion. Let us look more closely at the religious side of things. The provisional government, from its earliest days, was known as the Exovedate and its members as Exovedes (Exovidat and Exovide in French). The words were coined by Riel from the Latin words *ex* – 'from' – and *ovile* – 'flock of sheep.' An Exovede was 'one of the flock.'

After his surrender, Riel explained the thinking behind the term:

That word I made use of to convey that I was assuming no authority at all. And the advisers of the movement took also that title, instead of councillors or representatives; and their purpose in doing so was exactly the same as mine: no assumption of authority ... [63]

The Exovedate, continued Riel, was not a government; it was merely a committee of self-defence. The métis had not committed treasonous acts; they had only resorted to the natural right of self-protection against an impending attack by the government. If the terms 'council' or 'provisional government' were occasionally heard, it was because the métis were not yet accustomed to the word Exovedate.

This tendentious statement need not be taken seriously. Riel was looking forward to his legal defence when he made it. What remains of the term Exovedate is the religious symbolism of the flock which it incorporated. Riel occasionally used the signature Louis 'David' Riel Exovede, but he was technically not a member of the Exovedate. However, he deliberated with them, proposed motions to them, and accepted the results of their voting. His own position was that of official prophet of the movement, established without a dissenting vote by the Exovedate in the following motion:

That the French-Canadian Métis Exovedate recognize Louis 'David' Riel as a prophet in the service of Jesus Christ the Son of God and the only Redeemer of the world; as a prophet at the feet of Mary Immaculate under the powerful and most favourable protection of the Virgin Mother of Christ; as a prophet under the visible and most comforting protection of St Joseph, the chosen patron of the métis, the patron of the universal church; as a prophet humbly imitating in many ways St John the Baptist, the glorious patron of the French Canadians and the French-Canadian métis.[64]

It is mildly ironic to be officially recognized as a prophet, but Riel had always desired the recognition of human institutions to accompany the charismatic authority of divine inspiration.

Riel played the prophetic role to the full during the Rebellion. Almost every morning he would bring new revelations to the Exovedate and to the people at large. 'The Holy Spirit has told me,' he would say, or: 'The Holy Spirit has shown me.'[65] Gabriel Dumont was certainly convinced that Riel was inspired by God. Until the battle of Fish Creek, he allowed Riel to overrule his desire for a guerrilla war. He afterwards explained: 'I yielded to Riel's judgment although I was convinced that from a human standpoint, mine was the better plan; but I had confidence in his faith and his prayers, and that God would listen to him.'[66]

Riel did not just act like a prophet to impress his followers. He filled his diary with a constant stream of revelations. Even the most mundane thoughts and observations were cast in revelatory form. For example: 'The Spirit of God made me understand that we should tie up the prisoners.'[67] His inner voice told him on 28 April that 'help is coming to us.' When a messenger arrived on 1 May with a letter of support from Poundmaker, Riel had him write in the margin next to this prophecy, 'fulfilled to the letter' and sign his name.[68]

Although Riel openly called himself a prophet, he did not lay claim to the more extreme titles he had used in 1876-8, like priest-king or infallible pontiff. But he did glorify himself through comparison to certain Old Testament figures. He prayed to God to reveal his mission to the world 'just as Your light showed the Hebrews the divine task of Moses.'[69] He also said at a meeting that the 'spirit of Elias' was with him (in Jewish eschatology, Elias is supposed to return to earth before the coming of the messiah).[70] These references to Hebrew prophets and patriarchs fitted Riel's view that the métis were a new chosen people, the modern equivalent of the Jews. As a prophet, Riel expected to triumph through divine intervention. His miraculous victory would be the sign needed to authenticate his new religion in the eyes of the world. The military weakness of his strategy was its religious strength, because it required a miracle to work.

The rebel flag was in essence a plea for miraculous deliverance. It was a banner to which was attached a large picture of Our Lady of Lourdes, which had belonged to the Riel children. The cult of Lourdes, with its many miracles and supernatural cures, was well known to the métis through their French missionaries. There was a local shrine to Our Lady of Lourdes, and it was through her intercession that Charles Nolin's wife had allegedly been healed only a few months before. If Mary could perform medical miracles, why not pray to her for a military miracle? On the back of the picture was a poem composed by Riel, asking for her help.[71]

Riel never carried a gun throughout the Rebellion. At the battle of Duck Lake, he carried the figure of Christ borrowed from the crucifix of Father Touze's nearby chapel. He held it high to encourage his men, just as Father Leflèche had done when the métis fought the Sioux in 1851 at Grand Coteau. Riel called out the volleys: 'Fire in the name of God the Father almighty; fire in the name of God the Son; fire in the name of God the Holy Spirit.'[72]

When Dumont decided to engage Middleton at Fish Creek, Riel accompanied the expedition, which made slow progress because he compelled them to stop periodically to say the rosary. Riel turned back after the first day's march, when a messenger arrived from Batoche asking for more men to help guard the prisoners. Gabriel was just as glad that Riel left; he wryly commented afterwards that now he could make better time because 'we weren't saying the rosary any more.'[73] During the battle, Riel was at Batoche, where the firing was audible. He stood and prayed with his arms extended in the form of a cross. Two strong men helped him keep his weary arms up, as Moses had been helped during the battle with the Amalekites.[74]

After Fish Creek, Riel decreed four days of fasting and penance to placate God's wrath. God told him that He was going to get angry with the métis for they were 'too negligent ... not vigilant and obedient enough.' They had 'said "yes" too quickly,' that is, they had embarked on the Rebellion without fully understanding God's will. They had been too attached to their horses and to 'gambling on the detestable races'; that is why God had allowed them to lose fifty-five horses at Fish Creek. But 'four days of fasting is enough to turn a nation of dwarves into a nation of giants.' When the fast was over, Riel thought his people were morally uplifted, ready to face the enemy again.[75]

Riel continued to pray for miraculous deliverance as Middleton drew inexorably closer. He saw the greatest moment of his life approaching, a veritable Armageddon. He wrote in apocalyptic language on 6 May:

Here I am, squarely arrived at the time God has marked in the order of things to come. With my own eyes, I saw all the signs of the times which were shown us before now. I did not want to believe that they were really signs of the times. But finally I had to recognize what they were. Yes, before me lies the time identified in many ways, the time announced with all the signs that are supposed to accompany it, just as we are told in the scriptures.[76]

Before the battle of Batoche, a Canadian cannon fired a signal to the steamer *Northcote*. Riel told his men it was the thunder of God, and that lightning was about to strike the enemy.[77] He prayed during the fighting and led the women in the rosary. Until the end, he put his hope in a miracle. Half an hour before the surrender, Patrice Tourond said to him, 'Work your miracle now, it's time.' Riel sank to his knees and lifted his arms in the form of a cross. He spoke: 'All together, let us say three times, very loudly, "My God, have pity on us!"' Others fell to their knees and repeated the words. Riel continued: 'My God, stop those people, crush them.' He called two men to hold his arms up, as in the previous battle.[78] From beginning to end of the Rebellion, Riel was more prophet and miracle worker than political leader.

RELIGIOUS REFORM

Riel had begun the Rebellion by announcing that 'Rome has fallen.' The split with orthodoxy was officially ratified on 25 March, when the Exovedate passed the following motion:

That the commandments of God be the laws of the Provisional Government. That we recognize the right of Mr Louis 'David' Riel to direct the priests. That Archbishop Ignace Bourget is recognized from today by the French-Canadian people of the Saskatchewan as the pope of the New World ... [79]

In dealing with Protestants whose sympathy he wished to gain, Riel emphasized the break with Rome rather than the establishment of a new pope. He drafted a letter to the English half-breeds which asked for their help in 'the enterprise against Rome,' but did not mention Bourget's name.[80] But Riel's own intention to elevate Bourget to the head of his new religion is confirmed by a diary entry referring to him as 'Ignace *Pierre* Bourget,' the 'bishop of universal jurisdiction.'[81]

It is not clear whether Riel held that Rome retained legitimate jurisdiction in the Old World but had been supplanted in the New, or whether he thought that Rome was completely erased as a spiritual force. Similarly, it is reported that Riel denied the infallibility of the pope; but it is not known whether this applied to Bourget as well as Leo XIII.[82]

Another motion prepared by Riel for the Exovedate (it is not known whether it was adopted) amplified the meaning of the break with Rome. It declared that 'our line of conduct' would be determined by 'the three admirable letters which Archbishop Ignace Bourget wrote to Louis David Riel,' thus establishing the religion as Riel's personal creation. It also specified that the name 'Catholic, Apostolic, and Vital Church of the New World' would be adopted – the name Riel had conceived in 1876-8. Finally it declared that 'if God wills it ... we ask no better than to be His priests and to constitute the new religious ministry of Jesus Christ.'[83] The members of the Exovedate would become a new priesthood, a point which requires further discussion.

The Oblate missionaries unanimously refused to co-operate with the Rebellion in either its political or religious aspects. They refused to administer the sacraments to those who took up arms. Riel, therefore, had to provide an alternative for his followers. A small chapel was established by the rebels, adorned with the figure of Christ that Riel had carried at Duck Lake, the flag with the picture of Our Lady of Lourdes, the letters of Bishop Bourget to Riel, and a copy of a Latin benediction given by Bishop Grandin when he had visited in September.[84] No descriptions exist of services conducted in the chapel.

Riel initially allowed the missionaries to continue saying Sunday mass and did not set up a competing worship. He himself attended mass at St Antoine on Easter Sunday, 5 April, although he corrected Father Moulin's sermon afterwards.[85] But he already was planning to change the sabbath from Sunday to Saturday, to judge by this entry in his diary: 'O my God! Grant me the grace to re-establish your day of rest, so that men will again honour the Sabbath day, as determined by Your Holy Spirit in the person of Moses Your Servant.'[86]

The Exovedate acted on 26 April, resolving that 'the Lord's Day be returned to the seventh day of the week as the Holy Spirit appointed through the action of His servant Moses.'[87] Friday, 1 May, was designated as a Special Easter celebration, and Saturday, 2 May, was the first Saturday sabbath.[88] With his own chapel and day of worship, Riel had to create his own ministry. His solution was to constitute the Exovedate as a (perhaps temporary) priesthood. On 3 May he wrote in his diary the following prayer, which may have been an ordination or consecration of the new clergy:

On each member of the French-Canadian métis Exovedate, send down all the charitable gifts of the priesthood, all the evangelical graces, all the wonderful fruits of Your Holy Spirit, that each Exovede ... may celebrate the solemn and consoling services of the true religion ... [89]

This resort to a lay ministry was supported by a theory of the Church and of the priesthood. Abandoning his ultramontane deference to the ordained clergy, Riel wrote that 'priests are not religion.' They are ordained only 'to support the spirit of religion,' and their authority exists 'only in as much as they are faithful to their mission.' If they stray from that, 'they have lost their position and their usefulness.'[90]

Riel 'clarified religion' by explaining that its essence was

1 to have great confidence in God and in Jesus, Mary, Joseph, Saint John the Baptist, etc.
2 to observe the commandments faithfully.
3 to pray unceasingly and to have devotion.[91]

These aims can all be attained by laymen without the direction of a professional clergy. This approach to religion fits well with what Riel repeatedly said during the Rebellion, that the Holy Spirit is in every good man.

The most pressing liturgical problem was confession for the métis going into battle. On 3 May Riel prayed that the members of the Exovedate might receive 'the power to forgive the sins of those who confess to them.'[92] He urged the métis to confess to himself or to members of the Exovedate. A day before the fighting started at Batoche, he told a group of men to kneel down and confess. He publicly admitted the sin of gluttony and asked for a penance. After some hesitation, Baptiste Boucher told him to say five Paters and five Aves. The third day of the battle of Batoche, Riel was heard to say, 'I'm fine today, my conscience is clear. I confessed to Boucher this morning. Do the same thing, confess to each other.'[93]

Riel may also have experimented with a new communion ritual. There are long prayers in his diary in which he blesses bread and milk in words reminiscent of the Catholic eucharist.[94] But it is unclear from the context whether the words were part of an actual communion service or merely a private blessing upon food to be consumed.

Some of these ecclesiastical and liturgical reforms – the name of the new church, the papacy of Mgr Bourget, the Saturday sabbath – were longstanding elements in Riel's program. Others – the attack on infallibility, the lay ministry, the new sacraments – appeared for the first time. It is uncertain whether these latter innovations stemmed from a well-considered new departure in Riel's thinking or were only a hasty reaction to circumstances.

At the level of doctrine, Riel also introduced a number of ideas which had not previously been part of his thought. The Exovedate in a formal motion adopted the universalist position on salvation, that is, that eventually all souls will be saved. The motion declared that 'hell will not last forever,' that such a doctrine was 'contrary to divine mercy.' Even if it 'should be prolonged for millions and millions of years,' hell would one day come to an end.[95] Riel also denied the Catholic doctrine of the trinity. He admitted the existence of three divine persons, but 'not in the ordinary sense.'[96] His substitute theory has not survived. Also, Mary was not the Mother of God, but only 'the mother of the Son of God.'[97] The Holy Eucharist was not literally the body and blood of Jesus Christ. 'You can't eat a man six feet tall,' Riel scoffed.[98]

It is difficult to reduce these 'heresies' to a common denominator. All they have in common is that they are outside Catholic orthodoxy but might be acceptable to some Protestants. They might have been part of

Riel's program of reaching out to Protestants in an ecumenical Church of the New World. They would also have simplified Christianity somewhat, perhaps making it more palatable to the Jews, whom Riel hoped to convert.

Finally worth noting is a motion of the Exovedate to rename the days of the week:

Monday to be named: Christ Aurore
Tuesday: Vierge Aurore
Wednesday: Joseph Aube
Thursday: Dieu Aurore
Friday: Deuil Aurore
Saturday: Calme Durore
Sunday: Vive Aurore.[99]

Riel later explained this action as an elimination of pagan elements lingering in Christianity. One is reminded of the Jacobin reform of the calendar, another symbolic exercise in world renovation.

OPPOSITION AND ACCEPTANCE

Opposition to Riel's religious innovations can be detected at three levels: among the clergy, the Exovedate, and the métis at large. From the beginning of the revolt, the missionaries were obstinately against Riel and tried to subvert the people, but he did not act against them until mid-April, when news of the Frog Lake massacre made him realize that he must take measures for their safety. Then the two objectives of control and security were fulfilled by a policy of mild house arrest. Father Vegreville, Fourmond's assistant at St Laurent, who had been very outspoken in criticizing the rebels, was detained on 10 April while visiting Batoche. After a 'trial,' he was compelled to sign the following statement: 'I promise to remain perfectly neutral and not to leave here without consent of the Provisional Government.'[100] He was then taken to reside with Father Moulin in the presbytery of St Antoine. Next to be brought in were the six nuns, Sœurs Fidèles Compagnes de Jésus, who ran a small school at St Laurent. They had attempted to flee to Prince Albert, in the company of Brother Piquet, but were forced to return by bad weather and mud. Riel offered to guarantee their safety if they would stay at St Antoine, and they were installed on the second floor of the presbytery on 19 April. Riel made some disparaging remarks about 'Fathers and Sisters who love comfort, and about the nuns who caused his sister's death.' (ie, Sara, the missionary nun, who died of tuberculosis at Ile-à-la-Crosse).[101] Father Fourmond was brought down from St Laurent the next day, haled before the Exovedate, criticized for his attitude, and sent to join the others.[102] On 4 May, Father Touze was ordered to leave the Duck Lake mission and come to St Antoine.[103] It was there, exposed to fire from both sides, that the four priests, Brother Piquet, and the six nuns were liberated by the Canadian militia. It seems that throughout the Rebellion, even during the period of house arrest, the priests were not prevented from saying mass or administering the sacraments to those métis who wished to receive them.

Conflict with the missionaries reached a peak around the time the Saturday sabbath was introduced. On 30 April Riel held an interview with them, in which they excommunicated him and his adherents. The priests were brought back the next day and harangued by the Exovedate from 9:00 AM to 2:15 PM. Vegreville noted that Riel denied the infallibility of the Church and the doctrine of the trinity. He called himself the Paraclete and declared he was reforming the Church like Christ and Moses.[104] Father Fourmond wrote: 'We are obliged, Fathers Moulin, Vegreville and I, to confess and defend our insulted faith, which draws upon us a deluge of outrages and the threat of exposing us to enemy fire, if we persist in refusing to bow to the tyrant.'[105] Father Vegreville added: 'We had to endure the most vile insults. There is nothing left but to beat us and put us to death.'[106]

There was both political and religious opposition among the Exovedate. Most interesting was the case of Willie Jackson, who, having been persuaded by Riel to become a Catholic, was baptized on the evening of 18 March. Jackson was greatly alarmed when Riel broke with Rome and told Riel he could not follow him into schism. Riel reacted calmly and did not try to coerce him. After two or three days, Jackson accepted Riel as his director of conscience, though he still had some inner doubts about 'the supremacy of his mission.' Jackson functioned as secretary of the Exovedate during this period. He and Riel were drafting a document about the land question when they stopped to pray for enlightenment. Jackson experienced a peculiar convulsion while praying, but still could not quite accept Riel's mission in its plenitude. The decisive day was 25 March, the Feast of the Annunciation. Jackson became convinced that day that Riel could signal to him telepathically. That evening he experienced something like a mystical transport. He walked three miles barefoot on frozen ground without harming his feet, which he took to be a sign from God. Jackson now thought in his enthusiasm that 'God wished me to go and live among the Indians partly by way of penance and acquiring a natural method of life [and] partly to become a bond between them and the whites.' He thus made an attempt to escape from the métis to join the Indians in the North. Some métis concluded that Jackson had lost his mind, others that he could not be trusted; so he was put under guard among the prisoners for the rest of the Rebellion.[107]

Riel's other problems with the Exovedate were less mystical. Charles Nolin did not favour the revolt and agreed to join only after he was threatened with death. He escaped during the battle of Duck Lake and fled to Prince Albert. Philippe Garnot, a French Canadian, was pressed into service as secretary only because he could read and write. Albert Monkman, a half-breed with English as well as French blood, tried to foment resistance to Riel and was put among the English prisioners.

Even among those members of the Exovedate who were politically loyal to Riel there was some feeling against his religious activities. Riel noted early in the revolt that Maxime Lépine did not seem to be paying careful attention to him, even though 'good sense shone in me ... [and] sparkled in my face.' Riel prayed that God would 'turn the entire army and Exovedate' against him. He asked for grace to treat him 'kindly and with humility, but sincerely and frankly,' that he might cease his 'campaign of opposition.'[108] When the Exovedate officially recognized Riel as a prophet, no one voted nay, but Moïse Ouellette abstained. Riel asked God to 'change the obstinate mind of Moïse Ouellette,' to make him acknowledge that it was permissible to leave Rome, and to make 'him devote himself entirely to the divine reform of the liturgy and to overcoming all the deficiencies in the religion which Rome has inculcated in the peoples of the earth.'[109]

None of the Exovedes voted against the doctrine of universalism, and only Donald Ross was opposed to changing the names of the days. But serious resistance to the Saturday sabbath was manifest. Ross, Ouellette, and Lépine all voted against the motion, even though the text was a compromise which invited the Exovedes 'who are not yet ready to vote for this resolution' to join 'when they can in good conscience,' and promised that their adherence would be accepted with good grace even if it was delayed.[110]

There was also opposition among the general population of the métis, but it is difficult to form any numerical estimates. Some, who like Charles Nolin were opposed to the whole idea of the revolt, escaped to Prince Albert. Others stayed to fight but would not have anything to do with the new religion. Isidore Dumont and Gilbert Breland allegedly said to Riel: 'If we fight it's not for religion but for our rights. You came for our rights but now you only speak of religion.'[111]

The reformed liturgy was clearly a stumbling block for some. On Sunday, 26 April, the day after adoption of the Saturday sabbath, a number of métis attended mass at St Antoine. A week later there were still people who preferred the traditional worship. Father Vegreville noted in his diary: 'Opposition to Riel; they are coming to mass in spite of him. He is threatening to kill Daniel Dumas. They are talking a lot about counter-revolution.'[112]

A more or less public debate was held 4 May between Riel and Fourmond at the request of a number of métis who were confused about religious issues. Riel presented his case forcefully, ending with a denunciation of the 'Old Roman.' Fourmond tried to counter with eloquence of his own, crying 'Long live the Old Roman!'[113] Only a few voices echoed this cry, including a man named Riguidel and his wife, who had worked for Fourmond at St Laurent; and they took to the road the next day to escape the displeasure of the Exovedate. For the rest, Riel had carried the day.

The only estimates we have of the proportion of métis who supported Riel and his religious reforms are very imprecise. Louis Schmidt said that most of the métis had 'a blind, unlimited confidence' in their leader – but Schmidt was not an eyewitness after the revolt began.[114] Philippe Garnot said that 'the majority had such faith in his prophecies that they would have thrown themselves into the water if the Spirit of God had said that to Riel.' He added that, in his opinion, there were not even ten unbelievers at Batoche. But Garnot also contradicted himself by affirming that many métis supported Riel only from fear, and that there were many desertions, 'almost all caused by the religious ideas which Riel wanted to establish.'[115] One must conclude that opposition was real but limited. A large number, probably a strong majority of the métis, accepted not only the Rebellion but Riel's religious reform. They prayed with him until the end and fought until all they had to fire was nails and pebbles.

How much of this support was political, and how much religious? How many of the métis would have agreed with Isidore Dumont, that they were fighting for their rights, not for Riel's reformation of the Church? There is no way to know. However, one can say that the new religion was Riel's personal project, not a true creation of the community. There might conceivably have been a Rebellion without him, but certainly no

'Catholic, Apostolic, and Vital Church of the New World.' The cult was crushed by the battle of Batoche. Once the métis lost Riel's inspiration, they did not try to keep his teaching alive. The North-West Rebellion was a politico-religious movement with a political emphasis among the followers but a religious emphasis for the leader.

But even if the métis would never have developed a doctrine like Riel's on their own, it was at least acceptable to most of them. This acceptance has been attributed to the use of coercion by the Exovedate and to Riel's manipulation of the simple piety of the métis. Such explanations were particularly advanced by the missionaries after the Rebellion, when they wished to load all the blame on Riel while exculpating the bulk of the métis.[116] But neither theory can account for the obvious devotion of the métis to their prophet. He seems to have touched a genuinely responsive chord in their souls.

Riel's relative success as a religious founder in 1885, as compared to his utter failure in 1876, was chiefly due to the difference between the métis and French Canadians as an audience. But it should not be overlooked that Riel's thinking had undergone considerable modification over the years. The core of ideas had remained the same: his own mission as prophet and that of the métis as chosen people, transfer of the papacy to Mgr Bourget, creation of a church of the New World, establishment of the Saturday sabbath in recognition of the special affiliation with the Hebrews. But much had dropped out of sight: self-glorification as priest-king and infallible pontiff, plus radical teachings like incest, polygamy, and the wholesale adoption of the Mosaic Law. And new ideas had appeared, like the lay ministry and certain doctrines of a somewhat Protestant character. The result of these changes was a creed which was far more able to attract support than the highly personal system of his years in the insane asylum.

7
Disappointment and Hope

The overwhelming defeat at Batoche did not destroy Riel's faith in his mission. The predicted miracle had not come to pass; but like many other prophets and true believers, he was able to accept the failure of his predictions without giving up his underlying convictions.[1] Indeed, the débâcle of Batoche projected Riel into a new phase of his mission, in which he sought to address not only the métis but all North America. He began to emphasize those elements in his teaching which might be most acceptable to the Protestant majority of the continent, while playing down aspects of specific appeal to the métis, French Canadians, or Roman Catholics.

SURRENDER

When Middleton's troops took Batoche on 12 May, Riel fled into the surrounding woods. Gabriel Dumont saw him for the last time that evening, and heard him say to his wife, 'I think that God wants me to die.'[2] Declining to escape to Montana with Dumont and Michel Dumas, Riel waited until he received a promise of safe conduct from Middleton. He sent an answering note: 'I will go to fulfil God's will.'[3] He surrendered the same day, 15 May.

There is no contemporary record of what Riel hoped to achieve by voluntary surrender. From his subsequent statements, one may infer that he wanted a highly publicized trial, preferably in eastern Canada, which he could use as a political forum to expound the claims of the métis and also to present his new religion to the world.

Riel spent the first day of surrender in the company of General Middleton. He spoke 'a good deal' about his religion, although Middleton did not get a very clear impression of it, remembering it only as a 'disconnected thing.' He did recall Riel saying that 'Rome was all wrong and corrupt, and that the priests were narrow-minded and had interfered too much with the people,' and also that 'religion should be based on morality and humanity and charity.' The general did not hear Riel claim to be a prophet or to be inspired by the Spirit of God.[4]

The evening of 15 May, Middleton turned Riel over to Captain George Holmes Young of Winnipeg, who had known the prisoner in 1870. He remained in Young's custody until delivered to the prison at Regina on 23 May. The two men conversed 'almost constantly and very freely' on both political and religious subjects. Riel mentioned some ideas which had played a role at Batoche. He referred to the infallibility of the pope, although it is not known precisely what he said. He mentioned the doctrine of universalism. He discussed the change which the Exovedate had made in the names of the days of the week, explaining it as a purification of the 'remains of paganism' from Christianity. But he was silent about much else. Young explicitly denied that Riel claimed to be a prophet, or that he spoke about dividing the North-West among different nationalities.[5] There is also no record that he talked about changing the sabbath from Sunday to Saturday, or about making Bishop Bourget pope of the New World.

Riel seems to have deliberately suppressed many of his views, and to have presented himself in a way acceptable to rationalistic Protestants. He wrote in Young's notebook: 'I have a mission, so has everybody for me. I understand my mission in this way, to bring about practical results.'[6] This neutral statement is a far cry from Riel's true view of himself as a prophet, reformer, and religious founder. Young concluded that Riel was 'unitarian in his belief' and was 'making a strong bid for the support and protection of the ultra-Protestants.'[7]

A similar impression was obtained by the Reverend C.B. Pitblado, a Presbyterian clergyman, chaplain to the expeditionary force, who traveled with Young and Riel for five days. Riel wrote 'Some Words on Different Subjects' on the rear flysheets of Pitblado's Greek New Testament:

1 I have a passion: I love truth, justice, and righteousness above all other things. I pray to God that my knowledge of truth, of justice, and of righteousness be certain and without error.
2 The conscientious reading of the scriptures is full of life and of consolation.
3 The word of Christ purifies our souls.

4 Let us live and die in perfect harmony with the Redeemer: and we will be saved.

5 A preacher who preaches humbly for the benefit of Paradise, is a precious existence before God.

6 I am an unprofitable servant of our Lord Jesus Christ.[8]

These remarks touch on typical Protestant themes, such as preaching and scripture reading, in which Riel had never previously shown a special interest.

When Pitblado asked him what the beliefs of his new religion were, Riel grouped them under eight headings:

1 We believe that all true believers constitute the true church. Believers in the Lord Jesus Christ are Christians, and all Christians make the church holy, Catholic and vital.

2 We do not believe in the infallibility of the pope.

3 We believe in the inspiration of the Holy Scriptures and the right of every man to read and learn the truths they contain.

4 We believe in a regularly ordained ministry. We would accept the ministers of all the denominations, Episcopalians, Presbyterians, and the Congregationalists in our ministry without reordaining ...

5 We believe in a form of church government. We prefer the Episcopate. We would like to see a head bishop for the Dominion or for the new world, who would be independent of Rome. We do not think that the affairs of the Church can be rightly administered so far away. In fact, Rome has ceased to be a Holy Apostolic See.

6 We believe there is one God. We believe in the Trinity, though not in the ordinary sense. ... There is the Father. ... the Son. ... the Holy Ghost, who is the only spirit dwelling in every good man. This is the spirit of holiness.

7 We pray to God, to Christ, to Mary, to the saints ...

8 We believe in the final salvation of all men ... [9]

This credo obviously differs from the teaching Riel had propounded during the Rebellion. There is no reference to Riel's prophetic mission, the Mosaic Law, the Saturday sabbath, and the priesthood of the Exovedate. Bishop Bourget, the pope of the New World, survives only as an unnamed 'head bishop,' who seems to be an administrative convenience rather than a pope in the Catholic sense. Part of the enumeration is obviously directed towards Protestants: the reference to individual interpretation of the scriptures as well as the acceptance of ordained Protestant clergymen. Some articles also have a distinctly non-denominational or ecumenical tone. The Holy Spirit is said to dwell 'in every good man,' and the Church is said to be constituted by 'all true believers' – '[b]elievers in the Lord Jesus Christ' – 'all Christians.'

Riel had shown traces of this ecumenism during the Rebellion, but not to such a marked degree. It is not clear whether his doctrine was at all times the same, the apparent differences being due to the audience whom he was addressing, or whether his thinking entered a new ecumenical stage after the defeat of Batoche. In any case, he had traveled far from the narrow and fanatical ultramontanism of a decade earlier, when he had written that a Protestant was 'a child of the devil.'[10]

IMPRISONMENT

Riel was placed in solitary confinement in the NWMP jail on 23 May, under the command of Inspector Richard Burton Deane. An Association Nationale pour la Défense des Prisonniers Métis was quickly organized in Quebec, and two rising young lawyers of the Liberal party, F.-X. Lemieux and Charles Fitzpatrick, volunteered to defend Riel free of charge. They were later joined by J.N. Greenshields of Montreal and T.C. Johnstone of Regina.

Riel was formally charged with high treason on 6 July. He saw his lawyers for the first time on 14 July, and was arraigned on 20 July before Judge Hugh Richardson. When Riel and his attorneys requested a delay to obtain witnesses, Richardson granted them one week. The trial opened in earnest on 28 July.

In the two months between his arrival in Regina and the commencement of his trial, there was little that Riel could do to help his cause except to write letters in search of support. He was initially rather cautious about revealing his religious beliefs. He wrote first to his mother, justifying the Rebellion as a form of self-defence.[11] He said nothing at all about his religious innovations, for he probably assumed that the contents of this letter would become known to the métis of Manitoba. Now was not the time to risk offending the Church. Similarly, he was totally silent about religion when he wrote to his old school friend Romuald Fiset, a leading figure in the Association Nationale. His long and tendentious letter developed a legal defence based on self-preservation, but said nothing about the break with Rome.[12] Again, Riel was writing to an audience, knowing that his letter would become a public document (it appeared in La Minerve, 1 July, 1885). Riel also wrote to James W. Taylor, the United States consul at Winnipeg, to request American help in obtaining a fair trial. This time also, not a word about religion.[13]

He was less reticent in discussing his religion with his jailer, Inspector Deane. He sent him a poem asking permission to publish his account of the recent Rebellion, including the religious aspect: 'Grant me to touch Rome/ Its Pope under shade.'[14] He also proposed to summon a photographer to take pictures of him in various poses: 'For instance, one sitting in my cell; a second one, while I take exercise, the chains on and between the two sentries; a third one, while I pray on my knees ... ' These photographs were to be printed like the holy pictures then common in the Catholic Church. Each picture would bear an inscription, such as the following:

1st inscription: I respect the bishop of Rome and I pray for him: but I have nothing to do with him any more. Allegiance to him, I think, means constant division and endless struggles with the other Christian denominations. At the same time, I maintain all my respect and my adherence to the episcopate and to the priesthood of the New World, believing as I do, that they will also leave off before long the Bee-shop of Rome. [ie, 'busy bee,' reflecting Riel's belief that Rome had become a godless city of merchants.][15]

This inscription shows Riel searching for a reconciliation with the Catholic clergy of the New World. He would maintain 'respect' for and 'adherence' to them, under the assumption that they would soon break with Rome. This was significantly different from his position at Batoche, where he had denounced the missionaries for not immediately repudiating Rome. Deane, keeping the prisoner almost incommunicado, would not grant either of these requests.

On 24 June, Riel wrote to Governor Dewdney to ask that his trial be held before the Supreme Court of Canada. He wanted an inquiry into his whole career, from the events of 1869/70 to the Rebellion of 1885. Such an inquiry would exonerate the Conservatives and show that the Liberals were responsible for the troubles in the North-West. [16] Three days later Riel wrote again in a similar vein, this time adding a few words about his religious reform:

I have just done an extraordinary thing, I well know, in causing the métis of the Saskatchewan to separate from Rome. But when the whole Conservative Party sees for itself that my political conduct is well balanced, perhaps they will not be the last to sympathize with what I have done, and even to help, as much as they can if circumstances permit, all the métis to separate from Rome, with the assent of the clergy.[17]

Again we see Riel's desire to legitimize his new religion by involving the Catholic clergy.

Riel continued this campaign to ingratiate himself with the Conservatives by directly addressing the prime minister. On 6 July he wrote a long letter setting forth what he had already written to Dewdney, plus several new themes. He pointed out that Gabriel Dumont was at large in the United States. If the métis prisoners were not granted 'fair play,' he would put into effect Riel's plan of offering the Canadian North-West to various American ethnic groups: Irish, Poles, etc. There would be such an 'immense current of opinion' that the American government would have to intervene militarily.

But, said Riel, he did not really want this to occur. His true desire was for a new world order dominated by an 'Imperial Union' of Britain and the United States. Like Rome and Byzantium, London and Washington would be twin capitals of a vast, multinational empire. Small nations like the Irish, the French Canadians, and the métis would be secure within this protective structure.

The political reorganization of the world would be accompanied by religious reform. The 'Imperial Union' would be strong enough to ignore the pope. Thus it could 'lift religion far above the sad state in which it is now held by corrupt Rome.' Furthermore, the new empire should select 'someone known for his profound wisdom, his virtue, his knowledge, and vast intelligence.' He should be elevated to 'high rank,' where he could 'enlighten' and 'guide' the Catholics of the realm, while also 'promot[ing] the interests of the most perfect harmony possible among the different Christian denominations of [the] Colossal Dominion.'[18]

It is not apparent whether Riel had anyone specific in mind for this new post of secretary of religious affairs (to give it a modern-sounding name). Bishop Bourget, always his choice for highest religious leadership, had died on 8 June 1885. Riel may have been putting himself forward; but when he wrote again to Macdonald on 16 July, he sketched out a different future for himself. He might well be elected premier of Manitoba after being acquitted in a trial before the Supreme Court. Then he would renegotiate the entry of Manitoba into Confederation, which would set an example of co-operativeness for the rest of Canada and the British Empire, smoothing the way for the coming Imperial Union. He would need a representative of the Crown with whom he could work closely, and he suggested that Inspector Deane would be a good candidate for lieutenant-governor of Manitoba.[19] Deane, far from being flattered, only concluded that his famous prisoner was 'cracked.'[20]

Riel's final letter in this series written to seek support before his trial was to Archbishop Taché. Riel had irretrievably broken with his former patron by instigating the Rebellion; but he was encouraged to try to regain his favour when Taché sent an old friend, Father Georges Dugas, to Regina to minister to the spiritual needs of the métis prisoners. Riel wrote on 24 July 1885, which would have been the first celebration of the feast of St Joseph, national patron of the métis.[21]

Much of the letter recounts Riel's life – his youth, his 'fall,' and the subsequent development of his prophetic mission. This material has already been discussed in several places. The chief interest of the letter in this connection is that it sketches out a new version of Riel's religious reforms, to make them more palatable to the Catholic hierarchy. Mention of the rapprochement with Protestantism is omitted; and Riel presents his religion not as a break with Rome but as an outgrowth of Catholicism resulting in two mutually co-ordinated and friendly branches of the Church, one in the Old World, the other in the New.

The Holy Spirit has indeed left Rome. But refraining from a personal attack on Leo XIII, Riel attributes the departure of the Holy Ghost to the sad condition of the city of Rome. The Italian revolution has swept all before it, depriving the pope of the Papal States and making him the 'prisoner of the Vatican.' Rome is only 'a city of tradesmen and merchants,' and 'the capital of a Brigand King.' The Holy Spirit came to dwell with Ignace Bourget, as of 8 December 1875. Now that Bourget has died, his successor is Taché himself. Thus Riel says: 'I proclaim humbly from the padlocked compound of Regina prison that you are the pontiff chosen by God to instruct, console, succour, guide, bless, and save the New World through the grace of Jesus Christ.' Taché's new title will be Pontifex Major Totius Novi Mundi (Greater Pontiff of the Entire New World).

This transfer of the papacy of the New World from Montreal to St Boniface symbolizes the role of the métis as chosen people and anticipates the ultimate residence of the papacy among them. But the time is not yet. After Taché dies, the Holy Spirit will return to Montreal where He will stay 457 years, counting from 8 December 1875. In the year 2333 AD the papacy will again come to St Boniface, which will be its last home. (In 1876 Riel had written that St Vital, his own home town, would receive the papacy; now he switched to St Boniface, Taché's episcopal see.) The Pontifex Major Totius Novi Mundi will reign there in glory for

1876 years until the Second Advent. The reader will recognize the numerology, based on the Book of Daniel, which Riel had developed a decade earlier.

Riel no longer speaks of a rupture with Rome; rather he envisages a co-ordinated relationship between the two churches of the New World and the Old. Leo XIII is invited to come to America to establish Taché in his new position, after which he will return to Rome to oversee the affairs of Europe and Asia.

The two churches, the one of the Orient, and the other of the Occident, the one European and the other American, successful because of their mutual help, will act separately without interference or opposition. ... the difference in their articles of faith does not come from malevolence, but from the will of God who reveals more to the New World than He had judged appropriate to reveal to the Old.

Riel also describes his immigration plan, adding new dimensions to it. Immigrants to the North-West will be drawn not from the ethnic groups of the United States but directly from the nations of Europe. On the soil of British Columbia and the North-West Territories there will arise a new Ireland, Italy, Bavaria, Scandinavia, Poland, even 'a new Judea for Jews who agree to recognize Jesus Christ as the only Messiah and to recognize you, you Monseigneur, as the leader authorized by faith.' Manitoba will be reserved for the métis, augmented by immigrants from Quebec and France.

Riel closes with apocalyptic predictions on European affairs. The French Republic, enslaved by 'the evil spirit which torments it,' will declare war against the Catholic states of Europe. After terrible struggles, a coalition of Italy, Bavaria, Poland, Belgium, and Ireland will at long last slay 'the monster of the French Revolution.' Then will appear a scion of the Bourbons, a descendant of St Louis, who will ascend to the throne of France. Returning the Papal States to the Holy Father, he will inaugurate an era of lasting peace. Riel, who considered himself a Bourbon, may have pictured himself in this role (the Comte de Chambord had died in 1883); but he does not openly say so.

TRIAL

Riel's trial took place over five days from 28 July to 1 August 1885. At the end, the jury of six needed only half an hour's deliberation to convict him of high treason. The jury recommended clemency, but under the law the judge had no choice but to impose the death sentence. Clemency, if it was to come at all, would have to come from the Crown.

I will not attempt to discuss the whole trial, which has recently been the object of several studies.[22] I will confine my attention to Riel's presentation of his religious views in his two speeches to the court, the first made before the jury deliberated, the second before the judge passed sentence. The speeches were not very successful because Riel attempted too much in them. He sought to review his whole career; to argue that the Rebellion was justifiable self-defence; to refute the contention of his attorneys that he was insane; and to correct certain testimony which he felt had not been properly cross-examined. And he tried to do all this while speaking English, which he knew well but not perfectly.

Religion appears primarily in Riel's demonstration, taking up more than half the first speech, that he was not an imposter or a lunatic, but a genuine prophet with a mission to fulfil. Let us examine the argument. 'I have not assumed to myself that I had a mission,' said Riel. He tried to show that his mission had been conferred upon him by the hierarchy of the Catholic Church. He referred to two letters from Bishop Bourget (14 July 1875 and 2 January 1876). He mentioned the words of Father J.-B. Primeau of Worcester, who had told him: 'Riel, God has put an object into your hands, the cause of the triumph of religion in the world, take care, you will succeed when most believe you have lost.' And he told how Father Eberschweiler had blessed him and Gabriel Dumont in Fort Benton, Montana.

At a second level of proof, Riel appealed to the events of his life to show how Providence had prepared and protected him for his mission. 'It has been a great success for me to come through all the dangers I have in ... fifteen years.' God had kept him from being wounded at Batoche. God was helping him at his trial, by inspiring General Middleton and Captain Young to testify that he was not insane, and by helping the prosecution to refute the testimony of those like Dr Roy, who said that he was insane.

Both types of proof – the approval of the hierarchy and the events of his life – may be called objective because they involve externally visible events. Riel almost completely ignored the mystical and visionary experiences which were the subjective proof of his mission. We know these were important to him, for he included them in the autobiographical sketch he produced for publication later that year. But at the trial he suppressed all mention of them, save for a brief reference to 'the spirit who guides and assists me and consoles me.' Probably he thought his mysticism would not be congenial to the jury, nor to the general public of North America whom he was addressing through the press.

Riel defined the nature of his mission in minimal terms. He repeatedly used the words which he had written in Captain Young's notebook: to bring about 'practical results.' The examples Riel gave, such as his work in Manitoba in 1869/70, gave the impression that the main thrust of his mission was the political defence of the rights of the métis. Again, he was suppressing something of importance – his vocation as religious reformer and founder.

He did admit to being a prophet, and claimed the title 'prophet of the new world'; but we must take a close look at his use of the term. In this context 'prophecy' meant chiefly 'prediction.' Riel said, 'I could see something into the future' and he gave several examples of how he had correctly forecast events.

This limited sense of prophecy differs little from sagacity or foresight. It is a human ability possessed by all in varying degrees. 'We all see into the future more or less,' said Riel. He went on to compare his own power of prophecy to the alleged capacity of the métis hunters to predict the future:

I have seen half-breeds say, my hand is shaking, this part of my hand is shaking, you will see such a thing today, and it happens. Others will say I feel the flesh on my leg moving in such a way, it is a sign of such a thing, and it happens.

This explanation, while perhaps not wholly false, was certainly misleading. Riel's prophetism may have owed something to métis traditions, but it was chiefly patterned after biblical models like Daniel or Isaiah. Riel did not see himself as a tribal soothsayer; he was the voice of God to a sinful world. His function was to reform doctrine and worship, ushering in a new age of spiritual perfection.

Not surprisingly, since he was being less than candid about the meaning of prophecy, he minimized the importance and dignity of the title. He suggested that to be a prophet was 'practical' because it had been accepted by the Exovedate and the métis. But it was as much a burden as an honour. 'I do not wish, for my satisfaction, the name of prophet, generally that title is accompanied with such a burden, that if there is satisfaction for your vanity, there is [also] a check to it.'

Riel said very little about the substance of his new teaching. He briefly mentioned his theory that Bishop Bourget had replaced the pope 'because while Rome did not pay attention to us, he, as a bishop, paid attention to us.' His major pronouncement on doctrine emphasized his ecumenical desire to reconcile Protestant and Catholic.

As to religion, what is my belief? What is my insanity about that? My insanity, your Honors, gentlemen of the jury, is that I wish to leave Rome aside, inasmuch as it is the cause of division between Catholics and Protestants. I did not wish to force my views, because in Batoche to the half-breeds that followed me I used the word, *carte blanche*. If I have any influence in the new world it is to help in that way and even if it takes 200 years to become practical, then after my death that will bring out practical results, and then my children's children will shake hands with the Protestants of the new world in a friendly manner. I do not wish these evils which exist in Europe to be continued, as much as I can influence it, among the half-breeds. I do not wish that to be repeated in America. That work is not the work of some days or some years, it is the work of hundreds of years.[23]

Religious themes played a lesser but still significant part in Riel's second speech. He began by thanking the jury for their verdict of guilty, for it removed the stigma of insanity. 'I cannot fulfil my mission as long as I am looked upon as an insane being. ... [T]he verdict against me today is a proof that maybe I am a prophet ... ' He then compared his sufferings to those of David, suggesting his hope for an ultimately triumphant outcome.[24] At the end of the second speech, he returned to the question of the authenticity of his mission. He called for 'a commission of doctors' to examine his life and writings, to determine whether he was a madman, an impostor, or a genuine prophet.[25]

Between the beginning and the end of the speech, there was relatively little about religion. Riel in fact made the speech that he had originally intended to give first, but which for some reason he had postponed. It was a long description of his entire career, going into both rebellions, the amnesty question, the claims of the métis, his theory of their aboriginal rights, and so forth. In passing, he clarified the present state of his thinking about immigration. He made it clear that an invitation to the American ethnic groups to cross the line and settle in the North-West, which would inevitably result in American annexation of that area, would be a last resort, in case there was no other way for the métis to gain their rights. His true preference was for immigration direct from Europe to found a 'new Ireland,' a 'new Poland,' and so forth. (This agrees with what he had recently written to Taché.) These new peoples would remain part of the British Empire, under the leadership of the Anglo-Saxon race.[26]

Riel's presentation at his trial of his religious views and of his utopian political schemes cannot be taken as an accurate expression of his thinking. He did not directly falsify his ideas, but he selected and emphasized according to what he thought an English and Protestant audience would want to hear.

ABJURATION

The full significance of the guilty verdict and the death sentence did not seem to register on Riel's mind immediately. The day of his conviction he drafted a long letter to James W. Taylor in Winnipeg, asking again for American help. Not until the end did he think to say in a matter-of-fact way: 'I was forgetting that I am sentenced to death.'[27]

Urged by Father Cochin and especially Father Fourmond, Riel signed a recantation of his heresies on 5 August. Several motives impelled him, including a desire to have the help of the sacraments while facing death, as well as the lingering hope that he might yet bring the Church to support his mission. The abjuration seems to have been only external. Riel subscribed to certain formalities, but in such a way as to leave intact his underlying belief in himself.

Fourmond visited him on 3 August and strongly pressed him to recant. Riel agreed in principle, giving this note to Fourmond:

Please write and compose yourself the formula which I should sign to place myself in perfect harmony with the good Lord and with the Church of Jesus Christ, of which you are an authorized priest [prêtre approuvé]. I will make that formula my own. *Obedience* is the bread with which I should nourish myself. And *to obey* at the present moment, on the question of my retraction, is certainly the action which seems to me the most difficult of all you could propose to my will. I, to whom *a bishop* has said in official letters, 'You have a mission which you will have to accomplish in all respects' – I yield to the priest, *to the authorized Catholic priest, because I know that he has direct authority over our will.* O Holy Spirit of God, give me your docility so that ... I will mortify myself, and, through the grace of Jesus Christ, I will conquer my rebellious will, in *submitting to the desire of your authorized priest.* [Italics added][28]

The italicized phrases indicate Riel's line of thought. His mission had been undertaken in obedience to the instructions of the clergy, especially Bishop Bourget. In spite of his break with Rome, he had always considered his work to be an extension of Catholicism, not a repudiation of it. Now God's will required a manifest submission to the authority of the Church. Riel would comply in the spirit of obedience but without, at the deepest level, rejecting the validity of his mission.

This is shown by another letter which Riel soon wrote to Fourmond and Cochin, after he had had a chance to examine the retraction drawn up by Fourmond. The text was 'opposed on a great number of points to what is revealed to me by the Spirit who influences me.' Nevertheless, he would sign because 'I wish to have the help of the sacraments of the Church, in which I have every confidence and of which I have great need. That is what makes me sign Father Fourmond's abjuration.'[29]

Much of the letter was taken up in discussing the twin origins of Riel's mission, private inspiration and clerical approval. He told the story of how he had asked Father Primeau in 1875 for permission to try to perform a miraculous cure of the crippled legs of Senator Morton. He had thought the miracle would be possible because of 'my close union with the authorized priest, my subordination to his authority, and my complete submission to his discretion.' He also explained that subsequent revelations had encouraged him to pray for the resurrection of Senator Morton after the latter's death on 1 November 1877. Finally Riel, assuming that his abjuration would be published, asked that this letter be published along with it.

Riel's intentions, though not totally explicit in the letter, may be inferred. He had long believed that God would authenticate his mission in the eyes of the world through some special sign, a dramatic miracle like the resurrection of Senator Morton. He had speculated on this theme in Montana while composing his system for eventual publication. He still retained this hope, as shown by a letter he wrote from his cell to Colonel Irvine. He explained how a revelation in Montana had commanded him to publish, and added:

... I have always believed that God would, at the publication of some of my writings, accomplish a miracle or something wonderful, so that all might see for themselves and be satisfied that I have indeed a mission given to me by the One whom we all adore.[30]

Riel perhaps hoped that by humbling himself in a published recantation, he might encourage God to perform the long-awaited miracle. His humiliation might be the prelude to his triumph.

Before signing the abjuration, he drew up still another statement which was meant to be a preface to Fourmond's text. It read in part:

The religious principle which made me have so much confidence in the word of Archbishop Bourget logically leads me to have the same confidence in the interpretation which the approved priest, my director of conscience, gives me of the episcopal word of Archbishop Ignace Bourget of blessed memory. Renouncing, then, all the special interpretations that I have made of my mission which my confessor and director does not approve, I re-enter the bosom of the Catholic, Apostolic, and Roman Church ... [31]

Note that Riel here renounced his own 'special interpretations' of his mission but not the idea of a mission as such. He was juggling words, trying to combine obedience and independence.

The text of the abjuration was rather pedestrian.[32] Fourmond was more concerned with dogma and ecclesiastical discipline than with the essential concepts of Riel's thinking. He was required to renounce 'my false mission of prophet, first cause of my errors'; but beyond that all the enumerated points were rather trivial. He had to affirm the orthodox Catholic teachings about the Trinity and Christology. He had to consent to various matters of Church organization, such as papal infallibility, the authority of the hierarchy, and the sole capacity of the clergy to administer the sacraments. He had to give up the doctrine of universal salvation and renounce the Saturday sabbath. Except for the last point, these ideas, which Riel had only recently adopted, were not at the heart of his teaching.

Nonetheless, Riel had qualms until the last moment about signing. On his own copy of the abjuration, he began to write, then erased a letter to Fourmond requesting 'absolution of the sins you would make me commit through your recantation in case it is I who have correctly understood my mission and you who have not.' After signing, Riel obtained the signatures of the priests on the following affidavit, which was witnessed and kept by Inspector Deane:

We, the undersigned, certify as witnesses the authenticity of the answers made by Louis David Riel and of his recantation, and of the authenticity of the document of his renunciation; and we declare ourselves responsible before God and man for the legitimacy of the questions which we have put to him and for the legitimacy of the recantation which we have required from him as ordained priests.[33]

The day afterwards we find Cochin writing in the same vein to Riel, who must still have been plagued by doubts:

With reference to the responsibility that you fear to have incurred by making that abjuration, you certainly do not incur it, and I am so sure of it that I do not fear to take it upon myself before God and man. The proof is that I helped to compose the abjuration, and that I signed myself as priest ... [34]

The abjuration itself was executed in quasi-legal fashion. To the document drawn up by Fourmond, Riel affixed the double signature 'Louis "David" Riel or Louis Riel.' Fourmond and Cochin signed as witnesses. Riel had also made his own hand copy of the abjuration, which he gave to Deane to keep after the two priests had signed it in his presence. This copy was nearly but not quite exact. Whereas the original was headed 'Abjuration made by Mr Louis Riel of all his errors ... ' Riel began his own copy, 'Abjuration made by Mr Louis Riel, whose name is also Louis "David" Riel, of all his errors ... ' The insertion of his messianic name 'David' into that copy of the text which would be outside the keeping of the Church was perhaps a significant gesture.

But this was at best a very private act, destined for the uncertain future. In the present, Riel's submission was complete to all appearances. A mass was held for all the métis prisoners, at which he publicly answered a series of questions based on his abjuration. He was then allowed to receive Holy Communion.[35] The founder and last adherent of the 'Catholic, Apostolic, and Vital Church of the New World' had returned to the 'Old Roman.'

CONTINUED REVELATIONS

Little space is required to indicate the subsequent course of Riel's life, at least its external aspects. His lawyers launched appeals, first to the Court of Queen's Bench in Manitoba, then to the Judicial Committee of the Privy Council in London; but both were denied. Then Sir John A. Macdonald, pressed by the French-Canadian members of his cabinet, appointed a medical commission to see if Riel was sane enough to be hanged. When the commission, which was privately manipulated by the prime minister, agreed that Riel was sane, the sentence of the law was executed on 16 November 1885.

In the three and a half months between conviction and execution, Riel did not leave his prison at Regina. He was allowed a certain number of visitors, including reporters; but his major human contact was with his confessor – first Father Cochin, then Father André – who came almost every day. There was a single last visit from his wife, mother, and brother Joseph in early September. In October came the sad news that Marguerite's third child, newly born, had lived only two hours – 'an hour to be born, an hour to die,' as Riel put it.[37]

These days were tedious, monotonous, and nerve-wracking; but Riel's inner life expanded to fill the void. He meditated, prayed, and wrote endlessly, so that we are better informed about the thinking of his last months than about any other period in his life. His overriding concern was to reconcile his prophetic mission with his return to Catholic orthodoxy, for he was in a submissive mood following his recantation. He began to keep a diary, opening it with this humble declaration:

Everything I will write in this notebook is subject to the approval of His Excellency Monseigneur Alexandre-Antonin Taché, Archbishop of St Boniface.

At the outset, I renounce anything in my writings which, in Monseigneur's opinion, deserves condemnation.

Submission and obedience to his authority is an essential condition of the true religion.[38]

He was careful to keep the diary within orthodox bounds during August. The words 'prophecy' and 'revelation' do not appear in the text. Riel affirmed that he had 'returned to the obedience of the Catholic, Apostolic, and Roman Church.' He would follow the 'logic of obedience,' which is 'infinite like the will of God.'[39] He prayed for 'perfect obedience,' to be submissive to the directions of the priesthood.[40] A bit smugly perhaps, he congratulated himself on his 'charity toward the Reverend Father J.-V. Fourmond, who humiliated me as much as he could' in the abjuration.[41] Riel went out of his way to note his acceptance of the Sunday sabbath, which he had wanted to repeal.[42] In all of this he was a model of docility.

But other entries in the diary make it clear that he had not wholly abandoned faith in his mission. He prayed that the speeches he had made before the court might have an 'immense effect' upon public opinion in Canada, the United States, and 'all countries of the world.'[43] He prayed for the support of both Liberals and Conservatives on this earth. He prayed that all the Irish, Bavarians, etc., would favour his colonization project; and for good measure he performed the Stations of the Cross that God might deliver from Purgatory all the souls of the departed of those same nationalities.[44]

Above all, he prayed for the support of the Catholic hierarchy. 'O my God,' he wrote, 'make Archbishop Alexandre-Antonin Taché and Bishop Grandin declare themselves in favour of my mission, openly and without reserve.'[45] He asked God to 'inspire Your pious bishops and devoted priests with renewed ardour and zeal for the movement which You are promoting through my inspired words and actions.'[46]

His obedience would be instrumental in winning the support of the clergy, for they would see he was working for the cause of the Catholic Church. In effect, Riel redefined his mission to mean not a break with the Church but rather assistance to the Church from within to help Her attain Her sublime destiny in the New World. The clergy, he wrote,

would be happy if the tide of current events carried them along, and by a marvelous series of uncontrollable eventualities, becoming ever more inescapable, miraculously gave them the reasons and arguments they need to maintain that my mission and theirs are one and the same; that my mission is an outgrowth of theirs; that consequently my mission, coming from Jesus Christ through their ministry, can in justice not be considered apart from their mission.

Then the Church, Riel's 'mother, will not be able to delay in embracing me openly and proclaiming ... that I am the fruit of Her womb.' She will be 'profoundly contrite' for having ignored his voice 'these fifteen long years.' Now she will praise him because he, 'little David in the service of the great King,' had tried 'to hold off the giant who was marching against all of us with his redoubtable strength and reputation.'[47]

Riel gave vent to this emotional outburst on 23 August 1885, as the agitation in Quebec on his behalf was gathering strength. Watching from afar, he overestimated the impact this pressure would have on the government; and he became more optimistic that he would escape the hangman. His spiritual self-confidence grew correspondingly, so that after he finished his diary for August, he wrote a new preface to it, in striking contrast to the humble tone in which he had opened at the beginning of the month:

Everything written in this book is inspired, but I have expressed it in common, ordinary language.

Divine inspiration made me write this book.[48]

Such words were tantamount to declaring that he was a prophet, although Riel was careful to avoid openly calling himself that in the August diary, which he probably hoped to publish under the imprimatur of the Church. But in spite of his abjuration and his effort to be submissive, he had never really ceased to experience revelations and to believe himself a prophet.

His spiritual advisers were fully aware of this. When Father Cochin visited him the morning of 11 August, he found Riel eager to discuss his nocturnal revelations. He had seen Bishop Bourget, who had assumed the form of a resplendent sun. Within the sun was visible a 'crooked path' (chemin croche), which represented Riel's mission. The priests may have imposed a detour upon him, but he was still following the path of his mission.[49]

Father Cochin was soon replaced as Riel's confessor by Father André, whose experiences were similar. On 14 August he reported that Riel

called himself another Moses, another Elias, a new St Peter sent to raise the Church from the abyss where it has fallen today. It is he, it seems, who will defend us one day against all the heresiarchs; then we will be raised to new heights. Above all, he will elevate the archepiscopal throne of Mgr Taché above all others in the Church.[50]

André noted later that month that Riel's retraction was 'really only external.' He still maintained that the Spirit of God had moved from Rome to Montreal, and that, Bishop Bourget having died, Taché was now 'the true pope.' A new revelation was that after Taché's death Father André himself would 'ascend to the pinnacle as pope of the New World.'[51]

It was the same in following months. Riel had 'revelations and political plans for the reorganization of the universe; for all peoples seem to interest him.'[52] He slept 'neither day nor night,' being occupied in transcribing the revelations of the Spirit.[53]

André tried to correct Riel, to 'reprove him for his foolish and extravagant ideas.'[54] Riel only replied that he submitted to authority, but that he could not 'stifle the voice that speaks in him and the spirit that commands him to communicate to the world the revelations he receives.'[55] In the end, André had to leave the 'field free' for Riel as long as he did not stray into outright heresy.[56] Whenever he threatened to contradict specific Church teaching, André would warn him back, threatening to withhold the sacraments if necessary.[57] Riel always submitted, although sometimes after spirited argument. Under this pressure from André, Riel in his last months produced a sizable number of revelations which, although novel, could not be considered heretical. I will discuss them under three headings: political, philosophic and cosmological, and religious.

Riel was still keenly interested in Canadian politics and the fate of the métis. Through the newspapers, he followed the agitation in Quebec, sometimes expecting it to effect his deliverance and ascent to power. He wrote that the Canadian state was like a 'half-broken, prancing mare.' 'She is hard to ride, but I will mount into the saddle and she will obey me.'[58] But at other moments he was pessimistic about developments in Canada. His mind turned to thoughts of American intervention, with which he had tried to bluff the prime minister in July. He had prepared a manifesto, calling for American intervention, to read before the court at Regina; but he had never used it.[59] Now he drew up a petition to Grover Cleveland, President of the United States, and sent it to James W. Taylor to be forwarded to Washington. The document argued that the North-West Territories were virtually Riel's own property, entrusted to him by the people in 1870. Now he was declaring them free and requesting immediate annexation to the United States. James W. Taylor should be appointed governor-general of these territories, while

with the merciful help of God's providence, if such would be the disposition of your good will and the favor of your government, I, the undersigned, humbly ask you to appoint me as first minister and secretary of the North-West under Hon. James W. Taylor.[60]

Riel also developed the speculations on a new world order of which he had confided something to Macdonald. 'Emperors and princes,' he wrote, 'will accept my ideas. They will apply them to fulfil my intentions, to do my work.'[61]

Riel foresaw close ties growing up between French Canada and Latin America. Spanish children would come to study in Montreal and St Boniface, while métis and French-Canadian students would attend school in 'New Spain.'[62] Latin America would have 'the divine mission of lending a strong hand to the Greater Pontificate in New France and in Manitoba.'[63] The United States would dominate the Western hemisphere. It was 'destined one day to inherit all the power and prosperity which Great Britain now possesses.' It would 'protect New France and the North-West against the malevolent powers who would like to rule them.' Having become 'extraordinarily powerful,' the government of the

United States would be used by Providence 'to chastise the countries of Latin America, after their continual wars render them guilty of great sins.'[64]

But if the United States was going to dominate the New World, all was not lost for England. God would leave her power intact if she showed clemency toward Riel and the métis. England should 'try the project of imperial union [with the United States], at least for the limited time of one generation.' It could be dissolved if harmony could not be established. The union would be most helpful to England, for she would need the power of America in the 'disastrous wars' that were about to break out against her. Imperial union would also benefit the United States by strengthening commerce. And it would provide a world structure of peace in which small nations such as Ireland could flourish.[65]

Riel had a special interest in France. The Comte de Chambord having died two years earlier, Riel now felt himself, as a descendant of St Louis, to be the rightful heir to the throne of France. He began a long prophecy on France with these words: 'He whom the world sought in the person of Henry V will be found in the Prophet of the New World, Louis "David" Riel, who through his mother Julie de la Gimodière is one of the princes descended from Louis XI [sic for Louis IX]. [66]

Riel observed that France was divided into three warring factions: the Republic, the Legitimists (Monarchists), and the Bonapartists. In the sight of God, none of the three was fit to rule alone. The monarchy was discredited by centuries of oppression, the Empire by political maladroitness, and the Republican by anti-clericalism. But each of the three factions also had certain strengths. The Royalists were men of 'good principles'; the Bonapartists had done well to think of holding a plebiscite every seven years; and the Republicans were pleasing to God because their statesmen conducted themselves without pomp and arrogance. The solution was a grand coalition, headed by a king from the ancient royal house:

God has revealed to me that His desire is to see at the head of France one of the scions of St Louis, who must be pious, devoted to the interests of the Holy Church, and truly filled with love for all his people. ... who will live according to the model presented by Jesus Christ Himself, the true King. ... and who will have no other title than that of *Exovede* [Riel's emphasis].

A unified France would attain the hegemony of Europe that had long been predicted by Nostradamus and other oracles. Germany was about to challenge England, but would in turn be vanquished by the 'universal domination' of France.

Although Riel's political prophecies are diverse and often contradictory, a common theme runs through them: the punishment of a sinful world in devastating wars, followed by a lasting world order under providential guidance. Riel showed some true political insight in seeing the coming coalition of England and the United States, and in predicting the German challenge. But his ideas far transcended politics in the ordinary sense. They were a millenarian vision of salvation, translated into terms of nation, state, and empire.

In the realms of philosophy and cosmology, Riel also considered that he had important things to say. Part of his mission was to 'explain the existence of God, creation, and even the plan of creation.'[67] He returned to the theory of 'essences,' which he had tried to develop in Montana. He specified that the essences were composed of 'monads,' which were really a form of electricity. Riel did not make much progress in these speculations, although he would have liked to take them further. 'I would like, ' he wrote, 'to be able to expound this revelation in all its beauty' – subject to the approval of Bishop Taché, for his mission now 'consisted above all in obeying.'[68]

Riel also wrote down a substantial revelation on the subject of the Deluge.[69] At the time of Noah there had been only three continents: Africa, Asia, and Europe. The flood was caused not only by prolonged rains but by tidal waves generated when God raised the new continents of America, Australia, and Oceania out of the ocean. God created the New World at the time He punished the men of the Old World for their sins. The Americas were a new start, a second chance for mankind. This supported Riel's teaching that in his own lifetime the focus of religious fervour had passed from the Old World to the New.

Riel wished to 'baptize' the entire universe by giving Christian names to everything within it. During the Rebellion the Exovedate had changed the names of the days of the week. Now Riel gave new names to the oceans, continents, mountains, planets, stars, and even the signs of the zodiac. Many names were drawn from Riel's family; thus the North Star was to be called 'Henrietta' after his sister. Others were called after friends or benefactors, like the planet Neptune, which was to become 'Catherine-Aurélie,' after a nun in Quebec with whom Riel was friendly. Still other names were those of historical figures whom Riel admired. The South Pole was to become the 'Pole Moreno,' after Gabriel

Garcia Moreno, dictator of Ecuador from 1861 to 1875.[70] Moreno had installed a semi-theocratic régime and had officially dedicated Ecuador to the protection of the Sacred Heart of Jesus (one of Riel's favourite devotions because of its connection with his sister Sara's cure).

This attempt to rename the universe was not just a curious pastime of Riel's captivity. He had done the same thing as early as 1876, when he first emerged as a prophet.[71] The new names stemmed from the desire for total transformation which is part of the millenarian vision of salvation. In the words of St Paul, 'the universe itself is to be freed from the shackles of mortality and enter upon the liberty and splendour of the children of God' (Romans 8: 21-3).

In the area of religious doctrine, Riel made one last attempt to harmonize his teaching with Roman orthodoxy. Late in October, he further extended the plan he had sent to Taché of having a double papacy in Europe and America. Now he made it clear that the 'Greater Pontiff of the New World' would be subordinate to Rome. He 'should always be loyal to the Holy Father. Let him live and die working for the Eternal City, Rome.'

Leo XIII ought to 'adopt Montreal or Ville-Marie as his favourite city in the New World.' He should cross the ocean to spend several months there. While in America he should hold 'an ecumenical council of all bishops of the New World.' He must strengthen the American Church for its coming struggles by appointing a supervisory council of 'sixty or seventy-two archbishops, bishops, archpriests, priests, deacons, and laymen of solid and recognized piety.' And he should nominate Taché as 'Greater Pontiff of the New World,' to be 'his agent to supervise the progress of religious affairs and of all matters of interest to the Church, and to report as best he can to the Holy Father, the sovereign pontiff of Rome.' Before leaving, he should also inaugurate Riel's plan of massive European immigration to the North-West.

After Taché's death, the American pontificate would return to Bourget's episcopal see of Ville-Marie. There it would remain 'for 457 years, counting from December 8, 1875.' It would then go back to St Boniface for an additional 1876 years, to reign 'in the splendour and glory of Tabor.' At this transition, the Pontiff of Rome would again come to the New World to consecrate his American subordinate.[72]

This scheme resembled Riel's earlier plan in all essential respects except for continued submission to Rome. Riel must have thought that it was only his repudiation of Rome, and not the whole thrust of his thought, which was unacceptable to the Church. Thus he tried to preserve the essence of his thinking while fitting it into the framework of orthodoxy.

There is no further mention in these months of the particular heresies which he had taught during the Rebellion and subsequently abjured: the denial of the Trinity, universalism, etc. Interestingly, however, he returned to much earlier levels in his thinking about which he had been silent during the Rebellion. He reaffirmed his story about the Hebrew ancestry of the North American Indians.[73] And he hinted that he still held his negative views about St Paul. Although Paul was 'a great genius' who 'knew how to win the hearts of men as a missionary, he was not so pleasing to God as a minister of the liturgy.' Riel had argued in his Beauport writings that Paul's rejection of the Mosaic Law was only a tactical device to obtain converts, but was not the true will of God. Now he wrote: 'When the time comes, the world will see what one must think of St Paul in order to please God.'[74] The words suggest that Riel still clung to his original project, conceived a decade earlier, of reviving the Mosaic Law as a 'conservative' bulwark against the 'liberalism' of the modern world.

In spite of his attempts at conformity, Riel considered himself a prophet to the very end. The restraint he had exercised upon himself in his August diary disappeared. His October diary is filled with 'prophecies' and 'revelations' of all sorts. And he still sought recognition. A steady stream of prophetic utterances left his cell to appear in the eastern newspapers. Scarcely a week before his death, he wrote to Judge Richardson to thank him for his third stay of execution, and he added: 'I sincerely pray to God that you may be amongst the first who will acknowledge me as the Prophet of the [New] World.'[75] On 14 November he requested the judge to allow him to be interviewed by a newspaper reporter; for he had revelations from God 'which are glorious to publish.'[76] And Father André, who was with Riel every day and accompanied him to the scaffold, testified: 'To the last moment he believed himself a prophet and never ceased to speak of his mission.'[77]

DEATH AND RESURRECTION

Riel's thoughts in this period were naturally preoccupied with death. His attitude oscillated between dread and resignation. At times he fervently prayed to God to deliver him: 'Jesus, who deigned to endure all the cruelties and ignominies of death, spare me please from the agony to which I am condemned.' [78] At other times he was more composed, willing to follow the 'logic of obedience' even if it meant death. He consoled himself that knowing the time of his death gave him the chance for spiritual preparation. 'Blessed be the judge who told me: "I have set the day of your death. ... Use the time I'm giving you."'[79] He would offer his death as a sacrifice in submission to 'divine discretion.'[80] If it was God's will, he would rather die than return to his family. He must trust in the Providence which had guided his career.

If Riel was willing to sacrifice his life, he also expected an appropriate reward. He saw himself as a canonized saint, and composed a little prayer to be said on the first Monday of each month to commemorate his execution:

First Monday of the month. Prayer in memory of St Louis [the] métis. O Louis, who through the goodness of God and to give us an example of obedience, wished to climb the scaffold on this day to bring to God the merit of your sufferings in life – now that you are near to God, be our advocate and carry to the God of Heaven and earth the little sufferings which we endure in the desire of following the path which you have so generously traced. We beg through our Lord Jesus Christ that you give us the strength to achieve the great work which you have begun for the welfare of the Métis people and of the whole world. Amen.

St Louis David, pray for us. (Three times) 300 days indulgence.[81]

Sainthood was a spiritual victory over death, but Riel also desired a literal, physical victory. He became convinced that he, like Jesus, would rise from the grave. Dr Jukes visited Riel the evening before the execution and left this report of their conversation:

We spoke by his own choice (he having begun by saying that he wished to speak to me again on this subject) on the subject of his resurrection, which he maintained would take place on the third day. I said that was a subject on which I could not agree with him as I had told him before, though I had never doubted his own sincere belief in it. He said I have already given you in writing some revelations to that effect, but I will give you another – 'When I was in Montana I saw in a vision three persons before me, one a priest, one my brother, and a third. They were talking of my death and the third person said to my brother – pointing to me – God will be with him and though he will die' (or, 'they will cause him to die') 'God will raise him up again on the third day.'[82]

The other revelations about Riel's resurrection mentioned in this passage probably include these sentences found on a scrap of paper in the Jukes Papers:

The 'Corps Beaux' [ie, 'Beautiful Bodies,' a pun inspired by the French name of the Crow Indians, *Corbeaux*] put Jesus Christ to death eighteen hundred years ago. They are going to put me to death, but God will resurrect me on the third day.[83]

The paper is marked 'in Montana.'

Thus Riel told Jukes not only that he expected to be resurrected, but that he had believed in it for several years. There is no confirmation of this in any of Riel's own papers; nowhere does he mention his own resurrection. But it is not improbable that he had long believed in it. When he had started to write a systematic book of philosophy in Montana, he had tried to show that resurrection was possible through the power of the 'active essences.' And he had been praying for the resuscitation of Oliver Morton since 1878.

It seems that Riel had confided in certain members of his family. An unidentified cousin has left a curious document which is the report of a vision or a dream. The cousin sees himself in the house of Roger Goulet in St Vital, where Riel's corpse reposes on a bed. Riel's mother and brother Alexandre are present; all are awaiting Louis' resurrection. Suddenly Louis arises in haste; but he does not speak, he merely goes to another bed. Alexandre throws a blanket over him, saying brusquely, 'Stay dead then, if you won't listen to us!' Louis then rises again and delivers some admonitions to his cousin and Alexandre, but he still says nothing to his mother. His brother Joseph and sister Henriette arrive on the scene. Louis now addresses the group, saying, 'Come see how Monseigneur's [Taché's] work has turned out.' He leads them to a nearby mill. Demonstrating that it does not run properly, he says, 'That's Monseigneur's work!' The cousin runs off to tell the people of St Vital the news while Louis follows, 'very agitated' and 'making predictions.' He takes a fifty-pound sack of flour and scatters it in the street to show that people must have a conscience as white as snow before approaching him. Louis returns to his bed at Goulet's house, where, surrounded by a large crowd, he seems to be in ecstasy. Suddenly a priest appears to give him benediction with the eucharist, while two little boys put incense in the censer. An additional detail is worth noting. At one point the cousin says to Alexandre:

Now we see the Son of Man. When Louis used to speak to us, he said, 'When the Son of Man returns, His heart will be hardened and nothing will be able to resist His arm, for His arm will be like a rod of iron.'

Indeed, throughout the vision Riel acts like the Son of Man coming in judgment. He shows no tenderness towards his family and friends, only an attitude of reproach and correction.

The Christological imagery of the Son of Man harmonizes with Riel's statement to Jukes that he would rise 'on the third day.' Jukes also recalled that Riel spoke of something like the great earthquake which, according to Matthew 27: 52, took place after the death of Christ:

Some days ago in conversation with me with reference to this subject he told me that the Spirit had said to him, 'I will not begin to work until the 12th hour,' that is, he explained, 'twelve hours after my death.' Referring to that this evening he said – twelve hours after my death wonderful things will happen. He had told me before in speaking of this that 'there would be a great shaking throughout the land, and that many would be slain,' tonight he said, 'one-third of the people will die. I pray the Almighty that you may be one of those who will survive.'[85]

It would not have been in keeping with Riel's beliefs for him to think that he was literally another Christ, as some prophets and religious founders have done. A more plausible interpretation is that he now saw his mission as the imitation of Christ. Since 1876 he had thought that his task was to found the third and last era of the Kingdom of God – that of French-Canadian-métis Catholicism, following Roman Catholicism as the latter had succeeded Judaism. Though his opinions had been forced to shift many times on specific questions, he had always clung to the idea of being the founder of a new era. In that respect he was already imitating Christ, who was the founder of the second age of the Kingdom of God. It was therefore only a short step for this imitation to include death and resurrection when circumstances seemed to require it.

Buoyed by this faith, Riel met his death courageously. On 15 November Father André had to tell him that tomorrow was the irrevocable day. Riel took the news calmly, replying in the words of the psalmist, 'Laetatus sum in his quae dicta sunt mihi, in domum Domini ibimus.' (I have rejoiced in the things which have been said to me, we will go into the house of the Lord).[86] Sheriff Chapleau came that evening at nine o'clock to confirm the news. A journalist who was present asked Riel if he was ready to die, to which he replied: 'I made my peace with God long ago, and I am as well prepared as I could ever be. But you will see that I have a mission to fulfil.'[87] He then asked the sheriff if he would have the opportunity to speak from the scaffold.

Father André forbade Riel to speak, arguing that he might say something that would disturb his union with God. His mission now was not to prove to the spectators that he was a prophet, but to demonstrate how a Christian should die. Riel submitted, impressed by André's additional argument that he should imitate the silence of Jesus, who uttered only seven words while He hung on the cross.[88] Riel spent the vigil of his execution with his confessor, awake the whole time. They prayed and discussed spiritual matters, while Riel wrote some last messages for family and friends. 'I have never passed a happier and holier night,' said André:

He [Riel] was joyful, and all night I noticed no shadow of sadness on his face. We prayed together, and afterwards, being seated, he placed his head on my shoulder and embraced me saying: 'How happy and content I am! I feel my heart overflow with joy.'[89]

At 5:00 AM Father André said mass in the cell. Riel once again made a solemn abjuration of his heresies. When he came to the divine motherhood of Mary (ie that Mary was the Mother of God, not just of the man Jesus), he broke into tears and begged forgiveness from Mary for having insulted her 'glorious prerogative.'[90]

The early morning hours were passed with Father André and Father Charles McWilliams, a former schoolmate from the College of Montreal, who had spent the last few days in Regina. Riel now wrote his last letter and gave it to McWilliams. It was a short declaration of loyalty to the Church. Riel repudiated anything 'too presumptuous' in his writings, subordinating himself 'to the good pleasure of my God, to the doctrine of the Church and to the infallible decisions of the supreme Pontiff. I die Catholic and in the only true faith.'[91]

At 8:15 the sheriff's assistant came to fetch Riel but could not bring himself to make the dread announcement. Seeing him at the door of his cell, Riel spoke: 'Mr Gibson, you want me? I am ready.'[92] He walked calmly out, accompanied by the two priests. They said the rosary as they walked, Riel carried an ivory crucifix mounted in silver which had been loaned him. In the poetic words of Nicholas Flood Davin: 'As fair a morning as ever dawned shone. ... The sun glittered out in pitiless beauty and the prairie slightly silvered with hoar frost shone like a vast plain sown with diamonds.'[93] But Riel paid no attention. He was preoccupied with his last preparations. Father André asked him a series of questions: Did he repent of his sins, did he forgive his enemies, etc.? He made the appropriate answers. The sheriff asked him if he wished to speak, and Riel glanced at André. When his confessor urged him to keep silence, Riel said he would not speak, as a sacrifice to God. He received absolution, prayed briefly for his family, then turning his eyes upwards, he repeated the prayer he had said in Fort Benton when Father Eberschweiler blessed him on his way back to Canada: 'My God, bless me according to the intentions of your Providence, which we love even when they are beyond our measure.'[94] He had regarded Father Eberschweiler's blessing as an important sign of the validity of his mission. Now he recalled it to give him confidence as his providential mission led him into the mystery of death.

He ascended the scaffold without flinching. He helped put the rope around his own neck. 'Courage, bon courage, mon père,' he called to Father André, who was dissolved in tears. After a few more prayers and farewells, the time had come. Riel and Father McWilliams said the 'Our Father' together in English; and on the phrase 'deliver us from evil,' the trap was dropped.[95] Louis Riel's mission was over.

8
A Comparative View

Biography is not the only approach to the study of Louis Riel. It is possible to throw additional light on his career by comparing him to other prophets and religious founders who have arisen in similar circumstances. Specifically, this means situating Riel within the field of millenarian studies. (The word 'millennium' is derived from the Latin words mille, 'thousand,' and annus, 'year.' It is literally a period of a thousand years.) In Christian theology, the millennium refers to the thousand-year period of perfect happiness associated with the return of Christ to earth in the Second Coming. According to the Book of Revelation (20:1-3), the devil will be bound for a thousand years while the Kingdom of God is established on earth. The millennium will not end until the Last Judgment, which puts an end to history altogether.

A slight extension of meaning makes the term millennium denote any anticipated period of perfect happiness on earth, whether or not it is the thousand-year kingdom of the Book of Revelation. Millenarian religions are those which expect salvation in the form of a millennium. According to Talmon's widely accepted definition, millenarian salvation is 'imminent, total, ultimate, this-worldly, and collective.'[1] Salvation is 'imminent' if it is expected within the foreseeable future. This might be tomorrow, or it might be years in the future. The specific length of time is not so important as the expectation that those now alive will see redemption. 'Total' salvation means the absolute abolition of unhappiness and evil, the attainment of a realm of peace, freedom, equality, brotherhood, and prosperity. 'Ultimate' means that the expected salvation is the final stage of history, that nothing will succeed it except the end of the world. 'This-worldly' implies a kingdom on earth, not in the spiritual world of heaven. Finally, 'collective' redemption is that which comes to the group as a group, not as a matter of individual reward.

Millenarian studies cover a broad territory, including topics such as Jewish messianism; the origins of Christianity; popular heresies in mediaeval Catholicism; Protestant sects like the German Anabaptists, Puritans, Jehovah's Witnesses, and Seventh Day Adventists; and religious resistance movements among 'natives' against their European conquerors. Riel seems to belong in two of these categories: Catholic heresy and nativistic resistance. Let us look at these two more closely.

Norman Cohn's well-known book *The Pursuit of the Millennium* describes millenarianism in the religious underworld of the Middle Ages.[2] Expectation of the Second Coming was an important part of popular piety. Inspired prophets were repeatedly able to mobilize marginal elements of the population, like landless peasants or the urban proletariat, in movements of total and imminent salvation. These popular cults appeared dangerous to both church and state, which co-operated to repress them unmercifully.

Cohn's book ends with the sixteenth century, but the millenarian tradition continues beyond that point. One example, contemporary with Louis Riel, may be cited. In 1878, in a backward part of Tuscany, a prophet named Davide Lazzaretti announced that Leo XIII was no longer the valid pope. He himself had become the 'Grand Monarch, Christ the Leader and Judge,' who would usher in the millennium. He descended from the mountains with a thousand followers, all wearing crosses on their breasts like modern crusaders. The prophet was killed when the crowd was dispersed by the police, but a cult was formed which has persisted into this century.[3] Similar examples could be provided from France, Spain, Brazil, or other Catholic countries.[4] Millenarian traditions have remained alive among Catholic populations until quite recent times, so Louis Riel would not be an anomaly as a prophet of the millennium, even in the late nineteenth century.

Vittorio Lanternari's *Religions of the Oppressed* is probably the best-known book about religious resistance movements of the Third World.[5] Lanternari has shown how, on all continents, native populations have created new religions promising millenarian deliverance from colonial domination. Among the Plains Indians of the United States there was the Ghost Dance, whose followers were convinced that God would destroy the white man and restore the Indians to an unparalleled abundance of buffalo.[6] Another instance is the Cargo Cults of the South Sea Islands, with their teaching that the white man will vanish, leaving his

'cargo' for the native to enjoy.[7] One could also mention the famous rebellion of the Mahdi of the Sudan, roughly contemporaneous with Riel,
which drew on millenarian traditions within Islam.[8] Also relevant are
modern cults like the Rastafarians of Jamaica, who believe they will be
transported to the promised land of Ethiopia, or the Black Muslims of
the United States, who expect God to destroy the white man in retribution for what he has done to the coloured races.[9]

A striking feature of these nativistic movements is religious syncretism. Although their founders have generally borrowed liberally from
Christianity, they have also drawn on indigenous beliefs and have often
rejected Christianity as the religion of the white man. The result has
been a rich diversity of creeds, ranging from almost purely Christian to
almost purely pagan.

This syncretism was absent from the teaching of Louis Riel, except in-
sofar as he may have altered his ideas when presenting them to the illiterate métis. Then he might conceivably have drawn on local superstition
or Indian lore, but there is no record of this, except for his brief allusion
in his trial speech to métis traditions of prophecy. Riel's ideas were developed from Christian themes. His new religion was an exaggerated
version of the ultramontanism that he had learned from the French-
Canadian clergy. He was probably also inspired by Catholic prophetic
literature on the margin of orthodoxy, as suggested by Nolin's reference
to St Bridget. And he may have derived some secondary inspiration
from contemporary Protestant millenarians in the United States. His
numerology is reminiscent of the Millerites, the Saturday sabbath recalls the Seventh Day Adventists, and polygamy brings to mind the
Mormons. In any case, all his important ideas have Christian rather
than pagan sources.

But Riel's situation resembled those of typical native resistance movements. He created a religion which promised deliverance to a small people whose identity was threatened by the expansion of Western civilization. He could speak the traditional idiom of Catholic millenarianism
rather than a more exotic blend of paganism and Christianity because
the métis were already firmly Catholic.

How well does Riel fit Talmon's definition? Did he promise
'imminent, total, ultimate, this-worldly, collective, salvation'? In one
sense, no. Riel never abandoned the conventional Christian notions of
individual judgment and salvation. He believed that man was composed
of a material body and a non-material soul, that the soul would be
judged on its individual merits after death, and that it would be rewarded or punished by God in the other world. This conventional escha-

tology is the opposite of the millenarian scheme. Riel modified it slightly during the Rebellion by preaching the doctrine of universalism; but this only affected the number who would be saved, not the nature of salvation itself, which remained otherworldly. If Riel was a millenarian, it was in addition, not in opposition to his orthodox Catholic views about redemption.

He did have a doctrine of the Second Coming. He taught that Christ would return to earth in 4209 AD, that is, 2333 years from the commencement of his mission in 1876 AD. But this was hardly an imminent event in Talmon's sense. To see Riel as a millenarian, I must introduce a nuance of terminology.

A distinction is often made between 'premillennialism' and 'postmillennialism.' The Book of Revelation is unclear about the crucial detail of whether the Second Advent will precede or follow the millennium. Premillennialists hold that Jesus must literally return to earth before the millennium can be established. There is not much that man can do except to preach the Gospel and wait. Deliverance is in the hands of the Lord, who may appear at any moment. Postmillennialists, in contrast, hold that human effort, in co-operation with God's grace, will spread the Gospel throughout the world so that men's hearts will be changed. The Second Coming will take place only after a long period – a millennium in effect – of peace and happiness. The return of Christ to earth will be a culmination, not an inauguration.[10]

Riel preached a postmillennial message whose leading ideas were stable even if secondary ideas changed from time to time. The message was that a new era had dawned in 1876 when he began his prophetic mission. It was the third and last epoch of the Kingdom of God. Spiritual leadership had passed from Rome to the New World. Montreal would be the first residence of the Holy Spirit in America, followed after 457 years by St Boniface. The métis would be redeemed from their present state of oppression. Strengthened by French immigration, they would dominate Manitoba, which would become the leading state in a confederation of new nations in the North-West. Catholics and Protestants would be reconciled, and world peace would be established after disastrous wars. The new world order would ensure the triumph of the true religion. As the culmination of these happy events, Christ would return to earth after 457 plus 1876 years.

This message conforms reasonably well to Talmon's definition of millenarianism:

1 The promised salvation was imminent. Indeed it had already begun

in 1876 and only needed a visible sign from God to be manifested to the world.

2 If it was not total salvation, it was certainly a radical transformation of life on earth. Riel's theocratic régime would have meant a sweeping, world-wide moral reform of a sort that most men would call utopian.

3 It was ultimate in the sense that it was the final stage of human history. It was penultimate with respect to the direct rule of Christ on earth after 4209 AD.

4 It was clearly a this-worldly form of salvation, taking place on earth under guidance from heaven.

5 It was collective inasmuch as the métis as a people would be the special beneficiaries of God's actions. They would receive the new papacy as well as political domination of the whole North-West. But if Riel's promise of salvation was collective, it was not exclusive, at least in its later formulation. He wanted reconciliation with old-style Roman Catholics, with Protestants, with Anglo-Saxons, with all of mankind. Providence had given the métis a special role in the economy of salvation, but only as a means of redeeming the entire human race.

Riel's religion was in many ways unique, a highly personal response to the frustrations of his own life. It was a religious compensation for the glory he had sought and missed in politics. Yet it also contained several elements which are common to millenarian movements, and about which a good deal is known. [11] Consider four areas where the resemblance of Riel's religion to other millenarian cults is most marked: the social conditions under which it arose, the personality of the leader, its doctrines, and Riel's attitude towards violence.

GENERATIVE CONDITIONS

To the extent that Riel's religion was a personal matter, it arose from the frustrations of his own life. To the extent that it was social, it stemmed from the métis perception that their existence as a people was in danger. The métis were threatened in several ways at once. Their traditional economy was destroyed by the disappearance of the buffalo, the decline of the fur trade, and the introduction of new forms of transport superior to their cart trains and boat brigades. Their language and religion were jeopardized by massive English and Protestant immigration. Their ownership of land was threatened – or at least they perceived it to be threatened – by problems with the survey and issue of patents. And the benign neglect of the Hudson's Bay Company in local affairs was replaced by the stricter control of the Canadian state.

This general setting is identical to the situation in which millenarian movements have arisen among colonized peoples around the globe. The pursuit of the millennium is activated by the threat of destruction to a people's way of life by forces over which they have no control. When the natives see the collapse of the world they have always known, they become susceptible to promises of a new world to come. Typically, the situation of cultural destruction furnishes the long-range background to the emergence of nativistic movements. The movements themselves are usually triggered by immediate events which bring matters to a head. Common causes have been war, famine, drought, plague, or other natural calamities.

This pattern applies to the two Riel Rebellions. The first was preceded by a disastrous famine caused by grasshoppers. The second followed the world economic crash of 1883. The métis themselves did not produce a great deal of grain for the national or world market, but they earned money by cutting wood, freighting, or performing other labour. When the supply of money ran short, they were almost as much affected as the white settlers. Their hardship was aggravated by an extremely bad harvest in 1884, caused by drought, insects, and early frost.

That the second Rebellion was millenarian while the first was not is due less to fundamental differences in their causes than to the intervening development in Riel's thinking. Great historical causes provide impetus, but the precise outcome of events is determined by individuals. There would have been no new religion without Riel; but without the malaise of the métis there would have been no one to listen to the prophet.

THE LEADER

The millenarian prophet or messiah is usually someone who has lived both in the world of his own people and in the greater world outside. In the Middle Ages, the millenarian leader was often an ex-seminarian, a disaffected member of the lower clergy, a runaway monk, or a widely traveled pilgrim. The leader of a modern nativistic movement has often been in close contact with the white man as a pupil in a mission school or a member of the native armed forces. Perhaps this wider range of experience shakes his trust in the fixity of reality and helps him conceive of a radically different world to come. His larger experience also makes him something of an outsider to his own people. There is enough of the stranger about him to exert a certain fascination, yet he is familiar enough to command loyalty. In short, the leader has usually been at the cutting edge of cultural conflict. His distinctive contribution is to interpret that conflict in new religious symbolism.

This composite portrait applies accurately to Louis Riel. Seven-eighths white, he grew up in the settled portion of the métis community which was closest to white ways. His family farmed and did not participate in the characteristic métis activities of the buffalo hunt, bull trains, boat brigades, or fur trade. He was sent at an early age to Montreal to acquire an education and to become the first métis missionary priest. Abandoning this plan, he tried to become part of white society by marrying a white girl and pursuing a career as a lawyer. It was only when these intentions were impeded that he returned to the West. After the first Rebellion, Riel wanted a career in Canadian politics, an aim which he pursued tenaciously until the 'amnesty' of 1875. Even after his unhappy experience in the lunatic asylums of Quebec, he considered settling in the white society of the eastern United States. Not until 1879 did he go to the frontier to share the roving life of the métis. There his experience and reputation made him their natural leader, since they were mostly illiterate and had no real conception of what lay east of the Red River. Neither wholly white nor wholly métis, Riel participated in both ways of life. He came to view himself as a human bridge – between native and white, French and English, Catholic and Protestant, British and American, human and divine.

There are two chief models for the millenarian leader to imitate: the prophet who announces salvation and the messiah who brings it. Riel was more prophet than messiah. Calling himself the 'Prophet of the New World,' he did exactly what a prophet should do (the role is clearly described in the Old Testament). He saw visions and heard voices, he made predictions about the future, he called men to repentance, he promised to work miracles. He was 'charismatic' in the strict sense of that much-abused term; that is, his claim to lead was based on the visible manifestations of the anointing of the Holy Spirit – miracles, revelations, prophecies, and sanctity. Riel slipped into the messianic role at times, as when he styled himself the redeemer of the Jews or when he speculated on his own resurrection. But whether as prophet or messiah, he was imitating models of biblical tradition and acting in a way typical of millenarian leaders.

DOCTRINE

Certain of Riel's teachings were typical of millenarian cults. We have seen how he constructed a genealogy for the métis, making them descendants of the Hebrews. Such fictional genealogies are common in millenarianism, and so is the fascination with the Jews. As the first Chosen People, the Jews provide an ever-ready model for prophets who wish to constitute a new people as God's elect in the present age.

Riel's infatuation with the Jews went to great lengths. He wished to revive parts of the Mosaic Law, including polygamy, a married clergy, the Saturday sabbath, and circumcision. He modeled himself on Hebrew examples: Moses, Elias, Daniel, and above all David. He would be the earthly messiah whom the Jews expected. To the end, he kept a place open for them in his colonization scheme.

Millenarians often drastically simplify reality by clearly dividing good from evil. The chosen people represent good, while evil is symbolized by some Antichrist-like figure or force. In Riel's earlier thinking, 'liberalism' played the role of Antichrist. Liberalism was not so much a specific political or religious theory as an all-pervasive tendency of men to prefer their own desires to the will of God. The doctors and nuns who kept Riel in the hospital were liberals; Sir John A. Macdonald was a liberal; Bismarck was a liberal; even Pius IX was tainted with liberalism. But in Riel's later, ecumenical phase, when the accent was on universal reconciliation, liberalism was no longer an omnipresent, diabolical enemy. Riel dreamed of bringing the French Republicans into an alliance with the conservative forces in that country; and he hoped for the support of both the Liberal and the Conservative parties of Canada.

Other similarities to typical millenarian doctrines were connected with the very fact of promising a millennium. Such a future is not easily attained. Riel, like most millenarians, foresaw a transitional period of wars and other calamities before the millennium would arrive.

While devaluing the present, millenarians often glorify the past. The millennium is pictured as a restoration and transfiguration of the past, as in the Ghost Dance, where the buffalo are expected to return in unprecedented abundance after the white man's destruction. But the past received relatively little emphasis in Riel's thinking since he saw it as only the prologue to a more glorious future. He did on occasion speak of the past of the métis in Arcadian terms. They had lived in a 'land of natural opulence'; they had been 'a simple primitive people of good faith, placed by Providence in a fortunate abundance'; they had been fed by the buffalo, 'as wonderful as the heavenly manna.'[12] But Riel had no illusions about restoring the past. He knew that the days of the fur trade and buffalo hunt were gone for good. He wanted the métis to settle down as farmers and gradually to adopt the benefits of civilization. However exaggerated and utopian his vision, he was engaged in a creative task: trying to evoke the future of a people menaced with destruction.

VIOLENCE

We have seen Riel's curious ambiguity about violence. Although he spoke belligerently, he was most reluctant to fight. This stemmed partly from the strategy of taking hostages and forcing Ottawa to negotiate, but there was another aspect as well. Riel expected that God would win his battles for him if it came to fighting. In this he was a true millenarian. He relied upon the intervention of God in human affairs to vindicate his cause. He was not a revolutionary in the modern sense, seeking to remake society by force.

Enough has been said to show that Louis Riel's new religion was a form of millenarianism. Students of that subject may wish to take the comparison further; but for my purposes, it is enough to show that Riel's behaviour as a prophet was not an isolated phenomenon. His style, his teachings, the situation in which his religion originated – all have many clear parallels among millenarian movements.

All psychiatrists and most historians who have written about Riel have treated his prophetic mission as a symptom of mental disorder. Indeed, Dr Lachapelle's original diagnosis of 'frustrated ambition' and 'delusions of grandeur' explains a great deal. But it does not explain everything. Riel was acting in much the same way as many other millenarian leaders. Faced with the annihilation of his people's way of life, he tried to create a new identity, a new life, and a new future. His insanity – if it may be called that – was a message of hope. Common conceptions of what is normal may suffice for normal times, but they do not encompass the range of human response to adversity. We need a broader view of sanity to comprehend the actions of men in dark times.

Notes

PREFACE

1 Dr H. Gilson and Dr Bourque, 'La Folie de Riel et la justice anglaise,'
  L'Union médicale du Canada 14 (1885) 561-4; Gilson, 'Etude sur l'état
  mental de Louis Riel,' *L'Encéphale* 6 (1886) 51-60; Daniel Clark, 'A Psycho-
  Medical History of Louis Riel,' *American Journal of Insanity* 44 (1887-8) 33-
  51; Clark, 'A Few Canadian Cases in Criminal Courts in which the Plea of
  Insanity was Presented,' *Transactions of the American Medico-
  Psychological Association* 2 (1895) 183-90; W.W. Ireland, *Through the Ivory
  Gate* (Edinburgh 1889); C.K. Clarke, 'A Critical Study of the Case of Louis
  Riel,' *Queen's Quarterly* 12 (April 1905) 379-88; (July 1905) 14-26; Gabriel
  Nadeau, 'La Folie de Louis Riel,' c1944, unpublished ms, BNQ; E.R. Markson,
  'The Life and Death of Louis Riel: A Psychoanalytic Commentary,'
  Canadian Psychiatric Association Journal 10 (1965) 246-52; E. Desjardins
  and C. Dumas, 'Le Complexe médical de Louis Riel,' *L'Union médicale du
  Canada* 99 (1970) 1656-61, 1870-8

CHAPTER 1: PREPARATION

1 Antoine Champagne, 'La Famille de Louis Riel,' *Mémoires de la Société
  Généalogique Canadienne-Française* 20 (1969) 14
2 BNQ, Dr Gabriel Nadeau Papers, memo of Alban Boucher, OMI, archivist of
  the Oblate order (Rome)
3 Henriette Riel-Poitras, 'Préface pour une histoire de Riel,' nd, HSSB
4 Riel himself used 23 October in his 'Compte-Rendu de ses activités,' ASB(T).
  He also gave this date to Evelina Barnabé, *cf.* PAM, Riel (1), No. 350, Evelina
  to Riel, 21 October 1878. 22 October is given in Henriette Poitras, 'Préface,'
  HSSB, and in a statement by Riel's mother, PAM, Riel (1), no. 599. The

baptismal registry at St Boniface has been destroyed, so the question cannot be settled conclusively.

5 Henriette Poitras, 'Préface,' HSSB
6 *Ibid.*
7 ASB(T)
8 Robert Gosman, *The Riel and Lagimodière Families in Métis Society, 1840-1860*, Parks Canada, Manuscript Report no. 171 (1977)
9 PAM, Riel (1) no. 599 (February 1886)
10 Antoine Champagne to the author, 13 November 1974
11 Henriette Poitras, 'Préface,' HSSB
12 Louis Riel to A.-A. Taché, 24 July 1885; ASTR. English translation in Thomas Flanagan, 'Louis Riel's Religious Beliefs: A Letter to Bishop Taché,' *Saskatchewan History* 27 (1974) 15-28
13 *Ibid.* 18
14 *Ibid.* 19-20
15 PAM, 'A Passionate Adventurer,' memoir of Alice F. Loomis
16 Two younger children, Henriette and Alexandre, also considered entering the service of the Church. PAM, Riel (1), nos 378, 387, 392
17 G.F.G. Stanley, *Louis Riel* (Toronto 1963) 22
18 Olivier Maurault, *Le Petit Séminaire de Montréal* (Montreal 1918). The curriculum is given on pp 219-22.
19 *Ibid.* 80
20 Riel to Taché, 24 July 1885, 'Louis Riel's Religious Beliefs ... '
21 Riel's grades, from the archives of the Collège de Montréal, are given in Gilles Martel, 'Le Messianisme de Louis Riel (1844-1885)', thesis (Paris 1976) 162 n21.
22 Dr J.-O. Mousseau, *Une Page d'histoire* (Montreal 1886) 6. *Cf.* Eustache Prud'homme, 'Louis Riel,' *L'Opinion Publique*, 19 February 1870.
23 Mousseau, *Une Page d'histoire* 9
24 The notebook is in PAM, Riel(2); published in *PJ*.
25 *PJ*, #30. *Cf.* Thomas Flanagan and John Yardley, 'Louis Riel as a Latin Poet,' *Humanities Association Review* 26 (1975) 33-45.
26 *PJ*, #32
27 *PJ*, #13
28 *PJ*, #2
29 *PJ*, #4
30 *PJ*, #28
31 *PJ*, #14
32 Martel, 'Le Messianisme de Louis Riel ... ' 195ff.
33 Louis Riel to his mother and family, 23 February 1864, PAM, Riel (1), no. 5

34 *Ibid.*, 21 March 1864, PAM, Riel (1), no. 6
35 Affidavit of John Lee in *L'Etendard*, 26 April 1886
36 *PJ*, #5
37 *PJ*, #6
38 *PJ*, #20
39 *PJ*, #29
40 *PJ*, #21; #16
41 Dr Daniel Clark, 'A Psycho-Medical History of Louis Riel,' *American Journal of Insanity* 44 (1887-8) 38
42 Daniel Clark, 'A Few Canadian Cases in Criminal Courts in which the Plea of Insanity was Presented,' *Transactions of the American Medico-Psychological Association* 2 (1895) 184-5
43 Diary of Ontario Hospital (Toronto), 1878-86, in the Archives of the Queen's Mental Health Centre, Toronto
44 Clark, 'A Few Canadian Cases ... ' 185
45 Letter from Clark in *Toronto Mail*, dated 23 August 1885
46 Riel to Taché, 8 January 1876; and Riel to Father Bolduc, 30 July 1876, ASB; Riel to Taché, 24 July 1885, ASTR
47 Riel to Taché, 8 January 1876, ASB
48 *PJ*, #33
49 E.R. Markson, 'The Life and Death of Louis Riel: A Psychoanalytic Commentary,' *Canadian Psychiatric Association Journal* 10 (1965) 246-52
50 Stanley, *Louis Riel* 29
51 *PJ*, #7
52 *PJ*, #8
53 *PJ*, #9
54 *PJ*, #10
55 *PJ*, #11
56 Cited in Stanley, *Louis Riel* 29
57 Charles Lenoir-Rolland to Taché, 26 August 1865, ASB
58 *PJ*, #17
59 Vandenberghe to Taché, 16 July 1865, ASB
60 *Ibid.*, 8 August 1865
61 Archives of the Grey Sisters of Montreal, Mother Jane Slocombe to the Superior at St Boniface, 13 September 1865
62 UNB, Riel Papers; *PJ*, #36
63 W.M. Davidson, *The Life and Times of Louis Riel* (Calgary 1951) 13
64 McGill University, McCord Museum, no. 4158, *PJ*, #37. The existence of this letter was not known to Stanley.
65 24 February 1866, ANQ, Collection Chapais; *PJ*, #38. Stanley used this letter

but wrongly dated it 1865, even though the correct date is plainly written.
66 Nd, ANQ, Collection Chapais; *PJ,* #39. Stanley dated this 1865, but the sense clearly places it after the two preceding texts.
67 Archives of the Grey Sisters of Montreal, Mother Jane Slocombe to Sara Riel, 13 March 1866
68 Mousseau, *Une Page d'histoire* 11; A.-N. Montpetit, *Louis Riel à la Rivière-du-Loup* (Lévis 1885) 34
69 Mousseau, *Une Page d'histoire* 11
70 Printed in the introduction to *PJ*
71 Stanley, *Louis Riel* 381 n46
72 *PJ,* #34; #35
73 Riel to Taché, 24 July 1885, 'Louis Riel's Religious Beliefs ... '
74 Riel to Taché, 8 January 1876, ASB
75 Sara Riel to Marie Riel, 25 January 1868, PAM, Riel (1), no. 8
76 Louis Schmidt, 'Mémoires,' *Le Patriote de l'Ouest,* 8 February 1912
77 Prud'homme, 'Louis Riel,' *L'Opinion Publique,* 19 February 1870
78 Riel, 'Compte-Rendu de ses activités,' ASB(T)
79 W.L. Morton, editor, *Alexander Begg's Red River Journal* (Toronto: Champlain Society 1956) 35. Alastair Sweeney, *George-Etienne Cartier: A Biography* (Toronto 1976), has suggested that Riel was sent to Chicago and St Paul by Cartier to gather intelligence about Fenians and French-Canadian *émigrés.* The theory is interesting, but the author offers no proof.
80 *Ibid.* 582
81 *Ibid.* 395-9
82 Sara Riel to Louis Riel, 7 September 1868, PAM, Riel (1), no. 9
83 Stanley, *Louis Riel* 53
84 Sara Riel to Louis Riel, 7 September 1868, PAM, Riel (1), no. 9
85 PAM, Riel (2), contains the bill of sale from François Larivière to Louis Riel, 23 January 1869. Riel bought another piece of land from the same man 24 June 1869. PAC, Riel Collection, no. 2
86 C. Lachance to Louis Riel, 14 December 1868, PAM, Riel (1), no. 10
87 Louis Riel to 'Monsieur,' 23 March 1869, *ibid.,* no. 11

CHAPTER 2: TESTING

1 G.F.G. Stanley, *Louis Riel* (Toronto 1963) 114
2 F.M. Viscount Wolseley, *The Story of a Soldier's Life* (London 1903) vol. 2 p 178
3 Louis Riel to William Dease, 15 January 1870, Winfred V. Working Papers, University of North Dakota Library, Grand Forks, North Dakota

4 Stanley, *Louis Riel* 158
5 G.F.G. Stanley, editor, 'Riel's Petition to the President of the United States, 1870,' *Canadian Historical Review* 20 (1939) 421-8
6 Joseph Royal to Louis Riel, 17 December 1870, PAM, Riel (1), no. 60
7 Louis Riel to A.-A. Taché, 8 January 1876, ASB
8 Riel to Jos. Dubuc, 27 April 1871, PAM, Riel (1), no. 89
9 Cited in Stanley, *Louis Riel* 174
10 Louis Riel to Julie Riel, 16 April 1872, PAM, Riel (2)
11 Mary Jordan, *To Louis: From Your Sister Who Loves You* (Toronto 1974) 85
12 PAM, Riel (1), nos 185, 186, 187, 188, 192
13 Sara Riel to Julie and Louis Riel, nd, PAM, Riel (1), no. 185
14 Sara Riel to Louis Riel, 9 March 1873, PAM, Riel (1), no. 193
15 Louis Riel to A.-A. Taché, 8 January 1876, ASB
16 Louis Riel to Sara Riel, 26 July 1873, PAM, Riel (2)
17 Riel, 'Compte-Rendu de ses activités,' ASB(T)
18 Statement by Riel's mother, February 1886, PAM, Riel (1), no. 599; interview with Riel in *Montreal Daily Star*, 22 August 1885
19 Jos. Dubuc to L. Riel, 17 October 1873, PAM, Riel (1), no. 220; Dr E.-P. Lachapelle to Riel, 29 January 1874, *ibid.*, no. 237
20 Louis Riel, *L'Amnistie* (Montreal 1874).
21 Louis Riel to Ignace Bourget, 25 November 1874. Printed in Léon Pouliot, 'Correspondance Louis Riel – Mgr Bourget,' *Revue d'histoire de l'Amérique française* 15 (1961) 432-3
22 Louis Riel to Ignace Bourget, nd; ADM, 874-2
23 Riel, 'Compte-Rendu de ses activités,' ASB(T)
24 Mason Wade, *The French-Canadians*, 2nd edition (Toronto 1968) vol. l, p 360
25 *Ibid.* 352
26 Ramsay Cook, editor, *French-Canadian Nationalism* (Toronto 1969) 98
27 'Report of the Select Committee on the Causes of the Difficulties in the North-West Territories,' *Journals of the House of Commons* (1874) vol. 8, appendix 6
28 A.-A. Taché, *The North-West Difficulty* (Winnipeg 1874)
29 Robert Rumilly, *Histoire des Franco-Américains* (Montreal 1958) 34-5
30 The minutes of the Suncook meeting, 29 July 1874, are in PAM, Riel (2), as are the minutes of the Woonsocket meeting, 2 August 1874
31 Alfred Désilets, Trois-Rivières, to Riel, 24 September 1874, PAM, Riel (1), no. 333
32 Riel to Charles Larocque, 21 January 1875, Archives of the Archdiocese of St Hyacinthe

33 Riel to Mgr Taschereau, 20 January 1875, Archives of the Archdiocese of Quebec

34 Wilfrid Laurier to Edward Blake, 31 December 1885, Archives of Ontario, Blake Family Papers. It is often asserted that this meeting between Riel and Laurier took place in 1877. [O.D. Skelton, *Life and Letters of Sir Wilfrid Laurier* (Toronto 1921) vol. 1, p 294] But Skelton, who gave no proof for his statement, may have been mistaken. Laurier's letter to Blake explicitly says summer of 1874. Riel was in Beauport asylum in 1877. It is said that he was allowed to tour the province while supposedly hospitalized, but this is inherently improbable. His presence in Canada was illegal and would have caused a major scandal if discovered. The only evidence for such trips comes from Skelton and the letter from Trois-Rivières mentioned in note 31, *supra*, the date of which has sometimes been read as 24 September 1877. But I think 1874 is a better reading and agrees with Riel's known trip to Quebec City about that time.

35 Alphonse C. to Louis Riel, 28 October 1874, PAM, Riel (1), no. 283

36 *Cf. Catalogue de la Bibliothèque de l'Union-St-Jean-Baptiste de l'Amérique: Collection Mallet*, 2nd edition (Woonsocket, Rhode Island 1935).

37 PAM, Riel (1), no. 284, Barnabé to Riel, 14 November 1874

38 Pouliot, 'Correspondance Louis Riel-Mgr Bourget' 437. I have used with a few changes the translation in E.B. Osler, *The Man Who Had to Hang* (Toronto 1961) 170

39 Riel to Bourget, 6 July 1875, ADM; Pouliot, 'Correspondance ... '

40 PAM, Riel (1), no. 315, Lachapelle to Riel, 23 October 1875

41 See several letters from autumn 1875 in PAM, Riel (2)

42 Louis Riel to Julie Riel, 21 October 1875, PAM, Riel (1), no. 313

43 Louis Riel to Senator O.P. Morton, draft, 31 October 1875, PAM, Riel (1), no. 316

44 Louis Riel to Fathers Fourmond and Cochin, nd, but c 3-5 August 1885, ASB

45 Louis Riel to 'Monsieur le Curé,' 9 December 1875, newspaper clipping in scrapbook *L'Affaire Riel*, AUSJB

46 Edmond Mallet to Rollo Campbell, 11 March 1887, AUSJB

47 PAM, Riel (2). Published by Hartwell Bowsfield, 'Louis Riel's Letter to President Grant, 1875,' *Saskatchewan History* 21 (1968). Additional notes by Riel on the same subject are in PAM, Riel (1); nos 557, 558.

48 Edmond Mallet, 'Notes on Riel,' c 1886, AUSJB

49 Riel to Bourget, 6 December 1875, ADM; Pouliot, 'Correspondance ... ' 438-40

50 Extract of a letter from Riel to an unknown recipient, published in the *Courrier du Canada*, Quebec, 11 June 1885

51 Riel, 'Compte-Rendu de ses activités,' ASB(T)

52 *Courrier du Canada*, 11 June 1885

CHAPTER 3: THE PROPHET IN CHAINS

1 Riel, 'Compte-Rendu de ses activités,' ASB(T)
2 Louis Riel to Fathers Cochin and Fourmond, nd, but c 3-5 August 1885, ASB
3 Interview with Riel, *Montreal Daily Star*, 22 August 1885. The dating of the vision is problematical. The newspaper account makes Riel say that it took place on 18 December 1874, a date which biographers like Howard, Stanley, and Osler have all accepted. However, other evidence about Riel's life shows no trace of dramatic visionary experiences until December 1875. Furthermore, Riel also said in the interview that before this revelation he had already received a letter from Bishop Bourget saying he 'had a mission to perform.' This almost surely refers to Bourget's letter of 14 July 1875. It is tempting to suppose that the *Star* made a typographical error and that Riel actually said 18 December 1875; but the problem cannot be resolved so easily, for on that day Riel had already left Washington for Worcester. The date of this vision must be left open, given our present knowledge of Riel's life.
4 Riel to Mallet, nd but c December 1875, AUSJB
5 Riel,'Compte-Rendu de ses activités,' ASB(T)
6 Riel to Cochin and Fourmond, nd but c 3-5 August 1885, ASB
7 Riel to Bourget, 6 December 1875, ADM; Léon Pouliot, 'Correspondance Louis Riel – Mgr Bourget, *Revue d'histoire de l'Amérique Française* 15 (1961)
8 Riel to 'Monsieur le Curé,' newspaper clipping in scrapbook *L'Affaire Riel*, 9 December 1875, AUSJB
9 Edmond Mallet, 'Notes on Riel,' nd but c 1886, AUSJB
10 Wilbur Bryant, *The Blood of Abel* (Hastings, Nebraska 1887) 64
11 Barnabé to Mallet, 29 December 1875, AUSJB
12 Robert Rumilly, *Histoire des Franco-Américains* (Montreal 1958) 82-3
13 Primeau to Mallet, 31 December 1875, AUSJB
14 *Le Travailleur* (Worcester, Mass.), 11 December 1885
15 Bourget to Riel, 2 January 1876, Pouliot, 'Correspondance ... '
16 Riel to Taché, 8 January 1876, ASB
17 All details involving John Lee come from his affidavit published in *L'Etendard* (Montreal), 26 April 1886.
18 Memo of Father A. Champagne, HSSB
19 Dossier no. 565 in the medical archives of the Centre Hospitalier Saint-Jean-de-Dieu (Montréal-Gamelin)
20 Riel, 'Compte-Rendu de ses activités,' ASB(T)
21 14, 15 Vic. c 84; Consolidated Statutes of Canada (1859), cap. 73
22 Dr Henry Howard, 'Medical History of Louis David Riel during his Detention in Longue Pointe Asylum,' *Canada Medical and Surgical Journal*

(June 1886)641-9. Published in French in *L'Etendard* (Montreal), 13 July 1886. Howard's account is implausible or internally contradictory on a number of points, so events for which he is the only witness cannot be accepted as entirely certain.

23 Henry Howard, *The Philosophy of Insanity: Crime and Responsibility* (Montreal 1882)

24 David J. Rothman, *The Discovery of the Asylum* (Boston 1971) 144-5

25 Tuke first published his findings in 1884 in the *Journal of Mental Science*, then in book form in *The Insane in the United States and Canada* (London 1885). All citations from Tuke are from this book, 189-206.

26 Howard, 'Medical History of Louis David Riel ... '

27 Tuke, *Insane in the US and Canada*

28 Howard, 'Medical History of Louis David Riel ... '

29 These records no longer exist. This information is taken from a letter of Dr Omer Noël, Medical Superintendent of St-Jean-de-Dieu, to Mrs Olive Knox, nd but c 1949, PAM, Riel (1), no. 626. Dr Noël had access to records now destroyed.

30 Riel to Bourget, 15 May 1876, ADM

31 Dr Omer Noël to Olive Knox, nd, PAM, Riel (1), no. 626

32 Riel to Bourget, 15 May 1876, ADM

33 Howard, 'Medical History of Louis David Riel ... '

34 PAM, Jos. Dubuc, 'Mémoires d'un Manitobain,' ms, 311-14

35 Riel to Bourget, 15 May 1876, ADM

36 *Ibid.*, 9 May 1876

37 *Ibid.*, 11 May 1876

38 Howard, 'Medical History of Louis David Riel ... '

39 *L'Etendard* (Montreal), 17 July 1886

40 Centre Hospitalier St-Jean-de-Dieu, Dossier no. 565

41 PAC, Justice, 217-18, are copies of affidavits relative to Riel's admission to and discharge from Beauport, issued 21 June 1885, by the Provincial Secretary of Quebec.

42 Lee, affidavit, 26 April 1886

43 *Le Travailleur* (Worcester, Mass.), 11 December 1885

44 Lachapelle to Wilfrid Laurier, 29 March 1886, newspaper clipping in scrapbook, *L'Affaire Riel*, AUSJB

45 Howard, 'Medical History of Louis David Riel ... '

46 Tuke, *Insane in the US and Canada* 205

47 Hôpital St-Michel-Archange (Beauport), Dossier no. 3697

48 Daniel Clark, 'A Few Canadian Cases in Criminal Courts in which the Plea of

Insanity was Presented,' *Transactions of the American Medico-Psychological Association* 2 (1895) 187

49 *Courrier du Canada*, 11 June 1885
50 Note by Riel, 22 May 1876. Sent to Bourget with his letter of 29 May 1876, ADM
51 Riel to J.-B.-Z. Bolduc, 30 July 1876, ASB
52 Jos. Bussceres to Riel, 20 August 1876, PAM, Riel (1), no. 323
53 *New York Herald*, 18 May 1885
54 An outing to pick fruit is described in ASB(T).
55 Riel to Clément Vincelette, 3 February 1877, typed copy, HSSB
56 Riel to Taché, nd, ASTR
57 According to Dom Benoit, *Vie de Mgr Taché* (Montreal 1904) vol. 2, pp 302-3, Taché left St Boniface 16 October, arrived in Ottawa 25 October, and stayed in the Province of Quebec until 11 December 1876.
58 ASTR
59 Taché to the Governor-General, Lord Dufferin, 14 November 1877, ASB
60 Sara Riel to Taché, 9 January 1877, ASB
61 Riel to Bourget, 20 April 1876, ADM
62 Sara Riel to Taché, 9 January 1877, ASB
63 Sara Riel to Julie Riel, 12 February 1877, PAM, Riel (1), no. 329
64 ASB
65 *Polémiques et documents touchant le Nord-Ouest et l'exécution de Louis Riel* (Montreal: Imprimerie de l'Etendard 1886) part 3, p 6
66 Clipping from *La Vérité*, Quebec, nd, HSSB
67 *QvLR*, 246

CHAPTER 4: THE NEW RELIGION

1 This chapter is an enlarged version of my article, 'Louis "David" Riel: Prophet, Priest-King, Infallible Pontiff,' *Journal of Canadian Studies* 9 (1974) 15-26.
2 ASQ, 144
3 Above all, the letters to Bourget in ADM; the essays and poetry in ASQ; and the long letter to Taché in ASTR, nd but c 1876
4 Bourget to Riel, 14 July 1875, Pouliot, 'Correspondance Louis Riel – Mgr Bourget,' *Revue d'histoire de l'Amérique française* 15 (1961)
5 *Montreal Star*, 22 August 1885. *Cf.* Riel's mother's statement of February 1886, PAM, Riel (1), no. 599.
6 Dubuc to Riel, 17 October 1873, PAM, Riel (1), no. 220

7 Lachapelle to Riel, 29 January 1874, *ibid.*, no. 237

8 Riel to Bourget, 1 May 1876, ADM

9 Riel to Taché, nd but c December 1876, ASTR

10 Ruth 4: 21-2

11 Riel to Bourget, 1 May 1876, ADM

12 Text of Riel, 10 March 1876, in an unidentified newspaper clipping, *L'Affaire Riel* scrapbook, AUSJB

13 H.W. Gerth and C.W. Mills, editors, *From Max Weber* (New York 1958) 328

14 Riel to Bourget, 15 May 1876, ADM

15 ANQ, Collection F.-X. Lemieux, typescript, 'La Folie de Riel'

16 Riel to Bourget, 20 April 1876, ADM

17 *Ibid.*

18 *Ibid.*, 1 May 1876

19 *Ibid.*

20 ASQ 25

21 Riel to Bourget, 20 April 1876, ADM

22 *Ibid.*, 1 May 1876

23 *Ibid.*, 15 May 1876

24 ASQ 118

25 ASQ 146-7. Riel is in error; Nehemiah had nothing to do with building the second temple.

26 ASQ 121-4

27 *Ibid.*

28 Mason Wade, *The French-Canadians*, vol 1, pp 367-70

29 *Cf.* Michel Brunet, 'Trois Dominantes de la pensée canadienne-française,' *La Présence anglaise et les Canadiens* (Montreal 1958).

30 Louis Riel to Paul Proulx (a cousin), PAM, Riel (1), no. 495. This is a hand copy which bears no date. A typed copy in ASB is dated 10 May 1877. The original is missing.

31 ASQ 124. But in another text Riel affirmed that the new era had begun on 1 May 1876. ASQ 41. The day on which Riel informed Bourget by letter of some of his most important ideas was 1 May 1876.

32 ASQ 27-30

33 ASQ 141

34 ASQ 50

35 *Diaries* 165

36 Riel to Bourget, 20 April and 1 May 1876, ADM

37 Although there is a certain similarity between this story and the beliefs of the Mormons, the correspondence is not really very close, as any reader of the Book of Mormon can easily verify. Riel need not have been inspired by

the Mormons; the Hebrew ancestry of the Indians was a common hypothesis in nineteenth-century America. *Cf.* Robert Silverberg, *Mound-Builders of Ancient America* (Greenwich, Conn. 1968) 50ff.

38 ASQ 107
39 ASQ 109
40 ASQ 104
41 *Ibid.*
42 ASQ 97-8
43 Mary Jordan, *To Louis: From Your Sister Who Loves You* (Toronto 1974)
44 PAM, Riel (2). *Cf.* 2. Samuel 13.
45 ASQ 116
46 ASQ 97
47 ASQ 92
48 There are differing translations of 1 Corinthians 7: 36ff. Riel used the version which refers to the father marrying his daughter (ie, to a suitor). Other versions refer to the state of celibate marriage between two partners. The Greek text is ambiguous.
49 ASQ 89
50 *Ibid.*
51 *Ibid.* 89-90
52 On Joachim and Joachimism in the Middle Ages, see Marjorie Reeves, *The Influence of Prophecy in the Later Middle Ages* (Oxford 1969).
53 *Cf.* n 31, this chapter.
54 ASQ, 135
55 Riel to Bourget, 1 May 1876, ADM
56 Jukes Papers, GI
57 Riel to Taché, 24 July 1885, ASTR
58 Miller's numerology is summarized in Sylvester Bliss, *Memoirs of William Miller* (Boston 1853).
59 ASQ 38
60 ASQ 31
61 ASQ 34
62 *Ibid.*
63 ASQ 36
64 ASQ 37
65 ASQ 144
66 ASQ 88
67 Riel to Bourget, 15 May 1876, ADM
68 Riel to Taché, nd, ASTR
69 *Ibid.*

CHAPTER 5: WAITING

1 Robert Rumilly, *Mercier* (Montreal 1936) 485
2 Riel to Taché, 4 February 1878, ASB
3 Riel to Bourget, February 1884 (draft), PAC, Justice 63-9
4 PAC, Riel Collection, vol. 3, p 1
5 Louis Riel to Julie Riel, 1 February 1878; Julie Riel to Louis Riel, 28 February 1878, PAM, Riel (2). For the power of attorney, 5 March 1878, see PAM, Riel (1), no. 648.
6 Louis Riel to Julie Riel, 21 April 1878, PAM, Riel (2)
7 *New York Herald*, dispatch of 17 May 1885. 'Condon' is Edward O'Meagher Condon. I have not identified 'Melody.'
8 F. Barnabé to Julie Riel, 25 September 1878, PAM, Riel (2)
9 BNQ, Dr Gabriel Nadeau Papers, anonymous clipping
10 F. Barnabé to Louis Riel, 6 October 1878, PAM, Riel (1), no. 344
11 *Ibid.*, no. 347, 14 October 1878
12 E. Barnabé to Louis Riel, 17 October 1878, PAM, Riel (2)
13 T. Glenn to Louis Riel, 29 October 1878, PAM, Riel (1), no. 352
14 *Cf.* a 'situation wanted' ad in the *Herald*, PAM, Riel (1) no. 348.
15 E. Barnabé to Louis Riel, 11 October 1878; F. Barnabé to Louis Riel, 11 November 1878, PAM, Riel (1), nos. 345, 353
16 Alexandre Riel to Louis Riel, 12 December 1878, PAM, Riel (2)
17 J.P. Shannon, *Catholic Colonization on the Western Frontier* (New Haven 1957)
18 William Davidson, *The Life and Times of Louis Riel* (Calgary 1951) 58, asserts that Riel and Ireland had met, but gives no proof.
19 Copy in PAM, Riel (1), no. 357; F. Barnabé to Louis Riel, 7 January 1879
20 Jos. Dubuc, 'Mémoires d'un Manitobain,' ms, PAM
21 George Woodcock, *Gabriel Dumont* (Edmonton 1975) 83-4
22 Hugh Dempsey, *Crowfoot* (Edmonton 1972) 91, 108
23 *Saskatchewan Herald* (Battleford), 24 March 1879
24 PAM, Riel (2)
25 E. Barnabé to Louis Riel, 12 March 1879, PAM, Riel (1), no. 363
26 *Ibid.*, no. 368; and PAM, Riel (2), nd
27 Louis Riel to Julie Riel, 2 May 1879, PAM, Riel (2)
28 Louis Riel, *Poésies religieuses et politiques* (Montreal 1886) 50
29 Louis Riel to Julie Riel, 15 September 1879, PAM, Riel (2)
30 PAM, Riel (1), nos 377, 384 are reports by Wood Mountain métis.
31 Louis Riel to Julie Riel, 12 October 1879, PAM, Riel (2)
32 GI, Edgar Dewdney Papers 1090
33 W.L. Lincoln, Fort Belknap, to Indian Affairs Commissioner, 15 November

1879; receipts of Indian Affairs Commissioner from Montana, NAUS

34 *Ibid.*, report by Col. Black, commander of Fort Assiniboine, 28 January 1880

35 *Fort Benton Record*, 19 December 1879

36 Louis Riel to Joseph Riel, 28 December 1879, PAM, Riel (1), no. 649

37 Jean L'Heureux to J.A. Macdonald, 1 November 1886, PAC, Macdonald Papers, vol. 110, p 44891. Also James M. Walsh Papers, PAM. Walsh's report was quoted extensively in J.P. Turner, *The North-West Mounted Police 1873-1893* (Ottawa 1950), vol. 1, pp 410-14, but the events were erroneously dated 1878-9 rather than 1879-80.

38 See two letters by L'Heureux to Indian Affairs Commissioner Dewdney, September 1880, PAC, Indian Affairs Records, File 34527. Also letters from Superintendent Crozier of Fort Walsh, 24 March, 29 March, 7 May 1880, PAC, Mounted Police Records, vol. 2233. George Woodcock, *Gabriel Dumont* 84, has attributed the actions decribed here to Dumont rather than Riel, but offers no proof.

39 PAM, Walsh Papers

40 L'Heureux to Macdonald, 1 November 1886, PAC, Macdonald Papers. Corroborated by Crowfoot, *cf.* John Maclean, *Canadian Savage Folk* (Toronto 1896) 380.

41 *Toronto Mail*, 2 March 1886

42 W.L. Lincoln, Fort Belknap, to Indian Affairs Commissioner, 4 February 1880, NAUS, Receipts of Indian Affairs Commissioner from Montana, L264

43 Louis Riel to 'Colonel,' 16 March 1880, PAM, Riel (1), no. 383, draft

44 PAC, Justice 2105-14

45 NAUS, Records of the Adjutant-General's Office

46 PAM, Riel (1), no. 516, O'Hanlon to officials of T.C. Power in Fort Benton

47 *Fort Benton Record*, 17 September 1880

48 PAM, Riel (1), no. 391; and Riel (2), Jean L'Heureux to Louis Riel, 2 February 1881

49 J.W. Schultz, *My Life as an Indian* (New York 1907) 381

50 J.P. Turner, *NWMP 1873-1893*, vol. 2, p 577

51 Henriette Riel to E. Barnabé, nd (draft), PAM, Riel (2)

52 Riel, 'Compte-Rendu de ses activités,' ASB(T); marriage certificate, HSSB

53 *Fort Benton Record*, 19 May 1883

54 Louis Riel to Taché, nd (draft), PAC, Justice, 38

55 PAM,Riel (2)

56 *Ibid.*, especially the notebook which also contains Riel's draft letter to President Grant, discussed in ch. 2

57 PAM, Riel (2)

58 ASB(T)

59 PAC, Justice, 2207-10, 2283-4, 2310, 2312, 2314-19, 2361-4, 2369

60 Louis Riel to Jos. Riel, nd, PAC, Justice, 137-8

61 Schultz, *My Life as an Indian* 382

62 Alexander Botkin, 'The John Brown of the Half Breeds,' *Rocky Mountain Magazine* 1 (September 1900) 19

63 PAM, Riel (2)

64 PAC, Justice, 2070-1

65 PAC, Justice, 38-9, 44-7, 63-9, 396-9, 400-3

66 *Ibid.* 44-7

67 *Ibid.* 63-9

68 *Le Messager* (Lewiston, Maine), 8 October 1885

69 PAC, Justice, 436-42, Louis Riel to his brother-in-law, 28 May 1884 (draft)

70 PAC, Justice, 2058-69. In *The Diaries of Louis Riel*, I mistakenly dated this material 1885 instead of 1884. *Cf.* ch. 5 plus the appendix, 'Description of the Manuscripts.' But Gilles Martel has established conclusively that 1884 is correct. *Cf. Le Messianisme de Louis Riel* 346-8 n 94.

71 *Diaries* 90-2

72 *Ibid.* 26-7

73 ANQ, transcript of speech by Gabriel Dumont, 24 April 1888

74 PAC, Justice, 459-60

75 Riel to Taché, 24 July 1885, ASTR

76 W. Bischoff, *The Jesuits in Old Oregon* (Caldwell, Idaho 1945), preface by David McAstocker, SJ, p xvi

CHAPTER 6: THE PROPHET IN ARMS

1 George Stanley, 'The Half-Breed "Rising" of 1875,' *Canadian Historical Review* 17 (1936) 399-412

2 Marcel Giraud, *Le Métis canadien* (Paris 1945) vol. 2, pp 1108-73

3 Louis Riel to Joseph Riel and Louis Lavallée, [?] July 1884, PAM, Riel (1), no. 418

4 James Isbister to Louis Riel, 4 September 1884, PAM, Riel (1), no. 413

5 Gilles Martel, 'Le Messianisme de Louis Riel,' thesis (Paris 1976) 389-401

6 L.H. Thomas, 'Louis Riel's Petition of Rights, 1884,' *Saskatchewan History* 23 (1970) 16-26

7 Testimony of Nolin at *The Queen* v *Joseph Arcand et al.*, Canada Sessional Papers (1886) no. 52, p 393

8 Testimony of Nolin, *QvLR* 213

9 Statement of Nolin and Lépine in notebooks of evidence about the Rebellion compiled by Mgr Cloutier, 1886, ASB

10 *Diaries* 41
11 *Ibid.* 32
12 Fourmond to Bishop Grandin, 27 December 1884. *Missions des OMI* (Paris 1885) vol. 23, p 276
13 Louis Schmidt, 'Notes: Mouvement des Métis à St-Laurent, Saskatchewan, TNO en 1884,' ASB, p 29786
14 *Ibid.* 29789
15 *Ibid.* 29789-90
16 *Ibid.* 29791-2
17 Grandin to Clarke, 4 September 1884, PAM, Hudson's Bay Company Papers, D 20/30, Receipts of Trade Commissioner, Winnipeg
18 Schmidt, 'Notes,' ASB, 29796-7
19 St Joseph was also Riel's private patron. See PAM, Riel (1), no. 6; PAC, Justice, 413.
20 Schmidt, 'Notes,' ASB, 29801
21 *Ibid.* 29808-9; statement of Nolin and Lépine in Cloutier, ASB
22 Jules Le Chevallier, *Batoche* (Montreal 1941) 55
23 *Ibid.* 55-6; Fourmond, 'Petite Chronique de St-Laurent,' PAA, Oblate Papers, D-IV-125
24 Riel's reply to the delegation, 5 June 1884, PAC, Justice, 459-60
25 Martel, 'Le Messianisme de Louis Riel ... ' 387
26 Dewdney to Macdonald, 19 September 1884, PAC, Macdonald Papers, 42897ff.
27 Testimony of Charles Nolin, *QvLR* 194
28 *QvLR* 362
29 *Ibid.* 369
30 Louis Schmidt, 'Notes,' ASB, 29808
31 *QvLR* 234
32 D.H. MacDowall to E. Dewdney, 24 December 1884, PAC, Macdonald Papers, 42958ff.
33 A. André to E. Dewdney, 11 January 1885, *ibid.* 42954ff.
34 André to Dewdney, 21 January1885, *ibid.* 42971; 6 February 1885, *ibid.* 42995. MacDowall to Dewdney, 14 January 1885, GI, Dewdney Papers, 1406
35 Macdonald to Dewdney, 20 February 1885, GI, Dewdney Papers, 545
36 *QvLR* 195, testimony of Charles Nolin
37 *Ibid.*
38 Cloutier, ASB; Martel, 'Le Messianisme de Louis Riel' 428
39 *QvLR* 196
40 *Ibid.*
41 'Petite Chronique de St-Laurent,' 1885, PAA, Oblate Papers, D-IV-125

42 ANQ, APP-1791, is the text of Riel's prayer. See also Father André's journal, 22 March 1885, PAA, Oblate Papers, D-IV-137.
43 *Diaries* 44-7, 50
44 Louis Schmidt, 'Notes,' ASB, 29813
45 *Diaries* 149
46 Schmidt, 'Notes,' ASB, 29813
47 *Diaries* 52
48 Schmidt, 'Notes,' ASB, 29816; Martel, 'Le Messianisme de Louis Riel' 435
49 *Ibid.* 29814
50 *Ibid.* 29816
51 *Diaries* 54-5
52 Le Chevallier, *Batoche* 58
53 'Petite Chronique de St-Laurent,' 1885, PAA, Oblate Papers, D-IV-125
54 Le Chevallier, *Batoche* 61
55 Willoughby's testimony, *QvLR*, 78-80
56 Le Chevallier, *Batoche* 69
57 Statement of Joseph Charette in Cloutier, ASB; Martel, 'Le Messianisme de Louis Riel' 444-5
58 Le Chevallier, *Batoche* 69
59 'Petite Chronique de St-Laurent,' 1885, PAA, Oblate Papers, D-IV-125
60 *Diaries* 78
61 Riel and Exovedate to Major Crozier, 21 March 1885, *QvLR* 373
62 George Woodcock, *Gabriel Dumont* 170, 192-3
63 Diary of G.H. Young, Douglas Library, Queen's University
64 PAC, Justice 105
65 Memoir of Philippe Garnot, PAA, Oblate Papers, D-IV-119
66 G.F.G. Stanley, editor, 'Gabriel Dumont's Account of the North-West Rebellion,' *Canadian Historical Review* 30 (1949) 257
67 *Diaries* 59
68 *Ibid.* 74-5
69 *Ibid.* 84
70 Testimony of Philippe Garnot, *QvLR* 236
71 PAC, Riel Papers, no. 49
72 Le Chevallier, *Batoche* 74
73 PAM, Papers of La Société Historique Métisse, interview with Dumont, c 1903
74 Exodus 17: 8-16; Stanley, *Louis Riel* 333
75 *Diaries* 72-6
76 *Ibid.* 82
77 *La Minerve*, c June 1885, undated clipping scrapbook, *L'Affaire Riel*, AUSJB
78 Statement of Elie Dumont in Cloutier, ASB

79 PAC, Justice, 722
80 *QvLR* 380
81 *Diaries* 63
82 Diary of V. Vegreville, PAA, Oblate Papers, D-IV-126
83 PAC, Justice, 737
84 Cloutier, ASB; Martel, 'Le Messianisme de Louis Riel' 469
85 Vegreville diary, PAA, Oblate Papers, D-IV-126
86 *Diaries* 61
87 PAC, Justice 887
88 Vegreville diary
89 *Diaries* 80
90 *Ibid.* 79
91 *Ibid.*
92 *Ibid.* 80
93 Statement of Maxime Lépine, Cloutier, ASB
94 *Diaries* 63-5
95 PAC, Justice, 731
96 *Winnipeg Sun*, Rebellion number, 3 July 1885, report of C.B. Pitblado
97 Testimony of Fourmond, *QvLR* 240
98 Statement of Jos. Arcand, Cloutier, ASB
99 PAC, Justice, 103
100 Vegreville diary
101 Le Chevallier, *Batoche* 178-82
102 *Ibid.* 182
103 Vegreville diary
104 *Ibid.*
105 Le Chevallier, *Batoche* 188
106 Vegreville diary
107 W.H. Jackson to his family, 19 September 1885, private collection of Miss C.E. Plaxton of Prince Albert
108 *Diaries* 60-1
109 *Ibid.* 61-2
110 PAC, Justice, 887
111 Cloutier, ASB; Martel, 'Le Messianisme de Louis Riel' 478
112 Vegreville diary
113 Le Chevallier, *Batoche* 190
114 Schmidt, 'Notes,' ASB, 29805
115 Memoir of Philippe Garnot, PAA, Oblate Papers, D-IV-119
116 *Le Véritable Riel* (Montreal 1887), pamphlet with contributions by several missionaries such as Grandin, Fourmond, etc.

CHAPTER 7: DISAPPOINTMENT AND HOPE

1 Leon Festinger *et al.*, *When Prophecy Fails* (St Paul 1956)
2 PAM, Papers of La Société Historique Métisse, interview with Gabriel Dumont, c 1903
3 Riel to Middleton, 15 May 1885, PAC, Justice, 932
4 *QvLR* 186
5 *Ibid.* 275-9
6 *Ibid.* 279
7 *Winnipeg Sun*, Rebellion number, 3 July 1885, 14
8 PAC, Library
9 *Winnipeg Sun*, 3 July 1885, 15ff.
10 ASQ, 100
11 Louis Riel to Julie Riel, 9 June 1885, PAM, Riel (1), no. 420
12 Riel to R. Fiset and F.-X. Lemieux, 16 June 1885, PAC, Justice, 1037ff.
13 Riel to J.W. Taylor, 21 July 1885, NAUS, Consular Despatches from Winnipeg, State Department Records
14 Riel to Deane, 8 June 1885, PAC, Macdonald Papers, 43186ff.
15 *Ibid.* 43192-4
16 Riel to Dewdney, 24 June 1885, PAC, Justice, 1074-7
17 *Ibid.* 1151-4, 27 June 1885.
18 Riel to Macdonald, 6 July 1885, PAC, Justice, 1232-49
19 Riel to Macdonald, 16 July 1885, PAC, Macdonald Papers, 43229-32
20 R. Burton Deane, *Mounted Police Life in Canada* (London 1916) 190
21 T. Flanagan, editor, 'Louis Riel's Religious Beliefs: A Letter to Bishop Taché,' *Saskatchewan History* 27 (1974) 15-28. The original ms was subsequently found in ASTR.
22 Desmond Morton, Introduction, *QvLR*; L.H. Thomas, 'A Judicial Murder: The Trial of Louis Riel,' in Howard Palmer, editor, *The Settlement of the West* (Calgary 1977); Robert Toupin, 'Fallait-il exécuter Louis Riel?' *Revue de l'Université Laurentienne* 1 (1968) 49-60
23 *QvLR* 314-22
24 *Ibid.* 350-2
25 *Ibid.* 370-1
26 *Ibid.* 355-7, 367
27 Louis Riel to J.W. Taylor, 1 August 1885 (draft), PAC, Justice, 1612
28 Riel to Fourmond, 3 August 1885, ASB
29 Riel to Fourmond and Cochin, nd, ASB
30 Riel to Irvine, nd, McGill University, McCord Museum, no. 20187
31 PAC, Riel Papers, no. 55

32 There are two copies, one in Fourmond's hand, dated 5 August, ASB, the other in Riel's hand, dated 4 August, AUNB.

33 Deane, *Mounted Police Life in Canada* 229-30

34 Cochin to Riel, 6 August 1885, ASB

35 Cochin to Taché, 7 August 1885, ASB

36 See Thomas Flanagan, 'The Riel "Lunacy Commission'': The Report of Dr Valade,' *Revue de l'Université d'Ottawa* 46 (1976) 108-27.

37 Louis Riel to Henriette Poitras, 26 October 1885, HSSB

38 *Diaries* 94

39 *Ibid.* 100

40 *Ibid.* 111

41 *Ibid.* 133

42 *Ibid.* 98

43 *Ibid.* 100, 105

44 *Ibid.* 126-9

45 *Ibid.* 101

46 *Ibid.* 108

47 *Ibid.* 134

48 *Ibid.* 94

49 Cochin to Taché, 11 August 1885, ASB

50 Cochin to Taché, 14 August 1885, ASB

51 André to Taché, 24 August 1885, ASB

52 *Ibid.*, 16 September 1885

53 *Ibid.*, 21 September 1885

54 André to F.-X. Lemieux, 31 August 1885, appended to the original text of *The Queen* v *Louis Riel* (Ottawa 1886) 204-5

55 *Ibid.*

56 André to Taché, 16 September 1885, ASB

57 *Ibid.*, 24 August 1885

58 *Diaries* 156

59 ASB(T)

60 Louis Riel to President Cleveland, nd, forwarded by J.W. Taylor to Washington, 12 September 1885, NAUS, Consular despatches from Winnipeg, Department of State records

61 *Diaries* 146

62 *Ibid.* 150

63 *Ibid.* 169

64 *Ibid.*

65 *Ibid.* 170

66 ASB, nd

67 ASB(T)
68 *Ibid.*
69 HSSB
70 *Diaries* 165-6; and F.-X. Valade Papers, PAC
71 Riel, fragment, nd, but 1885, PAC, Dewdney Papers, unpaginated shreds, vol. 6a
72 *Diaries* 166-9
73 *Ibid.* 165
74 *Ibid.* 163
75 Riel to Richardson, PAC, Dewdney Papers, 165-6
76 Riel to Richardson, HSSB
77 André to Taché, 16 November 1885, ASB
78 *Diaries* 114
79 *Diaries* 103
80 *Ibid.* 124
81 ASB(T)
82 Dr Augustus Jukes Papers, GI
83 *Ibid.*
84 PAM, Riel (2); Martel, 'Le Messianisme de Louis Riel' 622-5
85 Jukes Papers, GI
86 André to Taché, 16 November 1885, ASB
87 Le Chevallier, *Batoche* 267-78
88 *Ibid.* 268
89 *Ibid.*
90 *Ibid.*
91 *New York Herald*, 16 or 17 November 1885
92 Le Chevallier, *Batoche* 269
93 *The Daily Leader* (Regina), 17 November 1885
94 *Ibid.*
95 *Ibid.*

CHAPTER 8: A COMPARATIVE VIEW

1 Yonina Talmon, 'Millenarism,' *International Encyclopedia of the Social Sciences* (1968) vol. 10, p 349
2 First edition, New York 1957. Two further editions have been published.
3 Antonio Moscato and Maria Pierini, *Rivolta religiosa nella Campagna* (Rome 1965)
4 Brazil has been particularly well studied; see the literature cited in Maria Isaura Pereira de Queiroz, *Réforme et révolution dans les sociétés traditionnelles* (Paris 1968).

5 London 1963
6 James Mooney, *The Ghost-Dance Religion and the Sioux Outbreak of 1890*, abridged edition (Chicago 1965)
7 Peter Worsley, *The Trumpet Shall Sound*, 2nd edition (London 1968)
8 Peter M. Holt, *The Mahdist State in the Sudan, 1881-1898* (Oxford 1970)
9 Sheila Kitzinger, 'Protest and Mysticism: The Rastafari Cult of Jamaica,' *Journal for the Scientific Study of Religion* 8 (1969) 240-62; C. Eric Lincoln, *The Black Muslims in America*, 2nd edition (Boston 1973)
10 *The New Schaff-Herzog Encyclopedia of Religious Knowledge* (1910) vol. 7, pp 377-8, sections 10-11 under 'Millennium'
11 The literature is much too large to list. Major works in addition to those already cited are W. Mühlmann, *Chiliasmus und Nativismus* (Berlin 1961); G. Guariglia, *Prophetismus und Heilserwartungsbewegungen* (Horn-Vienna 1959); Sylvia Thrupp, editor, *Millennial Dreams in Action* (The Hague 1962); two special issues of the *Archives de sociologie des religions* 4(1957) and 5(1958); Bryan Wilson, *Magic and the Millennium* (New York 1975); Henri Desroche *et al.*, *Dieux d'hommes* (Paris 1969). The recent literature is reviewed in Hillel Schwartz, 'The End of the Beginning: Millenarian Studies, 1969-1975,' *Religious Studies Review* 2 (1976) 1-15.
12 'Les Métis: Dernier mémoire de Louis Riel,' in A. Ouimet, editor, *La Vérité sur la question métisse* (Montreal 1889) 80-1; Louis Riel to the Métis of the Battleford area, draft nd, *QvLR* 375

Index

DATE DUE

JUL 27 '88			
779847			
GAYLORD			PRINTED IN U.S.A.